want to **know . . .**

what today's teens are really thinking and doing?

why they are longing for connection, for "intimate encounters"?

what having an STD means, in the long-term?

why STDs and pregnancy aren't the only reasons
not to have sex outside of marriage?

where to tell your kids to draw the line on a date?

what you can do to protect your kids?

why a pure revolution applies to you?

what you can do to bring change
to your family, church, and community?

then it's time for you to enter the

pure **revolution**

read on!

time for a
pure rev

olution

DOUG HERMAN

Tyndale House Publishers, Inc., Wheaton, Illinois

Visit Tyndale's exciting Web site at www.tyndale.com

Time for a Pure Revolution

Copyright © 2004 by Doug Herman. All rights reserved.

Cover photograph copyright © 2003 by Paul Vozdic/Getty Images. All rights reserved.

Designed by Jacqueline L. Noe

Edited by Ramona Cramer Tucker

Library of Congress Cataloging-in-Publication Data

Herman, Doug, date.
  Time for a pure revolution / Doug Herman.
     p. cm.
Includes bibliographical references.
  ISBN 0-8423-8357-3
  1. Chastity. 2. Christian teenagers—Sexual behavior. 3. Sexual abstinence—Religious aspects—Christianity. 4. Sex instruction for teenagers—Religious aspects—Christianity. I. Title.
  BV4647.C5 H47 2004
  241'.66—dc22   2003015508

Printed in the United States of America

10   09   08   07   06   05   04
7   6   5   4   3   2   1

To Josh, Bri, and Luc . . . my three children.
I pray this book becomes the beginning of a new movement of purity that touches each of your lives personally. May it impact the lives of your future in-laws, that they raise your future spouse with courage, wisdom, and purity. May it empower you as you become adults. May it afford you a relationship that is pure and fulfilling . . . and bring to all of us the contagious laughter of yet unborn grandchildren.

**I have fought the good fight.
I have finished the race. I have kept the faith.**
—2 Timothy 4:7

table of **contents**

Acknowledgments

For the adults in Littleton, Colorado, who wept together
at the news of parties that were killing our teens equally
as much as the Columbine shootings had earlier.
Your rallying cry has been heard in countless
thousands of lives and will continue on.

For those golfing buddies who dared to dream
with me about what could be done to impact our teens
and their families, may you be highly blessed
(and may God correct your slice).

unlock your **passion!**

if you'd have told me 15 years ago what I'd be doing today, I probably would have looked at you with a raised eyebrow. Traveling 100 days a year away from my family, speaking at over 250 public high schools, concerts, and churches about sex and tragedy, and discussing STDs over lunch wouldn't even have been a blip on my radar screen. But one early winter day in 1991 changed many things, including my family and my life's focus. I'll never forget the doctor's words. . . .

"As you know, Doug," the pediatrician began slowly, "your daughter, Ashli, is on life support through the ventilator. Her lungs are now filled with fluid. We can possibly extend her life for two more days, with medication, but . . ." His voice trailed off. The social worker, nurses, and other doctors in the room shifted uncomfortably. No one wanted to pick up where our doctor had stopped.

"If you shut the machines off today," he continued, "she'll die in a couple of hours. If you don't, she'll suffer for two days and then die. What do you want to do, Doug? It's your choice."

A few friends were with me that day, but such a choice was mine alone. That afternoon my wife, Evon, was at home, still recovering from the effects of the flu. We had discussed our options if faced with this choice, so I knew what she would want me to say. But I was paralyzed nonetheless.

Our two-year-old daughter, Ashli, was literally suffocating from pneumonia, caused by infections that resulted from her battle with AIDS. She had contracted HIV, the virus that causes AIDS, from my wife, Evon, through birth. Evon had contracted the virus through a blood transfusion years earlier following the birth of our first child, Joshua. Although Josh and I had never contracted HIV, it was deeply affecting our family.

"Doug?" the pediatrician asked. "Are you okay? I know this is tough, but it's your choice."

I was frozen. But as I gazed into the doctor's eyes, I saw incredible compassion. Scanning the room, I saw nurses with whom we'd developed wonderful relationships over the past two years. The social worker who had guided us through Medicaid and other financial issues had sat in meetings like these before, but now her eyes watered, along with those of the nursing staff. Even the doctor surprised me as he wiped a tear, awaiting my choice.

My choice. *Shall I shut off the breathing machine today, or shall I let Ashli suffer two more days and then remove the machine on Sunday?* That was my choice.

The room seemed to shrink as I tried to force myself to answer their question.

And what was I deciding, really? I was not determining *how* she would die, nor was I choosing the process of her death—those were predetermined by this disease. But I *was* deciding the date and time. I knew that, for all the years to come, every Memorial Day weekend I would run my finger along her name, engraved on her tombstone, and see the date of my choosing. So the time of her death was my only choice . . . and the irony burned.

> Making the decision to have a child is momentous—it is to decide forever to have your heart go walking around outside your body.
> —Elizabeth Stone

You see, my wife and I never chose the HIV contraction—we just wanted to have a family. I had never made a choice to be involved in high-risk activities and then lie, failing to disclose that lifestyle on a blood donor form. Only the blood donor, whose blood ultimately infected Evon and Ashli, had chosen that. And with his choice, he had stripped away every choice of mine but one—To choose the date and time of my two-year-old daughter's death. And I chose it alone.

As the meeting dispersed, I called Evon and shared the decision. We cried and prayed. Evon was so ill she couldn't even come to the hospital to say good-bye one last time. Thankfully, she'd done so two days earlier. Later, standing by Ashli's bed, I tried to say good-bye. How does a parent end the life of a child he loves with his whole being? How can any parent who truly loves a child give up? Something within us causes us to want to keep fighting, to demand a cure, to increase the oxygen flow, to . . .

But there was no such miracle or solution for Ashli. Looking at her, my heart broke again. Two nights earlier I had vowed to her and to God that I would do anything in my power to prevent this from occurring in other families. Never would I want another innocent infant to die from this ravaging disease—from a horrible, lingering pain that slowly destroys the eyes, the spleen, the digestive system, the mind, the skin, and the lungs. Never should any parent have to turn away from their child and motion to the nurse that the time has come.

An hour and a half crept by. I cried until my body shook, and no tears remained to flow. Ashli was conscious but fully medicated while on the breathing machine. So I could only assume she could hear me speak.

"Sweetheart," I said slowly, beginning my good-byes to the toddler I loved so much, "I'm sorry about the pain. I'm sorry about the hurt, the suffering, and your short life. But I am *not* sorry you are my little girl. I'm not sorry we had two years and two months together. I'm not sorry that I love you. And I'm not sorry that I get to see you again in heaven someday."

I finally found the strength to stop crying. I leaned over my little girl and kissed her forehead. "I love you, Ashli. Good-bye."

I called the nurse in, and she shut off the breathing machine. Ashli took two breaths and died.[1]

After she died, the nursing staff wrapped her in a white blanket and carried her out of the room. I happened to be in the hall as they exited. "Do you want to say good-bye one more time?" the nurse asked me. I knew they were taking her body for an autopsy, so I said yes. As they unfolded the blanket for me, I saw what appeared to be a life-size version of a doll. As I unwrapped this doll's face, I saw my daughter. I leaned forward, kissing her cold forehead one last time. "Good-bye" was all I could whisper. There were not enough words, nor enough time, to say all the things I longed to say—and especially how much I loved her.

Driving home that day, I was broken. And I was angry. Although AIDS is not the only killer today, it killed my little girl. And then, eight months later, it killed my wife. Evon died the same way. Not once did Evon or Ashli choose this disease. Nor did they choose to be involved in any high-risk activity that might cause them infection. Yet AIDS still killed half my family. As I sat by my daughter's deathbed, and later my wife's, I hated that disease more than I have ever hated anything in my life. It was an ugly passion indeed. But that passion has also sparked in me something that can never be taken away.

Who Will Chose?

Over a decade has passed since my wife and daughter died. I'm remarried to a wonderfully classy woman. Two additional children grace our home and add to the continual laughter echoing off the walls. My heart has healed, but I've not forgotten. The grass has completely grown over Ashli and Evon's graves, yet still I trace their names and dates with my hands every Memorial Day weekend. Oh yes, the memories of their deaths continue to sting. But the raw pain and ugly passion have been replaced with something far more clarifying: resolve. Resolve to not sit by idly while this disease rampages our nation. Resolve to do something about it, personally.

What has come of this passion? Every week it flows from my heart and lips into the lives of thousands of complete strangers. In public, private, and parochial schools I stand before unknown faces—students whom I already love. As I share only a brief snapshot of my story, tears flow and my voice begins to choke. No longer is it because of my grief over Evon and Ashli. You see, I've fully grieved and have shared this story in over two thousand school presentations. Now the tears come as our souls connect and my passion grows to reach the teens in my audience.

"Listen to my heart for a moment," I'll say. In my hands are two color copies—Evon's and Ashli's death certificates, with AIDS listed as the cause of death on each one. "Ashli and Evon did *not* have a choice . . . *but you do!*" I lay the certificates on the gym floor. "Blood donation systems are safer than they've ever been. The *only way* you'd get that virus, or any infection, unplanned pregnancy, emotional pain, or skewed future plans is if you chose to be involved in high-risk activity. And you don't have to make that choice to love somebody. Or to have somebody love you."

> **Always remember, my friend: One man with courage makes a majority.**
> —Andrew Johnson

Students sit, stunned. Mascara streaks the cheeks of many girls. Boyish hearts are fully gripped as even tough male athletes listen with respect and introspection. The beautiful women on campus clutch their purses with both hands, eyes rapt with attention. Have they listened? Oh, yes. And have our hearts connected? Without question. But will they change their lifestyle? Will this one presentation touch them deeply enough to cause them to choose better for their future? Only they can answer. And only you, the people who care so deeply, who love them so deeply, can help.

> **Only you, the people who care so deeply, who love your teens so deeply, can help.**

That's the purpose of this book: To equip you with the information, stories, and strategies to help you assist those you know and love in making good decisions. Decisions for *life,* not decisions for death. Decisions that will change their lives through a *Pure Revolution!*

It Takes a Revolution!

If I say the word *revolution,* what picture pops into your head? A picture of a war? Or of something spinning? But I've also learned that *revolution* means a process to "roll back." So a revolution, then, is to "come to the original point, return, revolve."[2] I use this process every week in school presentations. It helps to keep me focused.

Before I'm announced to 2,000 screaming teens in an all-school assembly, I occasionally get a knot in my stomach. After all, let's face it.

There's nothing teens would enjoy more than heckling a middle-aged male speaker talking about sexual abstinence in a public school. I can see them, mouths drooling, cynical sneers on their faces, as they await my presence. As I peer out over the multicolored sea of faces in the auditorium, I force myself to "come to my original point."

So I select at random two girls and a young man. In my mind I envision them 10 to 15 years into the future. I can see these teen girls as young ladies—one as a succeessful career woman in her early thirties, the other as a mother whose life is filled with piano lessons, soccer practice, the activities of a school volunteer, and continual housecleaning. The young man I also see in the future—happily married and thriving in his business. Then I project them into the future in a different way. This time I project them as I last remember seeing my late wife—emaciated in a hospital bed, completely blind, partially bald, being fed by IVs, and barely able to talk as she was wheeled into ICU to be put on a ventilator. And I hear a voice inside me whisper strongly, *You must tell them again, Doug. They don't deserve the pain or the infection. They don't even know how their choices are affecting them! Look at that young man and those two girls. They will love you forever if you tell them the truth!*

I'm startled back to the present by the announcer's voice. "Would you give a warm welcome to our speaker, Mr. Doug Herman!"

Once again I know that I *must* share the message—with all the passion I can muster.

You see, I speak and write with fervor because I know the message is not about me—it never has been. It's about *you,* the one listening! I share information and my story because I want *you* to have a great future. I want *you* to have children who are happy, healthy, and thriving in the future. Mom and Dad, I want *you* to have grandchildren who are happy and healthy too!

So although I share my story, my passion, it is not because I'm trying to "beat" some personal agenda to death. It's because I believe, with all my heart, that you and your children deserve so much more. Rather than infections, disease, unplanned pregnancies, and emotional isolation, I want you and your teens to find contentment and health. Rather than parent/teen relationships that are strained and lifeless, you deserve the conversations and connection you have been praying for. Instead of leading that triple life—one at home, one at work, and one at church—where you come away feeling fragmented, you can live one life, with a purity of heart. Yes, it is possible—even when we live in a sex-saturated world that believes there's no way out. But the world is wrong. Thousands are already finding a way out! And they're already proving what I've found to be true: If we present a new revolution, we can return or revolve again, coming to the original point of purity.

Decisions in Duluth

But why spend your life, your time, and your resources trying to reverse the powerful urges of a society that longs to experience sexual freedom? Isn't it a part of our culture we should just accept? "Go with the flow," so to speak? With music, television, film, and clothing all promoting more sexuality in our culture, why would someone spend his life standing against a flow so strong that it buries you with prophesied failure?

I found the answer to that in Duluth, Minnesota, five years ago. I was at a crossroads in my life and ministry. Was it time to finally quit telling my story nationally and begin working full-time in the area for which I'd been trained—as a pastor? I wondered. I had a month to decide. And while I wrestled with that decision, I traveled to speak to teens once again at an all-school assembly at Duluth East High School.

Just before I spoke, the local youth pastor, Dean Bjorlin, and I arrived in the gymnasium with Dukes, the athletic director. "Let's pray first," Dukes said. We grabbed hands and asked God to do something amazing in that gym. After we finished, we watched students file into their preassigned sections. Over 2,500 ninth to twelfth graders brought the gym to life. The electric energy was stunning! In the thousands of presentations I've conducted, few were as exciting. You could sense the administration's power, pride, and confidence in their students (at that time they were recognized as the state's premiere hockey school), and it was contagious. As I shared my story with rapt energy, not only did the students hang on every word, they responded with force. At the conclusion of my presentation, I mentioned that they were welcome to attend another event that evening at a local church to hear the rest of my story, faith content included. You see, since I'm not allowed to speak openly about Christ in a public-school setting, what I present in schools contains no faith content. However, what I share in churches and youth concerts is hard-hitting and straightforward.

That evening over 300 teens filled the auditorium of Gospel Tabernacle. As I presented the gospel, teens were again captivated by the Spirit and the message. I offered them the chance to respond to this message of faith. To my left were five teen girls I recognized from Duluth East High. Four of them instantly stood to receive Christ as their Savior. They came to the front with the other 30 or so and we prayed. What made that evening so memorable was that I later learned these teens were for the most part unchurched. After I prayed, the band led the audience in music. As I stood and watched, a small voice whispered inside me, *I've created you for such a time as this.*

It was just what I needed. After sharing my story for seven years, I had become very tired. I was ready to put my presentations to rest. But now there was a greater reason to press on. Just as Queen Esther in the Bible had to risk rejection, the loss of comforts, and even her life for the peace and safety of her nation, I too sensed this calling. *For such a time as this,* I contemplated. Seeing these teens walking hurriedly toward the front of the sanctuary to meet this God they'd just discovered was real, a God who could cleanse and change their lives, renewed my own resolve. *For such a time as this.*

That evening God made my path clear. I chose to leave pastoral ministry behind and work in school systems across the globe to bring hope and purity back into the minds, bodies, and lifestyles of our teens.

> The only limit to our realization of a bright tomorrow will be our doubts of today.
> —Franklin D. Roosevelt

Why do I do what I do? Because I believe it's my calling. And I believe that God has miraculously protected me from HIV infection from the exposure to my late wife for a reason. I love this generation of teens and their families, and I don't ever want to see other families devastated as mine was.

So from that evening on I've been determined: I'll lead this revolution as needed. After all, God has clearly lined up the qualifications I need to speak to a broad audience. How many male speakers and authors do you know who have met all this criteria: one who has a personal story of AIDS killing his family, who is educated about HIV, who was asked to leave his church due to his wife's and daughter's AIDS infection, who is compassionate to the gay communities and yet a Christian minister promoting sexual abstinence and purity? Mm-hmm. I don't believe in coincidence. Let's try *providence.*

But I want to be entirely clear. In my bold words about my qualifications, it's not pride you sense. It's confidence. Confidence in God and in his plan for me. I didn't *do* any of this. I didn't chose or want my story. But I do know what it is like to have an STD kill those I love. And no one should have to experience that. I also know what it's like to fail my own standards, and I've wrestled with that as well. And that breaking of my spirit has created an even deeper compassion and a new realism within me.

Just as I was sickened by how few Christians responded to those who were HIV-positive, gay or not, in the late eighties and nineties, so I am sickened now by the attitudes of an apathetic culture that allows our teens to die slow deaths. I will not stand by and watch. Will you?

Ripple Effects

A dear friend of mine in our neighborhood of Littleton, Colorado, shared with me a story a couple of years back. As a youth pastor at a local church, Todd Shulda finds himself immersed with teens. He hears their stories continually and sometimes shares them with me.

"Doug, you remember Angie?"[3] he asked.

I nodded and smiled.

"Well, when the football players from one high school transferred to another high school to continue playing with their coach who had moved, many of the students from their new school hosted a welcome party for them."

Todd paused, and I scrutinized his eyes to see what was wrong. They were watering. "At this party, there was a lot of drinking involved. And a lot of sexual activity—explicit sexual activity. Angie was involved and hosted the party." Todd's heart was breaking as he talked. You see, he'd met me just after I'd buried Evon. He knew that I spoke internationally about this issue, and we both fought professionally for the lives and souls of teens. Now he was telling me what was occurring in *our* neighborhood. These students were choosing death–and they didn't even know it. We cared deeply for Angie and her friends. They were walking into a death-trap . . . and calling it a party.

Again I was angry. After sharing this story with adults from our church, we found 75 adults willing to volunteer to help create an event that would inform and educate parents and teens about these sexual choices and the consequences. In the southwest Denver area in one week we conducted a parents' meeting, held a physicians' breakfast, created and aired a commercial for MTV on the cable networks in our area, held all-school assemblies in every local high school, and concluded the week with a concert featuring national artists and comedians. This "Pure Revolution Project" reached over 13,000 teens, 500 adults, and 50 physicians. We knew that every high school student we saw at Southwest Plaza Mall had heard our message. It was total saturation.

The various networks in our community were challenged to work together for the good of the community and the good of the teens. We provided a venue for the faith network to express faith at the concert, and over 50 teens responded to invitations for a relationship with Christ and expressed a desire to have someone pray with them in their struggles. What a rich week!

But there is no revolution without a conflict. Our local church's elders were not thrilled with an event growing in size as ours was, especially one that was not based within the church's control. So it withdrew its name from our Web site as a supporter. Some Christian parents were angered that we would talk about sexual abstinence to teens at all. They didn't feel their teens were ready to hear about sex or would ever choose to be involved in any sexual activities outside marriage. Others were angered that our information at the public school dealt only with physical health and did not address spiritual life. Some local school administrators would not let us in to present an assembly. "We live in a conservative community. Our kids don't do that," a principal informed the parent offering the program. Little did he know that it was teens from his middle school that shared with us stories of the oral sex "assembly line" parties that occurred in the afternoons.

Adults, listen to me, because what I'm going to say is crucial. Now is not the time to stick our heads in the sand and pretend none of these things are happening. Nor should we simply isolate our children from culture. Even if we try to shield them during their growing-up years—by homeschooling and other options—eventually they will have to engage this world as culturally relevant adults. So how do we raise children to be "in the world but not of it"? By addressing culture head-on and taking it back, that's how!

> **Now is not the time to stick our heads in the sand. We need to address culture head-on and take it back!**

Pure Revolution is not about *waiting* until marriage for sex. *It is much more than that.* Pure Revolution is a comprehensive approach to life restored to its original point. That means we need *pure relationships*—where families will once again truly connect and communicate. We need schools where *pure education* addresses all issues of life—sex and relational—from choices and consequences to character development. And we need the church to wake up! We need to understand why we believe what we believe and to teach it rationally, relationally, and respectfully. This *pure renaissance,* or new birth, is holistic in nature, covering every aspect of our lives.

Pure Revolution is not only for individual teens; it's for all of us. It's time for American families to join together, to be purified in their thoughts, ideals, standards, and relationships through a Pure Revolution. There is so much that's fighting against us. Will you take an active part in turning back the tide of evil that is impacting our children, our families, our communities, and our nation?

> **If we work together, together we can scale any wall—no matter how high, how thick.** —Anne Ortlund

If that sounds overwhelming, this book will show you how very doable it is. But first, *Time for a Pure Revolution* will help you understand how and why our world has become the way it is, how the meanings of sex and love have changed over the years, and why *now* is a crucial time to fight for our kids. This book will also give you a sneak peek into the hearts and minds of today's teenagers, as well as proven strategies for talking with your teens about sex and love, and practical ways you can make a unique impact on your kids and your community.

Different Opinions, Similar Heart

At a recent youth conference, I was addressing a room full of 80 youth leaders from various churches. Only halfway into my talk, I mentioned the names of individuals whose "contributions" in American society were key to the promotion of the sexual revolution. When one name was mentioned, an adult exploded from his silence. "What problem do you have with her? All she wanted to provide was birth control to prevent young single mothers from pregnancy, a quick trip into poverty." The discussion over the founder of Planned Parenthood created quite a stir in that room (we'll address it more in chapter 3, "The Great American Love Story"), and rightfully so!

I realize that many of you will agree with what I express in this book. Others, however, will not. In fact, some of you may have purchased this book to see what the buzz is all about. But please listen to my heart for a moment. Regardless of your position or opinion—be it theological, political, or educational—I'm pleading with you to listen from a position of passion. I'm passionate about this message because it's a message about life. I'm not as concerned about someone's *rights* as I am about they're being healthy and being alive.

Look at it this way: When my child gets on her bicycle and begins shooting down the driveway toward the street, there are times when I scream at her and grab her by the arms, stopping her. Why? Certainly she has a right to ride her bike. It's her home too, and I did say she could leave and ride to her friend Simone's house. But what she failed to see was the car speeding around the corner up the street. As a concerned adult who gave her permission to ride to her friend's house, I had to grab her to stop that process, saving her life. In a sense, I contradicted my permission for a time to keep her alive. My biggest concern was not whether or not she had the right to ride her bike, but her safety. I love my daughter and want her to live. Don't you feel the same way about your kids?

Teens deserve life. Families deserve a future. And that's why I'm fighting for life in this book. I will even step on someone's "rights" for a time, if it causes them to avoid death. So you see, my heart is tender and compassionate. Let yours be also. Let's agree to set aside judgment for a time. Even when you may disagree with a perspective here, it may only be another color to balance the spectrum of light desired to illuminate those in the dark. So read with an open mind and heart. Be honest with yourself. You can dissect my strategies later. But for now, unlock your passion and connect with me first as we fight for the lives and health of our teens and their families . . . *together!*

Teens deserve life. Families deserve a future.

pure **beginnings**

there's something enchanting about a garden, wouldn't you agree? Maybe it's the beautiful colors or the variety of scents emanating from such a rich bouquet. Perhaps it's the unique design, textures, and the restful allure that captivates our souls and stimulates our imagination, just as it must have fascinated Adam and Eve back in the original Garden.

Few things are as pure as an innocent beginning. And if we are to understand what God really wants for us in our quest for purity and our longing for connection, we need to know his plan and design for humankind in its original form.

If we are the creation, then we were created. A Creator formed us. And we find in the Book of Beginnings—also known as Genesis—that this Creator was a sole God. And yet he also had plurality in his essence— God the Father, Jesus the Son, and the Holy Spirit—revealing the importance of community.

The Book of Beginnings reveals how the Creator knelt down and began forming man[1] from the earth. The soil was a good place to begin life. After all, every living plant drew nourishment from its richness. As the Creator shaped, the animals must have watched, fascinated. This was another creation, a pure beginning.

Imagine seeing flesh and bone take shape in the hands of that Creator. And looking at this perfectly formed body, you and I would call it good. No, we'd call it *magnificent!* This was the prototype of humankind, perfect in every way. But the brow of the Creator was certainly creased. For something was missing—the human being was still dead.

> **The prototype of humankind was perfect in every way.**

It's All about Life

Until the Creator breathed life into man's body, it was useless. It only resembled his handiwork and shaping. But once man was fully alive, the Creator could see his reflection in this creation.

The first man must have come to life with amazement. Can you imagine what it must have been like for him? Fully adult and fully conscious, Adam arrived. Unlike a baby born today, who can't remember his birth (and for that I say, "Thank you, God!"), this man was able to think, talk, and recognize. It's another of God's wonderful mysteries—that, as God, he can create anything, and in any time, stage, or development that he chooses.

Next, God named Adam, giving him an identity. Adam's identity didn't come from what he did—his career, economic status, etc.—since he'd lived only an hour. Nor was

> **Every noble work in life at first looks impossible. Just ask God.** —Thomas Carlyle

that identity determined by a group he associated with, since he was the only human. Instead his identity was found within, in his soul and spirit. He was a child of the Creator. And this relationship and identity fulfilled and completed him.

Not Good to Be Alone

The Creator enjoyed his relationship with Adam. And Adam enjoyed it too. As the first person on the earth, he probably had a blast naming all the animals and other parts of creation. And I'm certain he tasted each of the fruits and vegetables before naming each one. His life was full, and he was happy.

In the cool of the evenings God and Adam walked together. They talked together. We can only guess what intimate conversations occurred between them. Maybe they spoke of the creation of the world. Perhaps Adam learned the keys to farming crops from the one who designed them. Most likely they discussed the interactions among the created animals as well, including pregnancy and birth. Peering into his reflection at the water's edge, I can imagine Adam wondering about his own young. Would he have any? And what about his mate? Later, maybe he expressed his heart to the Creator about companionship, and the Creator said, "This is not good."

Not good? How can anything made without sin in a garden of perfection be "not good"? But the Creator answered this question himself. "It is not good for man to be alone."

You may have questions here. And so do I. Why didn't God create companionship along with Adam in the first place? Why is it not until *later* that the Creator says, "This is not good"? I believe it's because he wanted Adam to establish what it meant to be a leader first, while developing a deep desire for someone to connect with. Adam needed to see the *blessings* of companionship. And to fully appreciate that, Adam needed to be completely alone and independent first.

You see, God could not complete his work in Adam until Adam had experienced life without human companionship. And that experience itself prepared him for a new relationship.

What was true back in the original Garden holds true today too. There comes a time in all of our lives when we must move out of our parents' home and live on our own. That goes for our kids too. We all long for our children to become independent from us, but not disconnected. At least *most* of you want that! That's natural. And that change in the parent-child relationship was also designed by the Creator. But do we want our grown-up children to be single forever? Or do we long for them to be happy and content in a marriage, where they may have the opportunity to birth or adopt children—and therefore learn even more about unconditional love? Such a match is also part of a larger design.

> What you teach your children is your gift to them. What they make of themselves is their decision—and their gift back to you and God.
> —Author Unknown

But sometimes we forget that living "as a single," like the first man on earth did for a while, can also be important and valuable.

Single and Celibate

Celibacy. What comes to your mind when you hear that word? Perhaps you think of a priest or monk, banished from a relationship with others due to a religious commitment made on a foggy, gray day. Or maybe *celibacy* evokes a picture of Mother Teresa, a person devoted fully to God and committed to love the "unlovable" people around her.

Or perhaps you think of celibacy as "the gift nobody wants," as a good friend once told me. And you know what I've found? He's not too far off! I've spoken with scores of single adults and teens who find themselves on a journey through this valley of singleness. They ply me with questions about relationships and hammer me with queries about the theology of God's role in the interpersonal connection. But under the surface, most of them are longing for a soul mate, someone to walk alongside them.

Is celibacy the gift nobody wants?

The truth is, few people like to be single. Well, let me rephrase that: Few people like to be *alone. Single* may be the posh marital status for some, so long as their activities are filled with friends and their bed rarely has a cold side. But is this right? Where do we find a pure relationship?

If you want to make a single adult angry, simply share with them the formula that goes something like this: "If you want to find the perfect man or woman for you, then you need to learn the power of contentment. See, being content is the essence of loving yourself in a godly way. Once you find that you don't *need* a relationship but simply *want* one, then the right person will come along—maybe they've been there all the while!"

Although there is truth in that response, the search for connection is often much more complicated. Too easily we who are married or happily connected to another will share our advice with a "single." But then we leave and go home to our spouse. Meanwhile, the sole sojourners surrounding us continue their journey. They open their sails wide and await God's winds to direct them to a deep place of contentment, even if no one is on board with them. At times this aloneness or loneliness can be incredibly painful, causing many things to surface, both good and bad.

Over the past couple of decades, singles have been finding the road to relational contentment increasingly littered with garbage and obstacles. Buried under the surface of that road are land mines that threaten the very existence of the single. Whether dodging emotional pain, strange invitations to connect, or even diseases, the journey has become perilous. As a result, many singles are looking beyond themselves for guidance. Teens and adults alike are turning to faith to guide them. "Undoubtedly, the push towards chastity is being led by the religious, who have the most to gain as they consider the darkest details of the afterlife," writes reporter Rebecca Fowler for a Sydney, Australia, newspaper. "But it is not their exclusive preserve."[2]

Fowler writes about two women discussing their newfound celibacy in London. Nicola Baxter, a 29-year-old drama teacher, explains that she had endured three consecutive relationships with 30-something professional men in which each ending was a bit more disappointing. As a result, she now abstains from sex in her relationships. "It's really refreshing," Baxter says. "Just removing it as an option and concentrating on other things. I'm sure you learn to focus that energy elsewhere. And you no longer feel a freak. I've got friends of both sexes who feel the same. Just for now, I'm happier going home with myself."

And she should be. Young men and women need to "concentrate on other things" if they are single. That way their minds won't be needlessly pounded by the continual question of where their soul mates are hiding. In fact, the usually less complicated lives of singles is a great time to connect, reconnect, or connect more deeply with the Creator, allowing his message and life purpose to flow through them. Even Baxter, who would not put herself in the "faith camp," claims that "being celibate for three months has given her a more spiritual sense of life. She is convinced the energy she might once have put into sex and boyfriends is now focused elsewhere." Good for her!

Not Only for Christians

So is celibacy strictly a Christian phenomenon? No, observes Fowler. "Outside Glasgow's central mosque, boys in traditional Islamic dress play football while their veiled mothers wait for them in the car park. Inside, a group of young men who call themselves 'the circle' have arrived for their weekly meeting to discuss the Koran. Those who are single do not have girlfriends and expect to have arranged marriages. Those who are married remain celibate during Ramadan between sunrise and sunset, and consider adultery a crime worthy of stoning."[3]

So "purity in a single life" is not some Christian's intellectual property. But to *be* a Christian requires purity in single living. Sadly, we are having to look harder today to find that standard.

Celibacy isn't just a "Christian" phenomenon.

If it is so hard to remain single and pure, not only in physical expression but in thoughts, character, and relationships in general, what should singles do? "It is better to marry than to burn with passion," the apostle Paul instructed.[4] So for generations, young men have stepped into marriage to escape the fire, only to find another heat burning at their core. What were they to expect? They were escaping the temptations of lust rather than developing the strength to conquer them. And without that strength in a marriage, affairs are imminent.

But that's just the men, correct? No! In most circles, men have certainly secured the role of sexual predators on the run, but women have fought for their right for flight as well. Just take a look at the periodicals at the newsstand, where more than one try to mask the stigma associated with women who have had multiple sexual partners. For too long it's been a symbol of "strength and virility" for a man to have many women in the parlor of his history. In fact, the greatest king in the history of Israel accumulated many wives. No, I'm not describing Solomon. I speak of his father, David. It was this accumulation of wives, by the way, that was David's initial sin against God's instruction.[5] This sin gained strength until it consumed David and led him to seduce Bathsheba, a married woman. Ultimately, David's lack of self-control led to many deaths and further division within an already war-torn kingdom.

It's not okay to have many wives—or lovers. Period. The innate drives in man grate against it. Why are most singles so curious about how many sexual partners the person they are dating has had? Part of that may be competition. But it's also the God-given longing to be solely connected as *one*.

Glamour magazine featured an entire article by writer Lynn Harris to advise women who are questioned by men about the number of their sexual partners. She quotes "specialists" in sexuality, specifically Paula Kamen, author of *Her Way: Young Women Remake the Sexual Revolution*. "Today, women see their number more like an astrological sign than as a reflection of their morals," says Kamen. "As in, 'I'm a nine, which means I'm bold yet circumspect.' So the real question isn't, 'What's your number?' it's 'Does your number reflect the way you see yourself (or the way you'd like to)?' Most women say yes."[6]

In efforts to make themselves feel better about their history and sexual experiences, many try to amplify the positive. Paula Kamen continues her report: "'I don't have an issue with my current number, which is 27,' says Karen, 32, a scientist in Washington, D.C. 'I don't think I'd have as much confidence if I hadn't experienced the things I have.' It all adds up to a woman who's comfortable with her sexuality."[7]

My heart breaks for Karen because 27 also represents a number of noncommittal moments. She's been used and not committed to. Her decisions to have sex also place her in a category of high risk for physical pain and even death (more on STDs later). And just because someone doesn't currently feel regret doesn't mean that, given time, regret won't be a natural response.

> All the sexual conquests in a single's life will never measure up to those breathtaking moments married couples regularly experience.

The truth is, all the sexual conquests in a single's life will never measure up to those breathtaking moments married couples regularly experience. In that same issue of *Glamour* a married woman shared her "number"—one. She was a virgin when she married at age 18, and she had been married for 12 years. This attractive, healthy-looking blonde had practiced abstinence as a single and now reports on the bliss of married sex: "'I've had more sex than most of my single friends, and I've been with only one person,' affirms Hillary happily, a 30-year-old lawyer in Canada who has been married for 12 years."[8]

In contrast, a woman pictured holding a sign displaying the number 43 purposefully posed with the wind blowing her brunette hair across her face, thus hiding her identity. I wonder . . . why? Is it pride or regret?

The *Glamour* writer's own bottom line when it comes to connecting with so many men? Ms. Harris tells you straight out: "When I meet the guy who makes me want to quit counting, I'll do so without regret." But when she finally does meet him, perhaps she'll do so with regret because she wishes she'd have waited and had higher standards until he came along. And maybe he'll be wishing the same thing too.

Whose Face Is It?

Of course men and women alike want to be with someone who is sexually stimulating and exciting. But a man also wants to be certain that when he is with someone (especially if he is considering the long-term relationship of marriage), that he is the *source* of that excitement in the bedroom. It's important for him to know that it is his face you are picturing in moments of ecstasy. More so, it's very important to him that it is *his face* you envision when thinking back to the best sex you've ever had.

What if God wants me to be single forever?

The same *Glamour* article also quotes New York City psychotherapist Sharyn Wolf, author of *Guerilla Dating:* "If your number is five, he might freak out because he can envision their faces. If it's 55, he might freak out because he can't." And a woman feels the same way about a man's "number."

This is why marriage is so powerful. If you've waited until marriage to have sex and you've only been with your spouse, whose face but theirs will come to mind? It is a *pure* image indeed!

Single Until . . .

But what if God wants me to be single . . . forever? That question has terrified many. It may help to place that question with these as well: *What if*

God calls me into the ministry? Or, *What if God calls me to be a mission-ary and live in poverty?* Now, none of those callings are negative. But if God is *not* calling you to those, they will sound awkward or have a nega-tive slant. You see, God gives us the desires of our hearts.[9] As long as you place him first, your heart will settle into a rhythm of life, and the choice or calling God gives you will only be one you desire: single or married, ministry or not, mission field or homeland.

It reminds me of couples who discussed my remarriage following the death of my first wife, Evon. "I don't think I could ever remarry," they say to me. "Good!" is my only reply. For them to be comfortable with the idea of marrying someone other than the spouse they are currently mar-ried to is perverse. Only when their life path crosses that bridge is that op-tion available to them. And only then is it viable to be comfortable thinking that way.

If God wants you to remain single for the rest of your life, it will not be a problem for you. Your comfort with that life choice will be an inspi-ration to many!

But loving and connecting are not to be equated with being married (although if you *are* married, I highly advise love and connection!). Our own teens desire this connection and love.

In chapter 9 I'll share about the importance of love and connection between teens and their parents. In that context I discuss it as a protec-tive measure preventing them from drug and alcohol abuse, sexual activity, and other be-haviors. Here, however, I want to discuss a teen's basic need for love as an unmarried in-dividual. In fact, all of us, no matter what age or stage, have these needs. And the meeting (or not) of these needs has largely shaped us to be who we are relationally.

> **The greatest single need any person has is to be loved.**
> —Author Unknown

True Intimacy

What exactly does the word *intimacy* mean? We see intimate apparel sold in stores. We see an intimate kiss portrayed between two unmarried peo-ple in a movie. As a Christian, I work hard to develop an intimate relationship with my heavenly Father. I'm intimate with my wife, too, and I hold my kids' faces in my hands in the most intimate of ways.

So if it's not clothes and if it's not confined to married couples or even earthly relationships, just what *is* intimacy? I learned the hard way, when I removed my late wife from life support. As I walked into Evon's room, I saw my withered bride on the respirator. In the same way that I talked with my daughter Ashli before she died, I began to speak to Evon. Whether she could hear me or not, I do not know for sure. But I think so since a tear streamed down her face. It was the most intimate experience we'd ever had.

You see, intimacy isn't about bodies. It's a soul-to-soul connection. The depth and expression of love I shared with my bride before she departed for heaven was genuine. And intimacy is this connection.

Every human being craves intimacy. Have you ever heard someone say, "We fell out of love"? Baloney! You never fall in or out of love. If you fall into something, it's usually a trap or a hole! No, you grow love. And when you remove intimacy from a growing relationship (remember, that soul-to-soul connection), your love becomes routine action. Feeling flees first, followed by a sense of caring.

Intimacy isn't about bodies. It's a soul-to-soul connection.

Who can show us what intimacy is, more than our intimate God? After all, he made us. And he loves to connect our soul with his; it's why he sent his Son, Jesus, to die for us. Jesus' death and resurrection paid the price for our failures, washing us clean from our past. Once purified, we can again connect our hearts to the heart of our Creator. Now *that* is an intimate connection! For that is how you were made and why God longs for you to know him. He already knows you, and he is in love with you!

Intimacy is crucial to families too (we'll talk more about this later). The soul-to-soul connection between moms and dads must be authentic and vulnerable. True intimacy allows the other person to roll up his or her sleeves and reach into the private recesses of your life. Your spouse may not be pleased with what he or she finds in those secret places, but because love is based on commitment, he or she will love you regardless and not reject you. That acceptance and intimate connection is vital to moms and dads remaining together.

Children need intimacy too! "Intimacy for younger children is much easier since they are less inhibited to reveal themselves," writes Dr. Margaret Meeker, a Christian pediatrician who has spent her medical practice discussing issues of health, sexuality, and emotional development with children and teens. "For example, toddlers cry easily ('I am afraid') and readily hug ('I need affection'). Parents see the emotion (fear, for example) revealed, determine that the child's need to have his fears calmed is real, and thus embrace him by giving him a hug."[10]

Oh, but let's talk about teenagers. When children mature into teens, it gets much more dicey! As teens are growing into adults, they crave freedom and individuality. However, they never relinquish their need for intimacy. No human ever does. So how do we navigate this turbulent time and stay connected, soul-to-soul? In her book *Restoring the Teenage Soul,* Dr. Meeker gives poignant insight.

> By the time adolescence creeps in, however, enough rejections have occurred over the years that teens raise their defenses and forbid certain parts of their selves to be revealed again, lest they feel painful rejection once more. Intimacy requires vulnerability. One cannot be received if one is not first opened and revealed.
>
> Thus, the first part of intimacy requires a sense of willingness on the teen's part to avail herself to being seen, to being opened for scrutiny. When the opening takes place ("I will allow you to see this part of who I am") and she has a pleasant experience ("You like what I have shown you"), intimacy has occurred.
>
> When children have pleasant experiences of connectedness and intimacy with parents and significant older adults, an increased sense of scrutiny and identity begins to emerge and flourish. But when they experience disconnection on the receiving end ("You don't approve of who I am and fail to embrace me") they are emotionally thrown off balance. [11]

This off-balance reaction causes teens to withdraw. They isolate their souls from you to ward off any future pain. Usually, if they get hurt but that pain only rarely occurs, they will reach out to you again. But if they continue to receive messages that say, "We don't approve of you and therefore don't accept you," it causes damage that cuts to the soul. And it's damage not easily forgotten or forgiven.

Parents, I know you love your teen. You wouldn't be reading this if you didn't care. But do your teens know that? I cannot overstate how vital your role is in their lives! They are surrounded by powerful influences, but when it comes to healing their soul, the restoration is in your hands. You can pray for them daily, but if you don't build true intimacy with them, your prayers are in vain. God wants you to connect soul-to-soul with them—just as he does with his children.

Sadly, I meet teens every day who do not have this connection at home. It's easy to find the lost heart of a teen when you speak about family and acceptance, as I do. Teens share openly with me about parents they love. They also vent when they feel disconnected. But that venting isn't always verbal. Sometimes they will go looking for that intimate connection missing from their fathers or mothers. In searching for the message, "I love you just as you are and want to embrace you," teens will often find others with unhealthy motives, whose actions seem to offer the missing connection. And in such turbulent times, teens may make decisions that will affect the rest of their lives.

> **Children need their parents more than anything we could buy them.** —Author Unknown

The longing for connection affects all of us. Why do you think we find magazines with sexual messages on the covers in grocery stores? Yes, sex sells, but it's more than that. Such ads appeal to our deep, heartfelt longing to connect with another person. It's how God wired us, from the very beginning when he created Adam in the first Garden. But when that connection "port" inside our souls refuses to risk rejection again, we move away from the deep intimacy for which sex was created. Making it more physical than holistic, we struggle to reduce the powerful multidimensionality of sex. To protect our hearts from getting broken, we refuse to acknowledge that sex is anything more than physical fun. In fact, we'll even allow someone from a major magazine to photograph us holding a whiteboard with the number of our sexual partners. It's all fun, it seems. Fun until we are alone . . . again.

So singles journey down this lonely path, hoping for a connection that completes them. They long for someone who fits their emotional, recreational, cultural, and family qualifications. One young lady I met in Tampa even uses a spreadsheet to evaluate the guys she meets. An ingenious idea no doubt, as this form weighs all aspects of their character and being. But who can measure up to her ideal?

Common Hot Questions

As single adults and teens look for another with whom to connect, they undoubtedly will court or date someone. In those relationships myriad questions arise. Here are some of the questions they ask me as they're looking for that connection, along with the guidance I suggest.

Q: *Is there a perfect match for me—only one person?*

A: Maybe you're wondering, *What if there is one person God has planned for me, but something happens and we don't connect? If God has only one person for me, my soul mate, can I mess this up and miss him?*

Perhaps it's because I've been married twice, but I personally don't think God is that trivial. I don't believe God has "just one person" for you. (This argument lands us in the theological debate of predestination and free will . . . sigh . . . but just hear me out.) I believe the person that you select to be your spouse is the one God has for you.

A cop-out, you say? Maybe. But the Bible offers foundational truths concerning our daily essentials, such as this promise: "Seek first his kingdom and his righteousness, and all these things will be given to you as well."[12] Another Scripture also guides us to "Delight yourself in the Lord and he will give you the desires of your heart."[13] That means as long as your heart is right and your mind has correct priorities, your decisions will be right.

But how will you know which decision is correct when there are more than one? Or which "date" is a potential spouse? Great questions. Many times when I was dating I found God saying no to me. It wasn't like a voice speaking out loud, but rather a gentle conviction in my gut. *No,*

Doug. Nope, not her. Her neither. Her? No way. Nope. The nos usually came because I myself knew that there were foundational issues between us that were not in harmony. But I also found God saying, Okay. Okay. Okay. Sometimes he lets you choose. And

As long as your heart is right, your decisions will be right.

then if you allow yourself to be guided by prayer, supported by a lot of godly counsel, and you make the choice based on faith, that choice is the right one. For me, it was that way with Evon. Then two years after Evon's death, it was that way with Stephanie.

Q: *I've been sexually active for so long. Why should I stop now?*

A: I understand that you may have very strong feelings for the person you're having sex with. And so many teenage girls and young women tell me, "If I stop having sex, I may lose my relationship with this guy!" But I want you to think about the relationship. How do you know that this guy loves you? You cannot say, "Because he says so," because anyone can just say the words. If you say, "Because he does nice things for me," I would bet he does nice things for others too. So why are you different? If you answer, "Because we've been together so long and it's almost like we're married," stop right there. Dating and having sex is entirely different than the lifelong commitment of marriage.

But if you've already gone against God's law of having sex before marriage, why stop now? Because sin, while fun for a season, is a sowing process. Every sin will reap fruit. The question is, how much fruit or consequences are you willing to bear? If you are single and have been sexually active, stop now—before there is unrepairable damage to your body, your mind, or your soul. You deserve the best, so don't settle for something "less than."

You deserve the best, so don't settle for something "less than."

Q: *How will I know when I've found the right one?*

A: When I was younger, I heard someone say that you'll know when you find the right person. How would you know? I wondered. So I asked the older lady who was my Sunday school teacher at the time. "You'll hear bells!" was her answer. What a crock! How many of you have exited the church doors and smiled at an elderly person when suddenly *DING! DONG! DING!* rang out? So much for the bell theory.

So no, you won't hear bells. But you'll know it's truly love when you do these things: Ask if he loves you, and he responds with "Yes." Ask if he'd die for you, and he responds with "Absolutely." Then, remove from your pocket or purse a piece of paper with an *X* and a dotted line on it and say, "Then sign right here that you'd die for me—you'd kill your single life for me. Marry me."

If he absolutely loses it and thinks you're crazy, you've not found the right one. If he is willing to marry you and add commitment and faithfulness *for life* to your relationship, then you've got yourself a keeper. And don't have sex until you sign that paper.

Q: *How far is too far?*

A: This is a question that singles need to decide—before going out on a date. And it's a question that parents need to decide—and then discuss with their teens before they even begin dating. But you know what? Every week I meet singles who haven't set any boundaries for appropriate behavior, so they allow themselves to be led further than they want to go due to the passion of the moment. And every week I meet thousands of teens whose parents have not given them any direction, so the teens are deciding the answer to this question on their own.

Before setting a limit or a standard for yourself or your teens, my suggestion to you is this: Read this entire book first. Some of the

> **The question isn't "How far can I go?" It's "How far can I go until *what?*"**

information you'll come across in this book may change your perspective.

But for now, in addressing this answer we must first address the *question.*

The fact that the question is even asked shows skewed thinking and improper intent. The real question singles want to ask here is, "How far can I go?" They want to know how sexually involved they can get. Moms and dads, answer this with a question: "How far can I go until *what?*" In other words, have them define what "too far" is. Maybe it's pregnancy. Then vaginal intercourse without *guaranteed* contraception is out, if that is your only concern. But what about sexual diseases or infections? Then genital contact of *any kind* should be avoided. (For more on this, see chapter 7, "The Real Facts about STDs.") If your concern is date rape or uncontrolled sexual arousal, then prolonged kissing and caressing should be deterred. Maybe they don't want to have a sexual addiction or to be continually bombarded by sexual thoughts (no, men do not think about sex every four seconds, as so many sources claim). Then pornography, as well as many television shows, movies, and music must be discarded. And mental self-discipline is required.

Do you see where I'm headed with this? Some of you are shaking your heads, thinking these standards will be impossible. But I'm here to tell you that the teenagers I speak with all across the country want to know how to manage these issues. They want to know what happens if you only have oral sex but not penile/vaginal intercourse. They may already be involved in sexual activities that are not listed as "sex" but still have serious consequences. So simply saying "Just say no" will never work. "Don't have sex" doesn't work either, since often we parents have never defined what *sex* is. All of this needs to be done before you can tell them "how far they can go."

Simply saying "Just say no" will never work.

When I'm asked, I'm willing to share my standard. I do it publicly in schools all the time. And as I do so, I realize that my 10-year-old daughter Brianna will soon have a boyfriend who will wonder, *How far can I go? Where is the line that I should never cross?* In the context of sexually transmitted infections, I say in powerful terms that the line you should never cross is . . . the tan line! Yes, that's right, don't cross the tan line. Because if the sun doesn't touch it, *nobody else's son better touch it either!* Of course, the teens in my audience laugh, and the girls applaud. But the answer is simple: To prevent sexually transmitted disease and pregnancy, there should be no genital contact of any kind.

There's a line you should never cross—the tan line!

Is that the only line? Of course not. But "the tan line" is a simple concept to understand and remember. However, there are other lines that can affect us much more deeply. We'll address those in later chapters.

Q: *What about masturbation?*

A: Can you believe we have to discuss this? This isn't devotional reading for Grandma! However, in seminars about sexuality, this is the most-asked question by Christian teens. So moms and dads, you have to address it.

What is masturbation? Simply put, it's self-arousal that can bring an individual to sexual climax (yes, you'll have to explain that too). Can masturbation be harmful? There are quality Christian leaders who disagree here, but I think you need to define again: Harmful to what? You cannot get an STD from yourself, so in that context, it's safe. And contrary to rumor, you won't go blind or grow hair in strange places from this either. But masturbation does have a powerful effect on the human mind, because it is the mind that must be fully engaged to bring about climax.

One religious writer and youth worker wrote that this activity, if done while focusing on God, can be an act of worship. "If the thought life is kept under control, the act becomes an experience of blessing from the Lord, rather than a shameful one. The sin doesn't come in enjoying the experience, but rather in abusing a gift that a loving and gracious God has given."[14] His theory is that since the mind is required for sexual release, just focus on pure things and thereby remove the sin and its associated guilt.

I appreciate his endeavor, but I'm a realist. I don't believe a young man is going to masturbate while thinking about Jesus in any pure fashion. Masturbation requires the mind and body to work in sync while entering stages of sexual arousal. When someone masturbates, unique chemical reactions occur within the mind. This is what makes it feel so good. Dr. Douglass Weiss, a sexual addiction counselor, explains the neurological activity. To set the stage, Dr. Weiss reminds us of the behavioral training of Pavlov's dogs.

When Pavlov's dog heard the bell and anticipated the reward, a neurological response was triggered and the dog salivated, preparing his body for food. The human male brain goes through a similar process when a man desires sex. During sex, chemicals called *endorphins* and *enkephalins* rush to the excitement center *(preoptic neuron)* of a man's brain, filling it to the highest possible level. The result is a "reward" of sorts. . . .

The *preoptic neuron* is the section of the brain where excitement and risk are experienced. Men who take risks such as skydiving, bungee jumping, or deep-sea diving utilize the same part of the brain as sex does. However, sex, by far, produces the greatest chemical release, making his brain and body feel their absolute best. That's why men love sex and why it's so appealing. . . .

Critical to a man's sexual success is understanding that whatever he *looks* at while having an ejaculation is what he will sexually connect or "glue" to. Whatever his eyes focus on when he sexually releases—a person, image, or object—will become etched in his brain as a photographic attachment toward that person, image, or object. I call it "sex glue." After a period of time having sex with the same person, when he sees her, he is going to feel attached to her.[15]

So here's the application and answer to the question. God created the process of sexual stimulation and climax for a reason. It was for husband and wife. If your child masturbates, he is having to create some visual image. And at the point of climax, he will begin to bond to that image. That can be detrimental to him down the road.

> **God created the process of sexual stimulation and climax for a reason.**

Think of it this way. Have you ever been sitting with Grandpa before the Thanksgiving meal when Grandma rounds the corner carrying hot buns, and Grandpa looks at her, elbows you, and says, "Isn't she hot?" "Grandpa!" you shout. "Not before the turkey!"

Well, Grandpa wasn't referring to the elderly woman your eyes see.

He was referring to the woman he is bonded to in his mind. And how many times do you think that bonding occurred in a 40-year-old marriage? (Go ahead, do the math!) That's a lot of connection. And that's why God created this neurological response, so that we'd bond with our spouse. When I travel away from my wife and kids today, I meet some very beautiful women. Certainly, they're attractive . . . but none of them is my wife. Stephanie and I have a connection that's both conscious and psychological.

When men or boys masturbate with images in their heads of women from next door, from magazines, or from Web sites, they begin to bond with that image or the multiplicity of images. They can also bond to images of violent sex with leather, blood, whippings, or defecation. Even if they think of an image that's not human, they can develop a sexual bond there also. If we encourage teenagers to masturbate and do not fully address these issues of image bonding, it can affect them powerfully and negatively later on.

Take your average newly married couple. During the first two years or so there is a megaboost of sexual activity. This is where the bonding is to occur, without issues of the past. Then the sexual activity plateaus into a regular schedule that needs to be comfortable for both. But if the man has masturbated for decades, what effect have these images, which have been etched into his mind, had? After a while, his wife no longer fully pleases him. While he can usually get aroused, he's beginning to find that he cannot fully climax. So he closes his eyes and thinks of someone (or something) else. Now, I have to ask you, is he truly making love to his wife?

So is it okay to masturbate? You're not going to get pregnant or an STD if you are alone (although masturbation with partners touching you is still dangerous). If you are married, I see no harm in masturbating so long as it is your spouse you think of and your spouse has consented. Is it a sin for a single person to masturbate? Only if you lust—and only you and God know if that is your true motive.

After sharing this with a very handsome single man in his mid-thirties, he asked, "Is there any hope? Can you get better?" I smiled and reassured him that there indeed *is* hope! Dr. Weiss discussed personally with me various therapies he uses with sexual addicts. It takes a lot of work and determination for those who want to reverse the bonding damage from their pasts. But it can be done—and is done—all the time.

Q: *Can I start over? If so, how do I start over?*

A: Many teenagers and single parents have asked if it's possible to start over once you've already been sexually involved. You will read it in every chapter here, but let me say it clearly up front: You can start over *right now*. Millions have done it, and so can you.

Some people call this *secondary virginity,* but to me that feels as if those people are coming in second place. I like the term *renewed virginity* for those who've been sexually involved and have recommitted to being sexually abstinent until marriage (or remarriage). Renewed virginity affirms that men and women have renewed their commitment toward purity.

> **You can start over *right now*. Millions have done it, and so can you!**

After speaking at Bear Creek High School in Lakewood, Colorado, the week of its prom, a young man approached me. "Mr. Herman, you talked about how those who had given away their virginity could start over."

"Yes, that's right," I replied.

"Well, not everyone has given their virginity away. Some of us, like myself, lost our virginity and it wasn't our choice."

My eyes burned and watered slightly as I reached out to squeeze this young man's hand. "You are right. And I'm sorry I didn't address that directly. I'm sorry that you had no choice in that incident. But you still have a choice to start over."

He squeezed my hand back and smiled. "Yes I do," was all he said before thanking me and turning to leave.

Perhaps as you are reading this right now, your eyes are wet like mine. If someone stole your virginity from you, let me say first how sorry I am. You didn't deserve that. Even if you may have been dressed a certain way, flirted, or simply trusted a relative or friend, what happened to you was not your fault. "Why then?" you may ask. "What caused them to do that?" Their action is the result of sin in this world. God gave each one of us the power to make choices, and sometimes people make very bad, very evil choices—such as what happened to you, without your consent. What that person did was very wrong, and you are not to blame. You did not cause that person to make that choice. But just the same, you feel used. And here you are now, reading and wondering if you too can start over. Is it possible to feel clean again when you've felt "dirty" because of what happened? My face breaks into a smile as I share this with you: Yes, you can! Today you have the power to make a choice, and God can help you stay strong in that choice!

Many people are asking, "But how can I start over?" They wonder if God really wants to get his hands dirty, just by touching them. But you need to know that no matter how you lost your virginity (whether it was your choice or not), God stands ready to embrace you, just as you are. He doesn't want you to try and clean yourself up first. So when you find yourself feeling rotten, unwanted, and dirty, ask God to join you right where you are, in the muck. For only God can give you true love and acceptance. As the Bible says, "God demonstrates his own love for us in this: While we were still sinners, Christ died for us."[16] That means cleaning is God's job. Your job is just to be honest. That means God wants to embrace you and clean out the corners of your life. If you find yourself involved in pornography or besieged by impure thoughts, don't run from those thoughts and then, once removed from that sin, pray to God. No, right in the middle of that sin, when you realize what's going on, call to Christ to enter into that setting with you. Ask him to embrace and purify you. Allow yourself to be honest with him; he already knows what's going on anyway. And he's waiting for you to connect the broken part of your life with the true life he offers you.

Today God offers you a fresh start. But you have to take it! You can start over by spending time talking with him honestly. You can read encouraging Scriptures that share how great God's love is:

For great is your love, higher than the heavens;
your faithfulness reaches to the skies.[17]

I will sing of the Lord's great love forever;

with my mouth I will make your faithfulness known through all
generations.
I will declare that your love stands firm forever.[18]

You can take three simple steps to change your lifestyle: You can throw away your pornography, delete your impure Internet sites, and change your e-mail address. If married, you can focus on your spouse. Gaze into her eyes during climax to begin bonding again. You can ask God to forgive you, and you can experience the freshness of a forgiven soul. Then you will finally connect soul-to-soul with God.

As you regain this soul-to-soul connection with God and set out on your own path to a Pure Revolution, you will be better equipped to help today's teens—like the teens in your home, in your school, in your church, in your community. Like the teens I meet every week who are crying out for love. Teens who may die emotionally and physically without the benefits of a Pure Revolution.

Craving Love

The results of today's disconnected society are clear. "We are a culture craving love," says Dr. Meeker. "A culture trying harder and more frantically to experience love with emotional depth and stability. We try so hard that we divorce and remarry, see the right counselors, and become involved in church and self-help groups to find help in receiving and experience love."[19]

What's really going on? I think we refuse to be dependent or reliant on others; we don't want to acknowledge our need for love. So in order to remove ourselves from the innate desire to receive, many of us struggle to remove the "receiving factor" of the equation. We trivialize sex, making it non-emotive. And by doing so, we violate the very core of how God made us—as beings who crave community and unconditional love.

Why do we crave community and unconditional love? Because God created us that way!

As parents, you will see this innate longing played out differently in the lives of your children. "I worried so much about the wrong things," said a stepmother of a 17-year-old. "I worried about him doing things the right way and meeting *my* expectations rather than simply accepting him and loving him. I realize now that I should have shown him my heart first. That I loved him unconditionally. That nothing he did or didn't do was going to change my love for him. That that belief was solid . . . before I worried about him doing something a certain way. I'm working on that now with him, but I need to get a handle on that for my younger children."

Dr. Meeker said it well:

Girls . . . are more relationally oriented. They need relationships with girlfriends and boys (as friends), and frequent verbal conversation is their usual medium for love expression. Hence, that's why we see extra phone lines in the homes of teen girls. Talking is an expression of love for them, and the arena for the discovery of self-perception. Conversation for teen girls is extremely healthy since it's often a place where love is returned.

Teen boys, on the other hand, may be more pragmatic and service-oriented in their expression of love. Wired with less relational needs, they may extend love to parents, friends, or girlfriends by mowing the lawn, finishing homework on time, hanging out together, or giving gifts. Their discomfort with [physical touch] renders them less likely to touch or hug a parent. As a matter of fact, *boys may outwardly disdain physical touch but inwardly crave it.*

Parents, please, keep hugging them, even if you feel they lack any interest in being touched. Astute parents can usually discern differences among children regarding their particular style of giving love. This requires objectivity, time, and intuitive observation, but finding your teen's particular manner of love expression pays off.[20]

And pay off it will, as your teen matures and discovers that love isn't just a feeling but a behavior. When teens feel loved, it's easier for them to feel, think, and then separate their feelings from their behavior. Parents,

know that going through this process will never be easy, for it will require a willingness on your part to allow and to help teens struggle with
hard emotional and intellectual issues and
sort out how one impacts the other. But it's
well worth the time and effort in getting a teen
on the road to "whole health." And it's the first
step for them to join you in a new perspective on life that's a Pure Revolution!

Love is a continual journey, not an arrival.
—Author Unknown

pure **identity**

imagine growing up in the Garden of Eden—a place that did not know the boundaries of shame and guilt. Eve never had to look at Adam and say, "I have nothing to wear!" She never had to get a tummy tuck or a BOTOX injection. She was happy with how she looked—and so was Adam. Adam didn't need to go to the gym to stay in shape. They didn't need to keep up with the Joneses or with the latest trends. And when they looked at each other, they saw beauty.

You see, Eden began in innocence—and so did the human race. Without sin, shame and guilt had no foothold. Everything was perfect and good. Relationships could be built without pretense or selfish lust. Issues that mattered were issues unseen—those of the heart. There was no evil. Nothing was twisted.

> Eve never had to get a tummy tuck or a BOTOX injection. She was happy with how she looked—and so was Adam.

This was our origin. Our birthplace. We began in perfection and purity. But if this was the original blueprint, then what went wrong? How did the beauty of sex become a marketing tool? Where did all these diseases and emotional daggers come from? Who let the evil in?

"Twisted" Enters

It's not the purpose of this book to delve into a deep study of theology and whether evil was created or God allowed it to be chosen, and if he did, where it came from. But it *is* important to realize we live in a world that is not right—a world that is not God's original intent.

Think about it this way. In Eden the world was beautiful, perfect. Adam and Eve's identity was never based on how they looked or what they did to fill the hours. Instead, they knew who they were because of *relationships*. Adam and Eve knew they were not the Creator. But looking inside themselves, they could see the fingerprints of God. They realized that all creation existed because of his mighty handiwork. Their identity flowed from an inner spiritual river that found its source in the heart of the Almighty.

But in today's world all that has changed. Now our identity is based on what we do, where we live, what we own, or whom we associate with. And what happens when these temporary sources are compromised or stripped away? We feel incredibly lifeless and shallow. But rather than turn to the author of our hearts, we work all the more to be the best, get the best, look the best, or know the best. Our society has become performance based. So what caused this change, this fall from innocence?

There's someone I want to introduce to you. I call him "Twisted." But beware—I call him that for a reason. Without a doubt, I believe Twisted exists today, and he's busily walking the earth. His work can be found at the apex of Eden's change from beauty to ashes. While he has no creative power (there is only one Creator), he can certainly distort what is good. Twisted is our enemy and the craftsman of the ash we slough through in our life's journeys.

Evil is here because man chose it (we'll talk more about this in chapter 3, "The Great American Love Story"). And man chose it because Twisted presented an alternative of "forbidden fruit," in contrast to the good that enveloped all of creation.

The choice of our foreparents has created a ripple effect that we feel the reverberations from even now. It's not hard to recognize that something is not right in this world! As I said in *What Good Is God?:* "Regardless of your definition of good or evil, bad is definitely on the rampage. If humanity carries the responsibility to care for Mother Earth and all the life she has birthed, shouldn't this be a happier place? If the 'force' within us is good, its power has somehow been short-circuited."[1]

We live in a world of ashes. And ashes are not what God originally wanted for us. But he has allowed it for a time. Until that time comes to a close, you and I need to fight against the wiles of Twisted and help others as we rediscover beauty and perfection.

The "Forbidden Fruit"

In many ways, it's still a battle about "forbidden fruit." When I speak to teens about sexual activity and ask them to postpone any sexual involvement until marriage, I receive a variety of responses. Many love the empowerment that comes from promoting the values of virginity. But some feel they have a *right* to be sexually involved, and to deter them would be discriminatory. How dare someone—even God—forbid sex before marriage? It's unconscionable!

This "forbidden fruit" isn't only for singles and teens. It can often tempt those who are married away from their spouse. Divorce rates resulting from marital infidelity reveal the powerful draw of someone who is "off limits."

When King David, a man after God's own heart,[2] sidestepped God's plan of marital fidelity and chose to sleep with another man's wife, he caused incredible pain—not only in his own life and the woman's life, but also in his relationships with his children. His action caused warring factions within a country that once had been connected. And those ripple effects are still being felt, millennia later.

Could "forbidden fruit" be something other than sexual in nature? Of course! Your neighbor's house or car, or even the longing for fame, power, or control could be such fruit. All these things are outside the context of what is rightfully ours, and yet we want them! *If only we can make this fruit available to all without consequence,* we reason. But that cannot happen. *Every* choice has a consequence.

However, such thinking shows that Twisted has made his entrance, leaving an eternal mark on each of us. Our deep inner nature longs for what we cannot have. We know what is right—for the most part—yet still we wrestle with conflicted longings.

Every choice has a consequence.

Is it impossible to overcome this drive of ours? Have we come from our Creator's hand, a marvelous creation "in his own image,"[3] only to fall into the animalism of sensuality? Are we now enslaved to our hunger and sex drives, impotent to control our destiny?

There is one who thinks so. And he works diligently in the lives and agendas of those who long to remove *forbidden* from our language. This being once longed for his own glory to be greater than God's. Cast down from eternity's home, he's now on the prowl, looking for vengeance, poised to damage God's greatest creation. With no creative power, he is forced only to distort what is. And what he offers has captivated many.

Some step into temptation fully aware of the dangerous traps surrounding them. Their overconfidence guarantees future pain. But there are others whose intentions are less defiant. With hearts torn from past wounds, they long to connect with another in purity. Looking for a new start, they try to ignore the consequences sprouting from the forbidden fruit they've already tasted.

Till Death Do Us Part

The wedding chapel is brightly decorated in white roses and lilies. The bridal party is assembled in their room. They tease the 27-year-old bride, Heather, who giggles nervously as she places the white veil over her face. There is no one more beautiful in the building than her. However, inside her mind and soul, there's anything but thoughts of white purity and feelings of calm.

Groomsmen laugh roughly as they tease Johnny, the groom. Some still have headaches from the night before and are looking for more ibuprofen to erase the pain. Others, including Johnny, are searching for ways to erase the memory as well.

As the wedding proceeds, the bride in white and the groom in sharp-pressed black make their vows. Heather has been through this before, and while her every intention is pure, she holds back her insecurity. *Will he cheat on me like Tony did?* she wonders privately. In her painful, two-year marriage to Tony, Heather never had children. She's grateful there was no child to be harmed in such a messy separation and divorce.

Johnny says his vows with all sincerity. He's not a bad young man. At 24, he's a bright salesman who has amassed some wealth. Truly in love with Heather, Johnny is excited about their future. But right behind him, seated in the second row, are his parents—both sets. He watched them divorce when he was 15, and the family's pain has never truly been resolved. Secretly he prays his alcohol use never escalates to the degree his mother's did. It destroyed her marriage and their family. His stomach turns slightly as he and Heather place rings on each other's fingers. *Be faithful to her only . . . as long as we both shall live,* he ponders. He thinks of the many women who have flirted with him, the flirting sometimes leading to other actions. Who would ever imagine that his most current fling, only three months ago, was with Mindy, a sales associate who is now sitting four rows behind his stepmother?

Because of the pain of divorce in both of their lives, Heather and Johnny had vowed never to split. They are certain that getting married and becoming a family will make them whole. And they are excited to add children to their new family.

As Heather and Johnny are pronounced husband and wife, they kiss. Turning to face their family and friends, they make their way to the back of the chapel. Their honeymoon will be a cruise in the Caribbean. As they leave the chapel, however, neither are aware of other facts that will affect their future. Not only have their past relationships and the innocent "flirting flings" begun making marks on their emotional and relational conditions, but physical consequences hide as well, awaiting discovery.

A few months prior to her tryst with Johnny, Mindy the sales associate contracted HPV. Mostly without symptoms, she doesn't even know it herself. But Johnny now carries this virus, and he'll never get rid of it. In fact, he won't even know he carries it for nearly a year. In that time Heather will contract it also.

Heather's marriage to the ever unfaithful Tony has done its harm as well. Pelvic inflammatory disease (PID) has scarred her fallopian tubes and uterine lining. It was caused by the three chlamydia infections Tony unknowingly transmitted to her and the gonorrhea she contracted while in college. Heather will probably be infertile.

Now, as the newly married couple runs through the shower of bird-seed to their car, they are excited. Both are certain their marriage has wonderful joys ahead. However, the sexual choices they made before this day will have tragic repercussions. Johnny and Heather truly have no idea what's in store.

Behind them, inaudible laughter roars through the now vacant chapel. Twisted has struck again, leaving his mark. His demonic joy is again manifest in another couple's pain. What could have been truly beautiful was ruined by cheap fulfillment that didn't satisfy long-term—it only hurt everyone involved.

Shallow Thinking

One of Twisted's favorite things to do is to confuse us about the truth. That includes skewing the truth about what beauty really is. Where can we find true beauty? Think about it this way: Have you ever tried to describe to your friends a person you felt wasn't *physically* attractive at all yet had a beautiful spirit? What did you say? Perhaps "He has such a wonderful spirit." Or, "She has the most wonderful personality!"

Is this a cop-out? I mean, is it skirting the issue of beauty by talking about personality instead? After speaking to countless thousands of teens and adults on issues of character, I've met some people who are strikingly beautiful. But if other people saw them at the mall, most would turn their heads, because these people are not attractive on the outside. So what's the problem? It's not the person who appears unattractive, but it is personal beliefs (aided by the wiles of Twisted) about what is beautiful. We all want to say, philosophically, that "beauty is in the eye of the beholder," or that "we see the beauty of each person." But the reality is that we often fall into Twisted's trap. We don't believe these "truths" enough to make them affect our own lives.

For instance, think about how much time you spend in front of the mirror or in the gym each day. Now think about how much time you spend working on your character and personality, integrating disciplines that produce the "fruit of the Spirit."⁴ Why, you wonder, am I bringing this up? To make you feel guilty? No, because I myself have to plead guilty—and that's why I'm taking a risk here and being honest. Often, I am ashamed to admit, when a physically attractive person walks by, I am drawn. When an unattractive person passes, I hardly blink or I stare for all the wrong reasons. Oh, how I long to be able to see past the exterior to the soul! But it isn't easy.

Recently I saw a movie entitled *Shallow Hal* with some friends. I expected to laugh a lot. But what I didn't expect was to find myself laughing at the expense of overweight characters on the screen. Worse, just three rows ahead of me sat some people blessed with pounds. I know they heard my laughter, and that breaks my heart. The movie presents every viewer with a challenge: What is most important to you? To value someone who is physically attractive yet whose character is shriveled and diseased? Or to value someone whose personality and character are so beautiful that you truly don't care if she is horribly burned from a fire or if she is 250 pounds overweight? If you've watched this flick, you realize that we all have to come to the point where we decide: Do I hug Cadence (the young girl in the burn unit whose face is distorted with scars) or not?

The movie was designed to strike a chord, and it was a direct hit for me. I exited that theater feeling very subdued. I kept asking myself, *What is more valuable for me? And do I act on that belief?*

What about you, as a parent of teens? What is most vital—their appearance or their soul?

What is most vital to you—your teen's appearance or his soul?

An experience with my son Josh brought this question home even more for me. Though my parents were wonderful, Josh is the one who really taught me how to parent. You see, my parents were raising me in the sixties and seventies. But raising a teenager today is far different. When Josh and I walked to junior high orientation as he began seventh grade, I placed my arm around him. "You realize this is weird for me," I said. He only nodded as we approached the ominous building. "I've never parented a junior higher before. And you know I'm going to make some mistakes. You'll make some too. But before we even begin, I want to apologize in advance for trying out what it means to parent a teenager on you."

As I stopped to take a breath, Josh looked up at me and grinned. I said no more but squeezed his shoulder before opening the door. I knew parenting an adolescent had just begun. Now it's six years later, and he's gone through a great deal.

When Josh wanted to grow his hair long and wear baggy clothes, I almost came unglued. That was not at all what I was like, nor was it my idea of how a young man should look. But Josh was not me. After gaining wisdom from Stephanie, Josh and I had a talk.

"What's most important to me, Josh," I began, "is not your appearance but your heart. If your relationship with God is good and your character is okay, then I don't care about your appearance. But as your parents, we still have the right to set boundaries on your clothes." The next year or so we had a long-haired, baggy-pants-wearing, thin young man whom we loved with all our hearts. Since then he's changed his style many times over. (We've never let him do anything permanent or invasive to his body, however. Diseases and other risks are regarded with respect in our home.) Through every style Josh experimented with, we looked beyond it into his heart, and we remained connected there. Our relationship with Josh helped shape my thoughts on loving someone for who they are instead of how they look. And that was a big step for me.

Three other people had a tremendous influence on me as well.

Seeing What's Real

My youngest brother, Dan, was battling a form of leukemia (AML) while my late wife, Evon, and daughter Ashli were battling AIDS. After Dan's second bout and rounds of chemotherapy, Dan, Evon, other family members, and I sat in my parents' living room. At the time, Dan was a senior in high school. Although he had been strikingly handsome as an underclassman, the steroids and chemicals used to correct his leukemia had ravaged his appearance. Initially, no one was willing to go to senior prom with him. Sitting there in his sweatpants and T-shirt, my bald and overweight younger brother eyed me and asked, "Can't they see I'm still me? I'm still Dan! Why can't they just accept me for *me?*" Our eyes watered as he shared his heart. He told how other high schoolers would see him coming and move quickly to the other side of the hall. Some would be laughing until he walked up and then the laughing would stop; they didn't know what to say. Dan was a wonderful man, with real emotions and a beautiful soul. He died eight months after I removed Evon from life support.

Evon shared with me similar struggles. One Sunday evening we were entering the church building where I was on staff as the youth pastor. You could hear the greeter ahead of us welcoming people and asking them about their son's game or their work. When Evon went to shake his hand, the greeter's disposition changed to one of genuine concern. "Evon, you look so good. How are you feeling?"

We entered the building and went into my office. "I'm so tired of this," she said. "I don't always want to talk about how I'm feeling. I know I've got AIDS. Can't they just ask me about Josh or my crafts? Why can't they just talk to me and not always think about my physical condition?" Good questions, indeed.

My Grandma Campbell passed away several years ago. She and my grandfather were dear to my heart. Her husband, George Campbell, was an incredible man, an astute farmer, and a creative inventor. (Go see some of his inventions at the museum in Aurora, Nebraska, sometime!) Old photographs reveal that my grandpa and I resemble each other. After Grandpa died and Grandma was placed in a rest home, my mother and I went to her house to clean it out and help get it ready for sale. While going through a photo album, I came across a black-and-white photo of a beautiful young lady. To be honest, her cute figure was quite sexy, and my heart leaped just a bit.

"Who's this?" I asked my mother.

"Why, that's Grandma," she said.

Yikes! I got a strange feeling from looking at *Grandma?* After laughing it off, I peered at the photo again. I recognized her eyes. Most certainly I could see what Grandpa had seen decades ago.

Later that day we went to the rest home to see her. We entered her room and talked with her for some time. As we did, I drew close and gazed deeply into her blue eyes. Do you know who I saw? The very same person my grandpa fell in love with before the Depression. When I looked past the wrinkled skin, the gray and white hair, and the frail bones, I found the beauty.

> You can't truly "see" someone's beauty until you've spent the time needed to look past all that *can* be seen.

My brother Dan was a beautiful man. Evon and Grandma were beautiful women. They are only three stunning examples of the truth that beauty is never found at a first glance. In fact, I don't think you can truly "see" someone's beauty until you've spent the time needed to look past all that *can* be seen.

Narcissus and Echo

Have you ever heard someone described as *narcissistic?* A mythological story from *The Metamorphoses of Ovid* reveals to us the origins for narcissism.

In this myth a seer is visited by Liriope, a nymph who had bathed in the river where Cesiphus, its god, had seized her in his embrace and seduced her. In time she gives birth to an amazingly pretty son and names him Narcissus. When she asks the seer how long her son will live, his answer is, "He will live long, if he does not know himself." She doesn't understand, but later it will make sense.

By the time Narcissus is 16 years old and fully a man, he has outgrown his pretty looks. Now he's truly gorgeous, with a "perfection that stopped the hearts of tender maidens . . . but none who yearned for him was favored, or even noticed. His pride was icy; his heart, cold."[5] Then one day when he is out in the woods hunting deer, a nymph named Echo hears him. Although she is unable to initiate speech, she can't help answering when someone else addresses her. But she can only repeat the last words she hears.

Having seen Narcissus, she is "struck by his beauty, enamored." She follows "along behind him, going from bush to bush, eager for yet a closer look at this marvelous creature."[6]

"Is anyone here?" Narcissus finally calls out.

"Here," Echo answers.

As they continue this type of conversation, Echo finally teases him into wanting to meet her. Finally, she appears from the woods, approaches, and "tries to embrace him, throwing her arms around his neck, but he flees as he always has. 'Keep away! I'd sooner die than have you touch me.'"

"Stricken, what can she say but, 'Touch me, touch me!' before she retreats into the woods . . . to hide her shame . . . ? She pines, dwindles away, grows gaunt in her grief, and her body wastes away to nothing."[7]

But Narcissus continues on his way, behaving in this manner to all, until someone he rejects petitions the heavens to "let him know how it feels to yearn without hope." One of the gods hears and grants the request.

One day Narcissus discovers a pond, a small and perfect body of water. As he kneels down to quench his thirst, "another thirst is born, an impossible longing for what he sees reflected in the water's surface. That face, that body, he adores, loves, yearns for with all his heart. He is smitten utterly."[8]

Although he realizes the trap and tells himself, *"Get up, turn away, forget it. What you seek, you have. It's merely an image, nothing. The face you see in the pond will be gone the moment you leave,"* he can't walk away. "That thought is unendurable, awful, as if he had contemplated murder."

Realizing there is no way to escape the entrapment of love for his own image, he finally relents, saying, "There's no other or easier way. We'll die with the same last breath." So Narcissus and his image weep together, "his tears falling downward, and the other's falling upward." As he begins wasting away "to a gaunt caricature of himself," Echo feels pity and love. As the stricken boy calls out, "Alas!" Echo gives back his word, along with her own grief. As he weakens further and calls out a last "Farewell," she replies with her own heartbroken "Farewell." And then they both die and descend into the depths.

While this myth is only a fable, the truth is still poignant. Narcissism is simply this: To love or desire yourself so much that even loss or expense to yourself or others around you doesn't matter. And that's one of the traps Twisted would love for you and the teens around you to fall into. He enters the scene once again, causing us to gaze at the forbidden fruit on the tree. "Eat of this and you will become like God yourself!" he offers you. "Your wisdom will increase. Your power and dominance will flourish. All will love and worship you! Eat of this fruit and fall in love with yourself. Worship your own desires!"

And this "worship your own desires" is going on all across our country, including in our schools.

Schoolgirl Discoveries

A few days after I spoke at a school in Tucson, Arizona, a young girl sent me this letter:

> *My name is Audra, and I'm sixteen years old. After the assembly you gave I was talking to some guys about what you had gone over with us and one of them said (the rest agreed), "Well, all he did was make it harder for the guys to get play." I was so mad at him. Of course I said something to him, but it seemed as though he didn't even care. I don't get it. I thought he was a really, really great and caring guy, but now I don't know how to look at him or any other guy. I've always had a hard time with trust. Hearing that comment from such a nice guy made me rethink the way I see guys. I know you said I deserve somebody who will treat me right and care for me, but how do I get over this trust issue?*

Audra had already built a lot of respect for this young man. To be a "really, really great guy" who had displayed moments of caring was attractive, sure. But with my presentation I had hit his area of dominance—his sexual and relational prowess—and shattered it. His reaction to my presentation revealed his true self. This "really great and caring guy" persona was just an image. The truth was, he was all about "getting play" for himself. And his friends agreed. In Audra's eyes, the image died. And she's right—she *does* deserve much more.

Figuring this out isn't rocket science (although I know some rocket scientists who could use this concept!). An eighth grader from Lakewood, Colorado, wrote:

Before you spoke at our school we never really took the time to get to know people for what's inside. We would just look at what was on the outside. We also never realized that in just one night of doing something stupid, we could throw our entire life away. It's great to see that an adult is actually trying to reach out and help us. Your work is very appreciated.

Parents, do you hear that? Teens *want* your involvement. They want adults to be powerful influences in their lives. But first you must change your own responses to the false images and twisted thinking. For even you may unwittingly be addicted to them—and sometimes those addictions can lead to drastic consequences. Just take a look at Rae's life.

The American Dream?

Top NFL player Rae Carruth[9] grew up in the rougher sections of Sacramento, California, without his biological father. As a result, he struggled to find examples of what it meant to be a man and treat a woman with respect. But as he entered high school, this athletic football player had no problem finding a girlfriend. When he met a young girl named Michelle, things got serious.

After graduating from high school, Rae found himself at Colorado University in Boulder, playing football for the Buffaloes. His string of girlfriends continued, even though he still saw Michelle, his girlfriend from high school. Michelle got pregnant when she was 18, only two years younger than Rae. Soon Little Rae was born into the kind of chaos a loving mother can only try to explain. By then Rae had another girlfriend—Amber. Although Amber knew of Little Rae and Michelle, it didn't deter her from wanting to be with Rae. She accepted money from him, birthed his child, and set up a home in Charlotte, North Carolina, where he'd just been drafted into the NFL.

Now in Charlotte, Rae's life was filled with fame, money, and the prestige that goes with being a top NFL player. But Rae was not content with several girlfriends; he wanted more. Among the many he lured to his bed was Cherica—only a year after Amber and Rae conceived their second child—and Cherica got pregnant.

Child support payments only added to the chaos of Rae's life. Due to injuries, his NFL career was beginning to crash. He realized that his finances were going to dry up quickly, especially when he calculated the child support payments he'd be making for the next 18 years for his four children. So he found a way out—at least he thought he did.

After meeting with a few rough characters and sketching out a plan, Rae and some hoodlums stopped Cherica's car on a remote highway. With Rae's car in front, preventing her from driving ahead, another car pulled beside her and fired six shots through the car door and into her pregnant body. As her car rolled onto the front lawn of a nearby residence, she grabbed her cell phone and wheezed out vital information that would be used to convict Rae Carruth of this crime. Cherica died, but the child in her womb lived.

So where did Rae Carruth go wrong? He was surrounded with pretty women who all longed to be in his bed, and he had lots of money. He should have been happy, right? After all, isn't that today's "American dream"—the one promoted on television commercials and in movies? Isn't that what life is all about? What's wrong with a little sex, anyway? Isn't it our "right"?

All this thinking, says Pitirim A. Sorokin, author of *The American Sex Revolution,* leads to a sex-obsessed society, which "unhesitatingly breaks both divine and human law, blows to smithereens all values. Like a tornado, it leaves in its path a legion of corpses, a multitude of wrecked lives, an untold amount of suffering, and an ugly debris of broken standards. It destroys the real freedom of normal love; and in lieu of enriching and ennobling the sexual passion, it reduces it to mere copulation."[10]

> What we obtain too easily, we value too lightly; it is the cost that gives value.
> —Author Unknown

There are dangerous consequences to openly engaging in sex prior to a faithful marriage. But some don't want to know the facts about those consequences. They ignore them, thinking they'll go away. Like Rae Carruth, they hunger for what they cannot have. Yet once that hunger is quenched, they find deepened appetites for more of this "fruit"—and

Twisted laughs harder. His message has come across loud and clear: *The forbidden fruit is ready for harvest. Go ahead. Take as much as you can.* And someone else has fallen into Twisted's trap.

But is this the kind of world we want for our children? A world of broken lives and shattered souls?

I, for one, am willing to shout, "ENOUGH!" Enough lies and pain! Enough forcing men and women to look a certain way to be considered desirable! And I've heard enough of Twisted's laughter as I gaze into the hollow, haunted, frightened eyes of teens or as I read news stories such as the one about Rae Carruth.

It is time that we see, believe, and share the real truth with others.

Does Pretty Always Mean Beautiful?

Pretty isn't always beautiful, but beauty is *always* pretty. When you realize the depth and character in that statement, you are on the road to some amazing discoveries. But realizing that truth is not enough. Your life, attitude, and actions must back up your belief as well.

After I gave a presentation in a public high school, a beautiful seventh-grade girl approached me. Her lower jaw and right cheek were zigzagged with light pink scars. "My friends call me Scar Face," she explained, saying that she had survived a dog attack when she was younger. My eyes watered as I reached out to hold her face in my palms. "Sweetheart," I whispered, "you are gorgeous. Your scars do not determine your beauty. They only tell a story of where you've been. We all have scars—some inside and some outside. They don't determine our future; they only share our history." I paused, then added, "You are very pretty, young lady."

> **Pretty isn't always beautiful, but beauty is *always* pretty.**

Why did I add that last statement? Because I know the difference between *pretty* and *beauty*. *Pretty* is what we see on the outside; it's a standard that varies from year to year and culture to culture. But *beauty* is eternal, spiritual, forever. I had reaffirmed her beauty, but I didn't know if she knew the difference between beauty and pretty. So I touched her scars and showed her that I was not afraid of them and not afraid to be seen talking with her. I wanted her to know I thought she was not only beautiful on the inside but pretty on the outside.

I pray that someday a young man will embrace that same beauty. Then to him she will also be pretty.

Each week I receive many e-mails from teens around the globe. Here is one of the most touching letters I've ever received from a young man. Read it yourself, and see his heart.

> *I've been dating a girl for six months. People who don't see her as a totally gorgeous person physically have asked me why someone who looks like I do would go for someone who looks like her. This upsets me because even if someone isn't the most drop-dead gorgeous person on the planet on the outside, she can be the most amazingly beautiful person on the inside (as I see her). I'm so glad you addressed that topic, because sometimes in high school people get caught up in how they look or act in front of people (mostly their outward appearance) and forget about looking at people on the inside for who they really are. Sometimes I wish people my age understood that better.*

Need I say anything more than a hearty Amen? This wise young man is only 14—a freshman in a public high school in California. But his letter—and many others I receive—prove that teenagers not only want to know the difference between pretty and beauty, they want to learn how to live with that knowledge. The best way to teach that is to integrate it into your own life. And the best way to start is by modeling the following concept daily.

Seeing Inside Out

If you want to teach your kids a concept that will stay with them for a lifetime and inform their decisions, small and large, it's this one: True beauty is wholeness. Why is this concept so crucial? Because until your kids can grasp the importance of being a whole person, they will never have the respect for themselves or others that the Creator wants them to have. They will never be able to experience true love, which begins and ends with much more than just a feeling or emotion. They will never understand that love is like a rose—it must be grown and then nurtured and cherished.

My wife and I discovered this in our relationship while working with flowers. One year I purchased some roses. After removing the plant from the plastic wrapping, I planted the root ball. Above the ground, all that could be seen was some thorny sticks with leaves. Was that a rose? Sure—it just hadn't bloomed yet. In time, with proper nourishment and care, I

> **Love—true love—is a rose that can brighten the gloomiest of days.**
> —William A. Ward

knew the plant would produce beautiful blooms that would come and go, spreading their fragrance to passersby. But that would take some work on my part. The other option would be to cease caring for the plant. If I did that, it would produce no blooms and wither and die.

Teens and parents often think that love is a feeling. But feelings come and go, like the blooms of a rose. True love is like the whole plant of a rose—the root ball, the thorny sticks, and the leaves—which needs commitment and care. Throughout the life of love, feelings (the blooms) will flower, and we should enjoy them. But the bloom is not the whole plant; it is only the fruit. We can kill love (the whole rose plant) by refusing to nurture it, or we can offer it sustenance to keep growing.

If we teach this to our children, they will finally be able to understand that *beautiful* means "full of beauty" rather than "looking pretty." Without that context, any teen will wonder at some time, just like my brother Dan did, *Why won't someone just love me for me, for who I am inside?*

So why not teach your kids the inside-out principle? Be creative, and find age-appropriate ways to show them the inner beauty of others. One example you can use with most children and teens is this: Write a list of people you enjoy being with and why. Focus on their inner-beauty traits.

With your younger children, you may want to plan an awards ceremony, giving homemade trophies with a presentation for their inner-character beauty. Or you could play Barbies with your daughter, as I have, and create an opportunity to teach this principle. We set up a four-couple wedding and had each "bride" and "groom" share why they loved one another—Barbie's figure notwithstanding.

But if you have teens, the best way to get the message across is verbally. Share openly with them why you love them and why you are proud of them. Don't list anything that they accomplish or an exterior quality. Instead, take some moments every week and tell your son, "I love you because you are the most kind young man I've met." Or maybe your daughter's soul needs you to say, "You are beautiful when you sing because I can hear your heart in the music, not just your voice."

As you live out the inside-out message regarding true beauty, you'll begin to see your children even more as God sees them. "Do not consider his appearance or his height," he says. "The Lord does not look at the things man looks at. Man looks at the outward appearance, but the Lord looks at the heart."[11]

So look at your teens through God's eyes instead of through your own fallible human ones. Turn aside from who you want them to be (how often we long for our children to follow exactly in our footsteps, whether in career, personality, etc.!) and allow them to be who they are in all their God-given uniqueness. Most of all, allow your teens to see you model this inside-out, unconditional love as you respond to others at home, at work, at the marketplace, and at church.

You see, it's inevitable that Twisted will continue his battle against our souls. But you, my friends, have a choice. You can entertain the fantasy of a twisted life, drooling (whether consciously or unconsciously) after the fruit beyond your own grasp. Or you can find renewed contentment and health in purity. If you want to help the teens around you, you'll first need to remove anything that is crooked or diseased in your own life. It won't always be easy, but the rewards will last a lifetime. So why not allow God, the grand Gardener, to prune you, making you even more fruitful? For if you do, that fruit of beauty and purity will be manifest in your children's own gardens, now and in the future.

pure **culture**

from the beginning, Twisted has been clever. Too clever for his own good, and definitely too clever for our good. Just listen to the way he weaseled Adam and Eve, the first humans, into choosing to go against God's orders:

> He said to the woman, "Did God really say, 'You must not eat from any tree in the garden'?"
>
> The woman said to the serpent, "We may eat fruit from the trees in the garden, but God did say, 'You must not eat fruit from the tree that is in the middle of the garden, and you must not touch it, or you will die.'"
>
> "You will not surely die," the serpent said to the woman. "For God knows that when you eat of it your eyes will be opened, and you will be like God, knowing good and evil."
>
> When the woman saw that the fruit of the tree was good for food and pleasing to the eye, and also desirable for gaining wisdom, she took some and ate it. She also gave some to her husband, who was with her, and he ate it. Then the eyes of both of

them were opened, and they realized they were naked; so they sewed fig leaves together and made coverings for themselves.[1]

Sure, you've heard this story before. And with ease I could reword it slightly to show you how the fruit can be sexual activity outside of marriage, contrary to God's plan for sex:

"Did God say you must not have sex at all?" the serpent asks.
"Of course we can have sex," Eve replies. "Just not with anyone but our mate, or we will die."

"Did God say you must not have sex at all?" the serpent asks.

Hissing loudly, the serpent then screams, "You will not die! God knows that your eyes will be opened to the wonderful pleasures of sex, and the joys of the flesh would be yours to openly offer to others. You will know others intimately, as God does."

So, created for relationships and intimate connections, Eve makes her move. A strange, new, and dark eroticism moves deep within her as she partakes of this "fruit." Her husband beside her does the same.

Okay, so I might be stretching Scripture a bit. But I'm trying to make a point. After the initial sin of eating the fruit, Adam and Eve didn't get a stomachache. You see, the original temptation in the Garden of Eden wasn't really about food. It was about stepping outside God's boundaries and sinning against him. The aftershocks of what seemed like such a simple act brought lifelong shame and awareness. For the first time in their lives, Adam and Eve realized they were naked.

The original temptation wasn't really about food. It was about stepping outside God's boundaries and sinning against him.

Twisted began his work in that garden, and he has continued it throughout the Bible and all of human history. The purpose of this chapter is to help you understand how Twisted has subtly continued his work and created philosophies that greatly affect not only our world, but you and your teen's daily lives and all the images you see.

The Gods and Sexuality

In the Bible we often read about Baal and the prophets of Baal. Who and what is this god? Alan G. Hefner states in his report that "the word *Baal* means 'master' or 'owner.' In ancient religions the name denoted sun, lord or god. Baal was a common name of small Syrian and Persian deities. Baal is still principally thought of as a Canaanite fertility deity. The Great Baal was of Canaan. He was the son of El, the high god of Canaan. The cult of Baal celebrated annually his death and resurrection as a part of the Canaanite fertility rituals. These ceremonies often included human sacrifice and temple prostitution."[2]

Do you again see the work of Twisted here? Before the birth of Jesus, this cult celebrated Baal's death and resurrection annually. Knowing ancient Scripture and the future impact that the Savior and Messiah would have on human hearts, Twisted presented a "deity," complete with a resurrection story, who required human sacrifice and prostitution.

The Canaanites weren't the only ones who worshiped Baal. The Phoenicians did too. In fact, Baal and his "cohort Ashtoreth, or Astarte, who is equivalent to the Greek goddess Aphrodite, were both Phoenician fertility symbols."[3]

Why is this history important? Why should you care? Because it was important enough for God to have it recorded in Scripture. And when you read the Bible, you need to see the context in which purity fights impurity. Then you'll understand what these other gods are and why God makes mention of them.

When God delivers Israel from Egyptian bondage, he gives them explicit directions as to how they are to act. In fact, in the book of Leviticus God specifically delineates what sexual practices are forbidden and how it should be handled when someone does commit these acts.[4] Why did God do such a thing? Because he was moving his chosen nation into the Promised Land and wanted them to be pure of sexual immorality.

So God told Moses, the leader of Israel, "You must not do as they do in Egypt, where you used to live, and you must not do as they do in the land of Canaan, where I am bringing you." God was very concerned about life and wanted to prevent death. That's why he told his people, "Do not follow their practices. You must obey my laws and be careful to follow my decrees. I am the Lord your God. Keep my decrees and laws, for the man who obeys them will live by them. I am the Lord."[5]

Maybe one reason God waited 400 years before releasing Israel from bondage in Egypt was to give these foreign nations time to repent. But their refusal to do so required them to be completely extinguished. This is why there were so many wars in the Old Testament. God could not build on impurity—nor could he establish a land for the people of Israel and a throne for their future kingdom in the midst of impurity. Idol worship was so enmeshed with sexual perversion that you could not separate the two. There is no middle ground for God. He requires holistic purity, *period.*

But the Israelites didn't take God's stance on purity seriously—at least not seriously enough. In Numbers 25 they stray from God's regulations: they get friendly with the pagan people instead of destroying them, and they end up worshiping the Baal of Peor. This Baal worship by the Moabite and Midianite cults was a "dramatization of sexual acts intended to incite Baal to lust so that he would have sexual relations with Anath, the goddess of love and war, and thus fertilize the land."[6] Twisted had seduced the Israelites, and their involvement in this sexual worship resulted in the deaths of 24,000 people at the hand of their angry God. That makes it pretty clear—yeah, God gets upset about sexual impurity!

> **There is no middle ground for God. He requires holistic purity, *period.***

In 1 Kings 18 we see the prophet Elijah confronting the prophets of Baal-Karmelos ("lord of Carmel").[7] Tired of the Israelites worshiping one god and then the other, Elijah gathers all the people and prophets to Mount Carmel (similar to most high places, or pagan shrines, as in 2 Kings 23:13-15, where most altars of the Baals were established) and shouts out, "How long will you waver between two opinions? If the Lord is God, follow him; but if Baal is God, follow him."[8]

When the people respond with dumb silence, Elijah proposes a power test between God and Baal. So each set of prophets sets up altars and lays their sacrifices on them. "The god who answers by fire—he is God," Elijah proclaims.[9]

The people agree to the test, and the prophets of Baal go first. True to any Baal worship, there is frantic screaming and chaos. Sexual activity mixes with the violence of self-mutilation. All morning the prophets of Baal carry on with these activities, shouting and calling upon Baal to act. But there is no response. About noontime, Elijah begins to mock them. "Shout louder," he scoffs. "Surely he is a god! Perhaps he is deep in thought, or busy, or traveling. Maybe he is sleeping and must be awakened."[10]

My face spreads into a grin as I see the demonic powers held at bay by . . . well, held at bay by the true God! Those perverted prophets cannot see it, though. So they continue their worship and rituals, shout louder, follow their normal custom of sexual perversion, and slash themselves "with swords and spears, as was their custom, until their blood flowed."[11] For the rest of the afternoon until evening, they worship, experiencing spiritual darkness and impotence.

Then Elijah steps in. He calls the people to watch him as his altar, wood, and sacrifice is soaked with gallons of water to make the test even more difficult and the results that much more incredible. Then he prays simply to the true God. An answer comes by fire, consuming the sacrifice, the wood, the stones, and the dust. It even licks up the water from the ditch! After that, the prophets of Baal are executed.

Why do I spend time sharing this story? Because it shows that God has proved, beyond any doubt, that he is far more powerful than any Baal. How exciting to see that, in the context of purity when facing sexual perversion! We must never forget the power of our pure God. Other Old Testament people fought for purity in the face of another impure god named Molech (also spelled Moloch):

> **What we don't remember will happen again.**
> —Sign at Dachau concentration camp

The statue was hollow, and inside there burned a fire which colored the Moloch a glowing red. Children were placed on the hands of the statue. Through an ingenious system the hands were raised to the mouth (as if Moloch were eating) and the children fell into the fire where they were consumed by the flames. The people gathered before the Moloch were dancing on the sounds of flutes and tambourines to drown out the screams of the victims.[12]

What horror to be a follower of Yahweh, the true God of Israel and the only true God, and watch child sacrifice in your nation! (See Leviticus 18:21; 20:2; and the judgment in Jeremiah 32:35.)

The New Testament shows that sexual perversion continued into the Roman cultures and Greek cities. The apostle Paul addresses it in his letters to church groups in Corinth, Galatia, Thessalonica, and Ephesus. The temple prostitutes were still very much a part of worship in these communities. Converts to Christianity who had grown up in that culture's pagan religions knew no other path. God's call to sexual purity and monogamy was new for many in the faith.

All this history shows strongly that God has always wanted to preserve life, especially through the wonderful gifts of sex and sexual expression. But as his original design demanded, it must *only* be between husband and wife in a marriage covenant entered into before God. Perhaps this original design is also why Jesus had to come from a virgin birth. Scriptural prophesies indicated that the Savior of Israel would be born of a virgin.[13] But why a virgin? Why couldn't the Savior come from a young woman who had been sexually active before? Why was virginity so important? Because the birth had to be *pure.* The mother had to be sexually pure. The father had to be purely divine, with no misunderstanding where the seed had originated. In fact, after Mary the mother of Jesus had conceived and spent a few months with her cousin, she returned to Joseph her fiancé. They were married and later traveled to Bethlehem for taxation (this is the beginning of the Christmas story).

> The Bible says Jesus was "born of a virgin," not "conceived by a virgin."

But it's intriguing that the Bible says Jesus was "born of a virgin," not "conceived by a virgin." That means Joseph had no sexual relations with his beautiful young bride until weeks after Jesus was born.[14] Yes, sexual purity and waiting until marriage (or later, in Mary and Joseph's case!) are important. And if "Jesus is the reason for the season," then it is only because he was divinely born of a virgin. And that virginity was preserved how? Through sexual abstinence. Some things (or people) are most assuredly worth waiting for!

How Did We Get Here?

Hundreds of centuries before Christ, nations were enticed into sexual immorality. Since then, wars have been waged over men's love of women, and countless scores of men who dueled to protect the honor of a fair maiden lie rotting in the earth.

Then the Americas were founded and people groups flooded this beautiful land, creating a nation with prominence and power. For the most part, the culture was incredibly family-based and conservative during the 1800s. But then things began to change. It's only when we understand how and why they changed that we can begin to combat those changes in today's world.

Sex O'Clock in America

When a St. Louis newspaper editor observed that the time was "sex o'clock in America," he was reading his cultural clock accurately. After all:

Open sexuality was spreading across the country like wildfire.
Young women were beginning to dress and act provocatively,
shocking their mothers, and aggressively seeking sexual
adventure. Sexually transmitted diseases were spreading to
epidemic levels. Pornography was becoming ubiquitous.
Authorities began teaching openly and explicitly how to enhance
sexual enjoyment while sex education debuted in public schools.
Others advocated for the normalcy of homosexual behavior, the
benefits of cohabitation, open marriage, and no-fault divorce.
Campaigns advocated the widespread use of birth control.[15]

So *this* is the sexual revolution of America. Do you know the date that the above description was originally written? 1913! That means the American sexual revolution occurred long before the famed movement of the 1960s and 1970s.

That editor was not alone in his assessment. In 1914 the arbiter of elite opinion, the *Atlantic Monthly,* lamented "the obsession of sex which has set us all a-babbling about matters once excluded from the amenities of conversation."[16] This is not just two opinions, mind you. One historian chimed in, stating, "Americans in the 1920s became obsessed with the subject of sex."[17] Even the distinguished Harvard sociologist Pitirim Sorokin claimed, "Our civilization has become so preoccupied with sex that it now oozes from all the pores of American life."[18] In 1956 he published *The American Sex Revolution* and noted that in earlier decades "homo sapiens [has been] replaced by homo sexualis."[19] An attack on the family was in full swing as saloons and brothels gained great capital successes, bringing financial motive to the corruption of politics and society.

The White Slave Trade and the Purity Movement

What happened to black slaves early in America's history is unconscionable. It certainly is a dark period in our history. It has made a significant impact on our world today and the relationships between races. However, slavery is not simply a black issue. It can move into other races and classes. For instance, in 1910 Congress halted the traffic in young girls, then noted as the "White Slave Trade." These young "kidnapped or destitute girls were often imprisoned in window-barred brothels."[20]

Together, "religious women and feminists joined forces to encourage a return to virtue, temperance and chastity that would safeguard the institutions of marriage and family."[21] This "virtuous women's coalition," also known as "The Purity Movement," not only targeted this White Slave Trade, but also "prostitution in general, promiscuity, poverty, child labor, drug and alcohol abuse, deleterious food and diet, disrespect for women, unsanitary conditions, and obscene literature."[22]

Looking over that list of targets from early in America's history, it's hard for me to comprehend how some people today are now able to pick and choose which of these vices they want, in order to massage their narcissistic souls or cushion their wallets. Friends, listen. The old adage is still true: *Hell hath no fury like a woman scorned!* If you get angry enough and are moved to action, you *can* make a difference. You *can* bring change! I'll show you simple ways to do that in chapter 11, "Drawing Lines in the Sand." However, in any good revolution, you first need to examine and understand its history before you can explain and change its course.

A Cultural Shift

So how did this overall cultural change from the 1800s to now occur—and why? "The complex history suggests that the sexual revolution has deep roots tied to the economic, cultural, and intellectual changes that greeted the dawn of the [past] century."[23] Since we can't study all these factors in this chapter, I'll give you some key factors that have brought us to the type of world we live in today.

Urbanization and industrialization were probably the most significant factors behind the sexual revolution:

> Nearing the early 1920s, over half of Americans now lived in cities, leaving their farms to work in factories. Middle-class families now lived predominantly in urban America. A young man who used to "come calling" on a young lady used to visit her in her parlor within close proximity of a supervising mother. Now however, urban apartment buildings failed to offer the luxury of a quiet parlor for time alone and fun conversation. Apartment living quarters were so tight with family—immediate and extended—that young couples could not find a quiet corner to visit. Therefore, courting, which traditionally took place in the home, had to take place elsewhere. The growing urban nightlife further facilitated the move of courtship away from the supervised parlor.[24]

With the family unit slowly fracturing and moving apart from rural areas where they had settled decades earlier into urban and suburban communities, the built-in social structure and supervision were diminished, leaving young men and women to rely on their own discipline, which was often untested. Men and women were also working alongside each other in urban companies and factories for extended hours; relationships were destined to develop. With these men and women away from their homes and spouses, their discipline was again tested. Sadly, many failed.

The Teenager and the Date

The old format of a young man calling on a young woman and sitting in her parent's parlor having engaging conversation was now on the outs. Because of those tight urban apartments, men and women would schedule times when they could go elsewhere and get to know one another. These scheduled *dates,* as they were called, became a new form of social meeting. "As a consequence, women were socializing with men under circumstances quite different than the intergenerational, female-controlled home environment provided by traditional courtship. Dating therefore created a new social situation where the young male gained control."[25]

Additionally, the invention and common use of technology and transportation brought extended liberties to these young couples. University of West Florida historian James R. McGovern notes, "The car, already numerous enough to affect dating and premarital patterns, the phone coming to be used for purposes of romantic accommodation, and the variety of patterns at the office or factory, all together assured unparalleled privacy and permissiveness between the sexes."[26]

In the 1920s, dating created a new social situation where the young male gained control.

The concept of the *teenager* wasn't truly formalized until midcentury. But because of renewed freedoms from family oversight, transportation and communication, and the invitation for permissiveness, this societal phenomenon became a galvanized reality. It soon developed a culture all its own. Capitalizing on the exuberance of post–World War II, musicians and marketing execs found in this age group a new source of economic wealth. Thus, the teenager was born and immediately became a target. Today, those crosshairs only target our teenagers with laser-point accuracy.

Moms and dads, do you see this incredible change that shaped our nation to be what it is? Our own parents and grandparents who were born in the first third of the 1900s were only children when this sexual revolution accelerated. The music and dress of that society became normalized for them. While many conservative families would never discuss sex or break marital vows, the initial cultural shift had begun. Parenting styles in American culture were about to be impacted by those parents' own history and previous lifestyles. And I believe Twisted was standing nearby, as he does now, pushing the momentum and whispering the ideas to bring about societal shifts not unlike his handiwork in empires centuries prior to ours.

The flapper personified the sexual revolution's attitudes and behaviors:

> Not to be outdone by the male of the species, the flapper displayed a "devil-may-care" attitude marked by unrestrained drinking, smoking, cussing, and petting. She wore dresses that revealed more of her legs, blouses that covered less of what they were supposed to hide, and sported short-cropped hair. She was unrestrained: she danced close, was freer with her favors, and made up her face in a sexually provocative manner. She was a revolutionary, a pleasure seeker.[27]

She was incredibly "preoccupied with sex—shocking and simultaneously unshockable."[28] The appearance of the flapper was not a huge debut. It morphed, albeit quickly, as a result of the permissiveness coupled with the woman's desire to take control. This sex-saturated society certainly was feeling the impact of its choices; less brides were tying the knot as virgins than ever before.[29] Although prostitution took a huge hit in the 1910s, "the weakening of prostitution between 1910 and 1920 was not the conversion of men to purity; it was the conversion of women to indulgence."[30] Becoming more indulgent and more aggressive, young women were tempting the men equally as much or more than the men were the women. Why should young men look to prostitutes when "the girl next door" would play for free?

Pornography, or "smut" as it was initially called, also played a major role in this cultural shift. Long before *Playboy* debuted in 1953, erotic stories were being published in magazines. *True Story,* which sold 2 million copies monthly, made its publisher a millionaire.[31] From the erotic story, stimulating pictures were introduced, including William Randolph Hearst's *Snappy Stories,* which featured as early as 1914 a swimsuit-clad woman on its cover. The next form of smut was more devious. In an effort to enhance the "arts," publications portraying nude models were created. "This thinly veiled attempt to make ogling into a high-cultured activity appeared in such publications as *American Art Student* and *Artists and Models.*"[32]

Finally, in the mid 1920s publishers cut to the chase and began simply printing the smut under titles as edgy as the rags. Cities were saturated with these publications. One writer reported that "out of 110 publications in a single store, 68 were either out-and-out smut or bordering the line."[33] Was he talking about L.A.? Nope—Steubenville, Ohio.

Four Individuals for "Honorable Mention"

It's unfair to pin the sexual revolution in America on any one individual, or even on a small group. But as we look at history, we can always locate various leaders who stepped up to the plate. The following four individuals added their own fuel to the raging fires of the American sexual revolution. Let's look briefly at each person's background, contribution to the sexual revolution, and the consequences their efforts have left us today.

Henry Havelock Ellis

James Reed, a noted historian of sexual theory, described Henry Havelock Ellis as "the world's leading prophet of sexual enlightenment."[34] In *The Modernization of Sex,* Paul Robinson explains that the two decades from 1890 to 1910 "saw a major transformation in sexual theory." He believes that "the central figure in the emergence of this modern sexual ethos was not Freud, as important as he may have been, but rather Henry Havelock Ellis. . . . Ellis stands in the same relation to modern sexual theory as Max Weber to modern sociology, or Albert Einstein to modern physics."[35]

Ellis published the multivolume *Studies in the Psychology of Sex*—the first six volumes from 1897 to 1910 and the seventh volume in 1927. His "authoritative" studies presented homosexuality as normal, based on his assertion that individuals are born with a sexual orientation rather than choosing it. In addition, he was a fierce critic of traditional marriages and a strong advocate of "trial marriages." He believed that what mattered between two people was the love shared, not a marital contract. "These trial marriages," he said, "are therefore demanded by prudence and caution because they enjoy [the] freedom of being more honest, and therefore disposable, if they are not satisfactory to both parties."[36] He also advocated open marriages, believing that husbands and wives would find it helpful to have open but discreet sexual liaisons with others and many at one time.[37] Thank you, Mr. Ellis, for the introduction of no-fault, unilateral divorce. Your contribution is still being wept over annually by countless thousands of teens with now-broken homes.

As one researcher states, "Even though few know the name of Ellis today, his name was a household word in his lifetime and he had a massive influence on the influencers. We have all witnessed the consequences of his ideas."[38]

Margaret Sanger

When I spoke at a religious conference in a seminar for youth leaders, just mentioning this lady's name got a vocal and diverse reaction. So who is she, and how do her contributions impact your teens today?

Industrialization and urbanization not only changed the method of how young people met and dated; it also changed the concept of and people's attitudes about having many children. In a farming community, more children meant more hands to work the land and therefore a better living. In one sense, it was a form of wealth to have many children. But when tight living arrangements plagued these large families and such great numbers of children could not work the farm to bring in revenue, concepts changed. Large families were now regarded as an economic liability. "The birth control movement also found its motivation in a growing feminism, which valued sexual self-determination and control over their fertility as the means to equity."[39]

Margaret Sanger is the premiere figure in the advent of birth control. She even coined the term *birth control* and advocated that women should "fight for [the] right to own and control her own body . . . to do with it as she desires—and it's no one's business what those desires may be."[40] Competing with birth control movement rival Mary Ware Dennett, Sanger, at the prompting of her lover, Henry Havelock Ellis, chose a more mainstream strategy to persuade the American public. She soon formed her Planned Parenthood Federation of America. As Mr. Reed explains, Sanger became the dominant runner in the birth control movement because she was now "providing social justifications for practices that had once seemed wholly personal and selfish."[41]

While I've been scolded for harshly evaluating Sanger's work, it would be good for my critics to realize that her so-called compassion for impoverished young women, which she displayed by offering birth control, was never based on her desire to create financial relief for the American welfare system. Sure, out-of-wedlock births are a leading indicator of poverty among single women. But Sanger's work was more about a woman's control of pregnancy and birth in order to have the freedom to be involved sexually whenever and with whomever they wished. In essence, her battle was to remove consequence.

> The real battle of Margaret Sanger—the premiere figure in the advent of birth control and the founder of the Planned Parenthood Federation of America—was to remove consequence from sexual choice.

Obviously, her plan has not built *discipline* into the lives of young men and women. Instead, contraceptive business has skyrocketed. Additionally, legalized abortion has produced income streams for many clinics. And with the onset of harvesting fetal tissue, who knows where it could lead? Yes, Sanger had to battle the Catholic Church specifically and the church in general to find ways to make contraception appear moral. "Helping impoverished women" was a nice spin.

Alfred C. Kinsey

Kinsey is the working title of a movie that is said to display the contributions of the "nearly forgotten groundbreaking researcher who conducted a nationwide survey of American bedroom habits in the 40s and 50s." Alfred Kinsey is described by the movie's writer as "the first to talk about what people actually did. . . . He spoke on the prevalence of affairs among men and women, and how your aunt, grandmother and mother masturbated." *USA Today* movie reporter Susan Wloszczyna claims that "though his findings fell out of favor during the latter Cold War era, there probably would be no Playboy or Dr. Ruth without his liberating effects."[42] Indeed, and I will present other developments based in this "nationwide survey" that have so deeply shaped other aspects of our public life, such as teacher training for sex education, why sexual offenders seem to go unpunished while victims have to pay, and the myriad of highly funded organizations that control public thought and information about sexuality in America.

Oh yes, Alfred Kinsey was an influencer. To learn Kinsey's history, it is probably best to begin with his upbringing. He was born in 1894 in New Jersey in a strict Christian home with a father who was very disconnected. As a young man, Kinsey prayed many times for God to give him guidance when dealing with issues like masturbation. But eventually he "was consumed by guilt."[43] He experienced the roaring twenties and the beginnings of the sexual revolution and observed closely as ordinary citizens began to overcome the "state sanctioned (or state ignored) 'commercial vice.'"[44] Soon he became a professor of zoology, and his doctoral dissertation on gall wasps earned him a place at Indiana University.

> Those who control what young people are taught and what they experience, what they see, hear, think, and believe . . . will determine the future course for the nation. —James C. Dobson

But how did a zoologist studying gall wasps become perhaps the world's foremost influencer on sexuality whose peers noted that his name was "mentioned in the same breath with Freud"?[45] While at Indiana University, students asked for a course in human sexuality for those who were engaged, married, or considering marriage. "The university asked a well-respected professor of zoology to coordinate the [marriage course] and felt that Dr. Alfred C. Kinsey, a Harvard-trained scientist known for his . . . exhaustive research on gall wasps, would provide a scholarly perspective to this sensitive subject."[46] Kinsey accepted this class. Due to a lack of scientific data on human sexual behavior and having no formal training in this area himself, he felt he was required to conduct his own research.

His formal sex research, under the cover of the "marriage course," began in 1938: "According to the University's official account, he was asked by the Association of Women Students to create the course. . . . John Bancroft, current director of the Kinsey Institute, . . . states that 'Kinsey's Mission' was to 'striv[e] for a greater understanding of the varieties of sexual expression and a resulting greater tolerance of such variability.'"[47]

Kinsey's research format was to take personal histories of married individuals' sex lives. His problems began when these conservative individuals didn't want to disclose the details of their very private sexual experiences. Kate Mueller, the Indiana University Dean of Women, shared in her interview with Kinsey biographer James H. Jones about her conflict with Kinsey. Concerned girls didn't want to reveal the intimate answers to Kinsey's 350 prepared and memorized questions—which included, for example, a question about the length of their clitoris.[48]

When Mueller insisted that the girls did not have to grant him interviews, Kinsey took his research into places where histories would be easier to access and he could collect them by the thousands. With no one but the inner circle of his associates aware of his work, he removed his studies from mainstream "American bedrooms" and went into the cells of convicted sexual offenders.[49] Those he interviewed were (or had been) married, including 785 who were also "widowed, separated, or divorced." To make it appear that the sample included a large married population, an ambiguous definition of *married* was adopted.[50] Adding to this sample many prostitutes, Kinsey was able "to present sexual promiscuity as 'normal,' including perversions such as sex with animals. Although he excluded 934 black women as unrepresentative of that population, he *included* 31 females who copulated with animals."[51]

Wardell Pomeroy, Kinsey's trusted friend and cowriter, wrote books

Today Alfred Kinsey is considered the world's foremost influencer on sexuality. However, his studies were not from mainstream "American bedrooms." They were from the cells of convicted sexual offenders.

in line with this theme for Planned Parenthood and the Sex Information and Education Council of the United States (SIECUS), which promote bestiality for boys.[52] Additionally, in a 1996 BBC telecast, Hugh Hefner, the publisher of *Playboy,* reported that "Kinsey was the researcher, but I was his 'pamphleteer.' The budding Playboy empire provided early and generous financial support for the Kinsey Institute."[53]

With sexual histories in the thousands (a minimum of 86 percent of the males were sexually aberrant), Dr. Kinsey was able to publish his two works that would shape the instruction, perceptions, and paradigm of sexual understanding: *Sexual Behavior in the Human Male* (1948) and *Sexual Behavior in the Human Female* (1953). The Rockefeller Foundation gave these works phenomenal exposure, funding large publicity and promotion campaigns.[54] Since these publications were perceived as professionally sound research sourced from typical American men and women and directed by a *Doctor* Kinsey, no one immediately questioned the supposed results. Yet all of today's sexuality education instructors in our schools have unwarily been influenced by these perverted "findings." What they've been taught as medically and biologically normal is actually anything but normal.

All of today's sexuality education instructors in our schools have unwarily been influenced by Kinsey's perverted "findings."

If you were to ask people at the Kinsey Institute today about their founder, they would agree with "Pomeroy, Christenson, and Indiana University (where Kinsey's sex-research operations were based) [that] claim that Kinsey was asexual, disinterested in sex, and celibate prior to marrying in 1921."

But in 1997, James H. Jones, a pro-Kinsey biographer *(Alfred C. Kinsey: A Public/Private Life)* who had also received support from the university, was interviewed for a 1998 British television program entitled "Kinsey Paedophiles." In that program Jones asserted:

> There is no way that the American public in the 1940s and the 1950s would have sanctioned any form of behavior that violated middle class morality. . . . Any disclosure of any feature of this private life that violated middle class morality would have been catastrophic for his career. . . . For Kinsey, life in the closet came

complete with a wife, children, a public image . . . that again he preserved at all costs. Kinsey's reputation still in large measure rests upon an image of him that he cultivated during his lifetime . . . the official mystique.[55]

As famed researcher and critic Dr. Judith A. Reisman aptly concludes, "had the public *known* that Kinsey, his team and his male population were sexually aberrant, the popular use of their data to change American law, education, culture and public policy would likely have come to the proverbial screeching halt."[56]

Instead, Kinsey's data is still influencing laws and education today. We live in a culture increasingly hostile to conservative, married, moral families. For decades now those who would stand up for what is right, true, and pure have either been uneducated about the facts or are afraid to speak lest they are attacked by militant sexual deviants.

Mary Steichen Calderone

In 1964 SIECUS was launched at the Kinsey Institute. Its objective was to promote Kinseyan ideology as sex education in schools. SIECUS (which now calls itself the *Sexuality* Information and Education Council of the United States) imprinted the new Kinsey variant standard on almost all sexuality education curricula. SIECUS's early leader, Dr. Mary Calderone (past medical director of Planned Parenthood), was the direct link between Kinsey's university-based research, Planned Parenthood's grassroots outreach, and SIECUS. SIECUS was a "resource center [operating] specialized programs to distribute information about human sexuality [through] learned journals, research studies, training materials for health professionals and sample classroom curricula."[57]

Not only was Dr. Calderone heavily involved in shaping the curricula for our health professionals and school systems, but her testimony also weighed in heavily in the *Roe v. Wade* decision legalizing abortion.[58]

In the 1980s *Time* dared twice to expose SIECUS founder and matriarch Mary Calderone and other sex educators who promoted the Kinseyan attitude of "anything goes," for and with children. "The April 14, 1980 issue of *Time* cited the SIECUS paper on incest, 'Attacking the

Last Taboo,' which claimed, 'We are roughly in the same position today regarding incest as we were a hundred years ago with respect to our fears of masturbation.' Concluded *Time,* SIECUS was part of an academic 'pro-incest lobby . . . conducting a campaign to undermine' the 'taboo against incest' and 'all other sexual inhibitions—the Kinsey Model.'"[59]

And it's not only incest that Mary Calderone wanted her organization to make common. A SIECUS brochure lays out its general goal to marginalize the difference between "sexual intercourse" and "having sex." It suggests "a partial list of safe sex practices for teens could include . . . massaging, caressing, undressing each other, masturbation alone, masturbation in front of a partner, mutual masturbation. . . . By helping teens explore the full range of safe sexual behaviors, we may help to raise a generation of adults that do not equate sex with intercourse, or intercourse with vaginal orgasm, as the goal of sex."[60]

We have seen the strength of this group's success in our schools. In fact, we've even seen it in our presidency, as former President Bill Clinton, after having oral sex with an intern, adamantly stated, "I did not have sexual relations with that woman." Not only is "that woman" a degrading, demeaning comment, but his words denote a blatant separation between what sexual intercourse and sexual activity really are—both Kinseyan at their core.

SIECUS is a communication and education organization, so you can easily find it in your schools or on-line. In cooperation with the SSSS (Society for the Scientific Study of Sex, also called "Quad S"), SIECUS has effectively moved from graduate schools to junior highs and into primary grades. Additional partnerships with Advocates for Youth promote student gay and lesbian clubs in our schools. An example of this work is found in one brochure written by SIECUS for Planned Parenthood. It's shockingly blatant in its message to teen boys, equating virginity with prostitution. "Do you want a warm body? Buy one. That's right. There are women who have freely chosen that business, buy one. . . . Do you want a virgin to marry? Buy

What are SIECUS and Planned Parenthood really saying in the brochures and curriculum placed in your local schools? Why not find out for yourself?

one. There are girls in that business too. Marriage is the price you'll pay, and you'll get the virgin. Very temporarily."[61]

Have you examined the brochures and curriculum that Planned Parenthood has placed in your local schools? It would benefit many of you to do so.

Organizations That Fueled the Revolution

Just who are these organizations that have fueled the sexual revolution in our nation? And how have they become so powerful? Researcher Judith A. Reisman identifies them, as well as key individuals involved.[62] Interestingly enough, these organizations organized, declaring *themselves* as the authority for education and accreditation! These self-proclaimed "experts" now have become interconnected, impacting more organizations that you know.

It's ironic. While our money states "In God We Trust," we turn to SIECUS to educate our kids about what healthy sexuality is. As your daughters and sons stand to recite the Pledge of Allegiance and proudly state, "one nation, under God, indivisible," we find the lobbying power of these deviants, cloaked in "tolerance," as they rip our nation to shreds with biases and prejudices that dwarf those of generations past. As your family stands for the pledge to our country's flag, hands covering their hearts in respect, there are individuals under the influence of Twisted who are aligning with others in an allegiance of immorality and impurity. Will you allow them to win?

> Ironically, our money states "In God We Trust," but we turn to SIECUS to educate our kids about what healthy sexuality is.

For decades such organizations have masqueraded as nothing more than houses of helpful education. But they are not. They have brought to us a culture of death—a culture that has strayed appallingly far from the guidelines set by our Creator. But God's rule hasn't changed: "The wages of sin is death."[63] Yes, forgiveness is available. But I know many young ladies who found forgiveness in the arms of God but who still remained pregnant or felt emotionally paralyzed in future relationships or had to combat the physical effects of STDs for a lifetime—sometimes a shorter lifetime than they'd ever imagined.

It's Payback Time!

In our apathy and ignorance, we have sinned. Twisted's payback for our sin surrounds us. Millions are paying his price annually in death: the death of innocence, the death of virginity, the death of physical health, the death of marriage and united families, the death of mental clarity, and the death of spiritual wholeness.

Today all of us stand at the funeral of purity. And each of us will respond differently. We can cry and leave for home, unchanged. We can become nauseous and be moved—temporarily—to action, but only until we "feel better" or our lives become numb in busyness. Or we can resolve to get our own payback against Twisted and make a difference—a *permanent* difference—in our country. For those who are willing to stand up and fight for our kids' sake, a revolution awaits!

It reminds me of one of my favorite scenes from the movie *Tombstone*. When Doc Holliday is asked why Wyatt Earp is so angry, some are assuming it's for the revenge of his dead brother. "Oh, make no mistake," Doc corrects them. "It's not revenge he's after. It's a reckoning."

As a Christian, I know that God—and God alone—holds the keys to vengeance. I also realize that the Day of Reckoning is not mine to direct. But I know something else: it was *people*, moved by the heated fires of selfish ambition, who brought about the day of impurity that we now live in. It was *people* who fought vehemently for sexual rights and recognition when God clearly forbids it. And it is *people* who have been sitting on their hands as young children innocently wander into the highway of adult sin.

> God has always worked through people first. Are you willing?

And know this: It will be *people* God uses to bring correction. Just praying for some spiritualistic form of mystical revival won't work. God is not waiting for us to build up enough mystical "faith" before we can manage to coerce him into delivering judgment and righteous correction. No. Since the Cross, God has always worked through people first. So the question is really, Will *you* allow God to work through you? Will you be one who steps forward?

In 1991, as I looked down at my daughter, moments before she died from AIDS, I chose to step forward. I chose to make a life commitment to defend our children and grandchildren against disease, unnecessary pain, and impurity. Today's dirty culture is one that longs to devour youth. Pediatrician Dr. Margaret Meeker concurs, stating, "Never has a culture been so anti-teen, so willing to strangle the life and soul out of healthy kids."[64]

Think of it this way: Every time your teen walks out the door (and even within your home!) he is in a war against sexual bombardment. But *you* can make the difference—as you join with others who have the same goal and commitment in mind. Their faith may not be identical in worship style to yours. But if you have maturity in your soul, you will see the greater prize and link arms. Father Benedict Groeschel, who runs the evangelical Grassroots Renewal Project in the United States, is one such person. He is a person I am willing to stand side by side with. "Half the people you meet on the bus or in a shopping centre, or even at church on Sunday, have had some genital sexual experience during the preceding few days," Groeschel says. "The single person lives in a world of continuous sexual bombardment. The media trumpets the message that sex brings happiness. If this were true, we would indeed live in an earthly paradise and the world would be 'happy valley.'"[65]

You can make the difference—as you join with others who have the same goal and commitment in mind.

But we are not in a cheap episode of *Happy Days,* nor do we live in "happy valley," where sexual paradise can be attained. This is real life. And the trail of death that originated in the Garden of Eden extends through history, reaching now to your own doorstep. None of us can hide from it.

So what can we do? Today, not tomorrow, is the time to begin fighting back. It's time for our own payback! I and numerous others are convinced that America's love story will not end as these sex information organizations have planned. We have already struck several deep blows to their schemes, giving them spiritual and naturally consequential hurdles to overcome. No longer are adults silent. We are fighting back for our children—and, wonderfully, we are also seeing teens rise to the challenge of staying pure in character and sex. And we are beginning to win! As we see more and more caring individuals, such as yourself, joining in, we are encouraged.

Yes, the history of the American love story *is* a sordid tale. But it's far from over, and the credits are not yet rolling. We have several chapters to write! Will you stand on the sidelines or be an active participant in the script?

Only as we learn the truth about sexuality and today's culture can we be informed enough to change our homes, our neighborhoods, our churches, our schools! How can we do this? First, we must get the information so that we're empowered. Then we can choose to move others to action with real stories in this real world. We can stand united with strategic resolve.

> **Example is not the main thing influencing others. It is the only thing.**
> —Albert Schweitzer

pure **love** AND pure **Sex**

the movie begins. . . .

it's a cold, snowy winter evening and a handsome young man enters Macy's on Times Square. While searching for a pair of gloves, he meets a beautiful young lady who also grabs the exact pair of gloves he was reaching for. Is this "chance meeting" destiny—or fate? They have a brief moment, an intimate encounter, yet they never kiss. They don't even exchange names. But the woman decides to tempt fate. She writes her name and number inside a used book and sells it to a bookstore without the man knowing its location. If they are destined to meet, she explains, then that book will find its way into his hands and he can call her.

In another movie an attractive blonde emits an icy persona. She eyes Mr. Bond with a steely glare and claims that she will never fall for his seductive play. Only minutes later, however, they are in his room, in his bed. He knows her name and sees her fully exposed. This too is an intimate encounter—or so it seems. But was there any real connection there?

What Is Intimacy Anyway?

In today's world, true intimacy isn't easy to find—even though the word *intimacy* is thrown around ad nauseum by marketers. Intimacy isn't a clothing line advertised in a catalog sent multiple times monthly to your mailbox by some unscrupulous woman named Victoria. Nor is it only a hot, sexy moment of seduction. Intimacy, as I shared earlier, is a soul-to-soul connection. Watch any of the *007* films, and you'll realize that James Bond rarely has these. Nor do intimate moments—although there may be many trysts—often occur at airport bars, corporate conferences, or national sales meetings.

But did you know a couple can have an intimate moment just by having a discussion? Courtship used to be that way. In the "old days," a young caller would sit in the parlor with the girl he was interested in. They would rarely touch (after all, who dared to do so, when a parent or guardian was usually watching carefully from the next room?). But talk? Oh, how they would talk. And they would get to know each other intimately. Instead of relying on sexual expression to be the "glue" of their relationship, they had to rely on conversation. The only way a woman was to find a man interesting was to enjoy his wit, his sense of humor, his understanding of her feelings and opinions, and how they interacted together. The young man took interest in her as he learned what she enjoyed doing for fun, her favorite foods, or memories that she cherished.

Think how different that was even from when you and I were teenagers. Remember all the folded notes we used to send, with questions like, "Do you want to go out?" or "Do you like pizza? Maybe we could share one sometime." Then we'd include cute little boxes with "Yes" or "No" answers so the person could easily check one or the other. Other times we'd choose a less risky route. We'd send our closest and most trusted friends to inquire whether or not that particular person "liked" us. These friends had to be trusted, mind you, because otherwise "the friend" might end up going out with the person *you* liked. But then, that was only junior high.

In high school things got much more complicated. Oh, yes. Remember the flirting, the Farrah Fawcett hair, and the Madonna and

Cindy Lauper clothing styles that aided our connections? The eighties and nineties music reflected our reckless abandon in relationships— well, at least that's how we acted publicly. In private, once we were on a date (now called *dating,* not *going together*), we felt that incredible rush of being with someone of the opposite sex. But to amplify that rush was the discomfort and wonder.

The girl might be wondering, *Will he put his arm around me? Will he try to kiss me? Is tonight the night?*

Similar questions raced through the guy's mind: *Should I hold her hand? How will she act if I put my arm around her? How can I make sure she won't reject me? What will I tell my friends on Monday? I've got to make sure they think I'm the man . . .*

Hmm. Suddenly I'm sick of reflecting! How about you? Even though I actually had a very pleasant high school experience, I certainly wasn't the most attractive or athletic guy on our very small campus. My popularity was marginal, although I was well liked by most. I imagine most of you would say the same. But when trying to help plan a high-school class reunion a few years ago, I found that very few of my friends wanted to go back in time. Why? For the same reason some of you are popping antacids right now as you reflect. You too have incredible regrets from the past. What we thought was an intimate moment that would end in magic was instead instant gratification that ended in mistrust and disillusion.

> Very few of us want to go back in time to our high-school years. Just why is that?

For the most part, the story continues today for our teens as it did for us. There are some who will look—or already are looking—for love in the arms of others. And we need to know what to tell them.

Does Sex Equal Intimacy?

Last spring I received a disturbing e-mail from Genie, a high-school freshman in Texas:

> *I dated a guy for almost 7 months, and recently we broke up. He's a junior and a really awesome guy. He never forced me to do*

anything that I didn't want to do. While we were dating, he had been in so many tragedies [deaths in the family, tornado hit his house] . . . and I was there for him through all of it. I am only 14, but I really do love him. And what really hurts is that he told me we would be together forever. His mother says that he's angry with the world, that he hates the world for what has happened.

I figured he wouldn't know how much I love him or feel bad for him, so why not show him? So we had sexual intercourse. But we didn't just have sex, we made love. I believe there is a difference. I wanted to wait for marriage, and we were going to because he even asked me to marry him. And then just after we made love, he was in a wreck. I think God did that because he was telling us something. So I prayed and told God that we will never ever do that again (until marriage) if he just lets us be together. I think my boyfriend wants to be with me but doesn't know how to handle everything . . . and neither do I. I need someone to help me get through this.

Genie, only 14, found a guy two years older who promised to marry her. She definitely had strong feelings about him, but there are problems in her e-mail. They just broke up, she explained. And because this guy had gone through so much, Genie reached out to him in compassion. He responded, and their love became sexual. After having sex, he was in a car accident—something she feared God caused as a warning. Listen to her pleading with God. She's willing to do *anything*, even practice abstinence, so long as the relationship is restored.

Did these two high schoolers have an *intimate* encounter? Were Genie's feelings genuine and real, or were they fake and masked by her boyfriend's lust and her own desire to please and comfort?

I believe her feelings were as real as she had experienced up to that point in her life. But the tragedy is that once sex enters the picture, the relationship will most likely never be restored. (We'll talk more about this later.) And Genie's disappointment and regret are also very real.

Take Tina as another example. She's from the same Texas high school as Genie. As you listen to her story, you can almost hear her personality and see her twinkling eyes as her ponytail swings in agreement to her opinion.

Last year I went out with this guy. I thought I was sooo in love, but I held out from having sex with him until about the last 2 or 3 months we saw each other. I knew we wouldn't be together again, but I wanted him to be my first, because I loved him so much. Which was SUUUCH stupid reasoning!! He was SUCH a jerk to me, he didn't deserve what I gave him!! He took something I can't ever have back—my virginity. He obviously wasn't worth it, but I, for some reason, thought he was. Don't get me wrong—we're still cool and talk when we pass in the halls. Or when I see him at a party, we'll just say hi or something. But now I have a new boyfriend, for about 4 months, and he's EVERYTHING I think I really deserve. He'd do anything for me. He's as in love with me as I was with my ex, and I want to be with him and I am. But it's like something's holding me back a little (having sex with my ex). I want to let go and give him my whole heart, but there's a little piece of me that just can't do that. It's killing me! I want to be with this guy as long as possible, but I don't have that same feeling as with my ex. Or, sometimes I do, but sometimes I don't. How can I let go of the mistake I made in the past and the fact that my ex hurt me? That's another thing I'm afraid of—getting hurt again—although I know my new boyfriend would never do that to me. I feel like I'm ruining the REALLY good thing I have now, without meaning to. And when should I tell my new guy about it? Because I know he has the right to know.

Wow, do you feel that? Can you sense Tina's lost and bleeding heart? Her feelings about her ex flip-flop from "I knew we wouldn't be together" to "I wanted him to be my first" to "He was such a jerk to me" to "He took something" to "we're still cool and talk."

Did Tina have an *intimate* encounter, or was it just sex? Reflect on that for a few minutes before you read on.

Did a light come on for you? Tina's choice to give her virginity to a guy who was willing to take it is causing her continued pain. Sure, she had sex. But she wouldn't be hurting so badly if something deep and intimate hadn't occurred. Her soul was engaged and embraced. Then something ripped a hole into her very core. Yes, this most certainly was an intimate encounter—even with this "jerk" she knew she would never have a long-term relationship with.

> ½ person + ½ person ≠ a whole marriage
> —A sign on a youth group leader's refrigerator

Because Tina and Genie longed for the acceptance and affections of others, they fell into an intimate encounter. But it wasn't the soul-to-soul connection they were longing for. And they're not the only ones who have mistaken sex for intimacy.

So how in their journey to find love can teens develop relationships with deep, long-lasting levels of healthy intimacy, romance, and sexuality?

Relationships, Expectations, and Romance

First we need to understand what we're all *really* looking for. As human beings, we were created by God with a need for community—a need to be "in relationship." But what does that really mean? And how does that form our expectations and the way we look at romance?

A Real Relationship

If *intimacy* is a soul-to-soul connection, then a *relationship* is the interaction between two souls who learn to relate to one another on many levels: first, as new acquaintances, then as friends and dear friends, and finally soul-to-soul. In a relationship, physical activity is optional. Of course, depending on the type of relationship, various forms of physical activity are appropriate.

When I was a child, I enjoyed working with my father in his garage or on house projects. With my friends today, I love eating at restaurants in Denver or screaming at a game. With my children, I play games—and strangely lose near the end of each! And with my wife, I enjoy a wide variety of physical activity, whether yard work, leisure travel, or intimacy in our bedroom.

A real relationship occurs on many levels, in various dimensions, and has no template. You build this bridge—from soul to soul—as you walk on it.

Expectations or Hopes?

Ugh. That's how I feel nowadays when I hear the word *expectations*. Of course I realize that we are often expected to do certain things in life. God himself expects us to live a life worthy of the calling he has placed on us. But because of the many relationship issues we must face, it seems that the very word *expectations* is a death knell to many.

Why not think about *hopes* instead? You see, in a relationship, if you place expectations on the person you love, only two things can happen—either the person will meet those expectations or the person will let you down. There are no other options and no pleasant surprises. And the higher your expectations, the greater the chance of disappointment. Conversely, though, if you lower your expectations, you feel as if you are settling for something "second best." Who wants to live a lifetime feeling like that?

So how can you grapple with these standards and the associated feelings?

If you are single and looking for someone to share your life with, I would simply encourage you to get "nonnegotiables" in your mind (even better, get them on paper, so you won't be swayed when somebody intriguing comes along!). These may be issues of faith, standards on how to raise any children you might have, or issues of finance or marital faithfulness, for example. But for other expectations you have—such as physical appearance, hobbies, or the ability to sing romantically while playing the piano in a candlelit room as he gives you a foot massage while you soak in a warm bath and he caresses your temple—well, maybe you can change those expectations to hopes ("negotiables"). For you women looking for Mr. Gorgeous in appearance, maybe Mr. Not-Too-Bad is exactly your fit. You can still set your hopes high for some of those "outside" qualities. But just realize

> If you are looking for someone to share your life with, separate your "nonnegotiables" from your "negotiables."

that if you find someone who doesn't meet them all, it's okay. When they're simply hopes, you won't be devastated—and you may be pleasantly surprised. But the most important thing is keeping the nonnegotiables intact.

The same is true for guys. But us men have "peripheral" issues that are a necessity at times, ladies. It may be important (at least at first) to have someone who is physically attractive to us (though not necessarily drop-dead gorgeous) and sexually in tune with our music. But as the relationship grows, you'll find that we men also enjoy the soul-to-soul moments.

We guys especially need to set our expectations in a reasonable zone. (Hint: This is the section of the book you wives can begin reading aloud to your husbands.) If we expect our wife to give birth to several children and still have narrow hips and breasts that don't sag after going from a size B to DD and back to B again—well, such thoughts are ludicrous. So remember, men, hopes—*realistic* hopes. Setting expectations for your bride to continue to look 26 when she's in her forties and fifties only guarantees disappointment. After all, do *you* look the same as you did at 26? One quick look in the mirror at yourself ought to bring you back to reality!

So when looking for a spouse, or continuing to develop our relationship with our spouse, let's set expectations on mutually agreed-upon issues. For everything else, let's make them hopes and not be so crushed if they are not fulfilled. For example, I don't expect my wife to dress provocatively and seduce me every evening—but there's always that hope!

The Dance of Romance

Ah, l'amour! If you are a hopeless romantic as I am, this topic is tough to address. That's probably because it would be like describing how to paint beautiful sunsets to an artist who sees those sunsets differently than you. We all need a good dose of romance in our relationships. But romance is not truly romance if it has selfish expectations tied to it. If the man, for instance, has ideas of candlelight and rose petals for a romantic evening but the woman has ideas of snuggling before a raging fireplace, each reading a good book or sharing fun stories, then someone's expectations are going to be dashed. Instead, why not learn to be adventurous adults again? Why not allow the Master Creator to flow through our creative soul, helping us find ways to provide fun and romantic times for our spouses?

Years ago when Evon and I got married, I thought romance was only a mystical ritual that we enjoyed en route to the bedroom. I even prayed for God to give me a special "anointing," since it was he who created marriage and presented us with the joys of sex. But as I've matured, I've come to understand that romance is not about leading up to and engaging in sex. It is about the heart and soul of two lovers dancing together in pleasant delight. The moves are not predetermined, and the outcome is unscripted. The joy of intimacy is in the dance of romance.

Romance isn't truly romance if it has selfish expectations tied to it.

For our teens to understand the context of healthy, loving relationships, someone needs to teach them. Who? Why, *you,* my friend. Your relationships and the dynamics involved cause them to form a worldview, or "intimacy view." They can only learn what is presented before them. So it is you who must rediscover these components afresh and implement them in your own relationships. If you live them out loud (within reason!), the young men and women in your care will develop a healthy and whole view of true love and romance—within the context of a loving relationship, where expectations are nonnegotiable issues, where hopes are still there but realistic, and where romance dances, pure and healthy.

Modeling It Out

When teaching about intimacy and relationships to teenagers, I like to use a model like the one below. These two balloons represent the inner hearts or souls of two people.

When we first meet someone, that brief encounter makes them an acquaintance. Nothing deep or permanent connects us; it's only a brief meeting. In our illustration, it's as if a small piece of thread wraps around these two balloons. If one person were to leave and be separated from that person forever, the thread would be easily broken and the loss (the severance of the thread) would not be that great.

But the more two people get to know each other, the more pieces of thread begin to tie them together. As the relationship progresses, the thread becomes string.

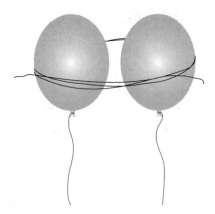

Each relationship experience with that person is represented by another piece of string. The more time you spend with this person, the more string bonds your hearts together. After many great experiences and wonderful times, a loss or separation now would be much more deeply felt.

Now these two people have an intimate heart connection, and the memories they have together will last them a lifetime, even if a separation were to occur. If these two are friends of the opposite sex and their relationship becomes one of a romantic nature, they begin creating a more intense bond that we will call a *cable*. This cable engages areas of passion not normally touched on by typical friends, regardless of how close they are. And this cable begins to bind the two all the more tightly.

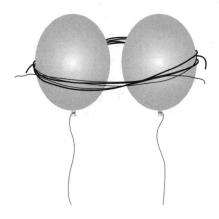

Now add sex to this romantic relationship, and the level of vulnerability is incredible. Not only will they remove their clothes and reveal the most private areas of their bodies, but they will allow another person to touch them there. More so, they will allow another person to become equally as vulnerable, and join those two areas of privacy. That moves the intimate encounter of two souls into yet another stage—a physical expression that is equal in intensity, vulnerability, and acceptance. As one soul opens and embraces the actions of another, so one body opens and receives the private being of that romantic friend. As hearts are spilled and emotions openly expressed in conversation, so life is spilled and one body pours into another. A bonding occurs here that's found nowhere else. Stronger than cable, this intimate encounter is like a *chain* that fastens two lives in a moment forever unforgettable.

At this point, without question, the two people are bound together. They have a relationship that began as acquaintances and developed into great friends. With a friendship worthy of honor, they moved into areas of romance and then sealed this relationship with the offering and accepting of one another sexually. And this is God's plan—if this chain bonding occurs within the bounds of marriage. Depending on the culture you live in, then, marriage should occur at the early stages of the romantic relationship, before there is any physical joining. This is the context of a loving relationship. And it's exactly how God designed it to work. For two people to become one, soul-to-soul, body-to-body, for a lifetime.

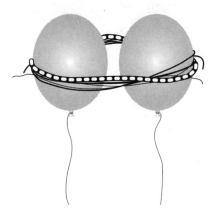

But pain comes when there is separation between the two people. It can be a separation because there is no commitment on one or both sides, such as adultery or divorce. Or it can be a separation because of the death of one person. Either way, in a relationship of this magnitude, separation brings immense pain. I can speak from experience. My late wife, Evon, and I were bonded in all these ways. But when she died, we were cut in two. No longer were we "one flesh." I was alone, and the experience was devastating. I looked and felt like this, torn and bleeding from the heart.

At that time my emotions seemed to bleed. Although I read many books on grief, there was no way to remove the cords, cables, and chains that had wrapped around my soul. Each one represented a memory, an experience that Evon and I had shared since the time I first saw her. The only path for healing in our torn relationship was for God to heal each and every cord. And that meant he had to take each hemorrhaging end and allow the life that flowed through it to cease.

This, then, is the process of grief—taking what was once an experience and interaction of life and accepting its death. You can never remove the cords, the cables, or the chains from your soul. They are a part of you. They live within your heart. For me, they are memories I guard and cherish. And only in time did I find a woman—my wife, Stephanie—with whom I could describe these memories. And with her I found acceptance and love instead of competition and a refusal to listen and share with me.

What about your life? For some of you, this really struck a chord (apologies for that pun). You may have gone through the death of your marriage through divorce. Whether originating from betrayal or even simple "flings" from the past, the memories are etched in your soul. Often, I've discovered, we attempt to bring healing to the bleeding strands hanging from our soul by trying to wrap them around another person. But the new relationship will never be the same as the old one. Our old strands will continue to bleed, and the new bonds experienced with this new person will only add to the confusion. In time this may lead to another relational separation. Alcohol, drugs, pornography, busyness—all these are feeble attempts to cover up a damaged soul. But until God truly brings healing, we will continue to bleed.

Often we are so tender inside from being hurt that we refuse to let anyone in. Sure, sex is okay, we reason within ourselves, so long as we only keep it on a physical level. But even if there is no string or cable between us, sex is still a chain. Out of fear of being hurt again, we try to run from any truly intimate connection. This can manifest itself in numerous hurtful ways in our own lives and in the lives of others. We cannot simply jump from acquaintance or stranger to sexual partner, thinking there will be no consequence. Each sexual experience is an intimate connection and has intimate effects. These are things we need to be aware of not only for ourselves, but we also must explain them to our kids.

Remember Tina? Reread her letter just one more time and think of the analogy I used about cords, cable, and chains. . . .

Hear her longing to be connected? The background of her e-mail revealed to me a relationship that stopped, and then started over and over. If only she could love him and have him love her . . .

Genie clearly fought the same longing. In an attempt to care for a guy and hold him close to her heart, she wrapped chain and cable around their souls. But without eternal commitment and proven faithfulness, the chain and cable broke. The bleeding began. Pain engulfed her until she heard an adult speak in her school about relationships and true love. Then she e-mails a stranger twice her age, hoping for any kind of help and guidance.

"Not feeling needed is hard to cope with, but feeling unloved cuts to a deeper level," says pediatrician Margaret Meeker.[1] How true. Tina and Genie both risked giving their souls to another and were needed for a moment. But when the need was removed, the "love" evaporated from their relationships. And their lives and emotions have crumpled into a heap.

Does this mean there's no hope? Certainly not. God is a God of love. He not only wants you to be intimately connected with others, he wants you to experience and enjoy the wonderful feelings of love and acceptance that come from a relationship in which he, the designer, is an active part. The key to this is finding one person with whom you can share your life. With that one person you can share your body, your soul, and every step you take from here to the grave. If by chance you find yourself like me and death takes your spouse, then know that while no future relationship is exactly like the one before, they may be equally exciting and beautiful.

Parents, your teens need to see how the relationships they engage in deeply touch them—for a lifetime. Is any teen's love "puppy love," as we were told years ago? Perhaps. But it is love, nonetheless. And they are truly getting more and more connected as acquaintances and friends. So explain to them and show them through your own actions how God wants to draw us together as Christians and unify us. Help them understand the bonding power of a romantic and sexual relationship, even if you are no longer married. If you are a single parent, you know the power of the bond because you've experienced it being broken. So share honestly with them your own heart and struggles. Your vulnerability with your teen will again wrap more cords around your soul and theirs. They may be uncomfortable for a moment, but that's okay. It's the proof that you've touched the privacy of their soul. So keep talking—and listening!

Love Is a Verb

Over the decades, musicians have written many songs about love. Some have claimed that love is "more than a feeling." Others—idiots in my opinion—sing about sex, asking, "What's love got to do with it?" Well, they're wrong—love has everything to do with it! I think DC Talk, a Christian rock group hit it on the head when they sang this song: "Love Is a Verb." Now that's the truth. If you really love someone, you need to act on that.

And that means, as parents, we are given the responsibility to raise our children and to see them grow into mature and responsible men and women. Physically, that's not too hard a job to accomplish, so long as you feed and clothe them. Children will mature physically with limited supervision. But just because they *look* mature doesn't mean they are. We have our work cut out for us to see our children mature as kind, loving individuals who will respect themselves and others and please God.

"What is happening inside the teen's heart is a maturing of love from a feeling to a behavior," says Dr. Margaret Meeker in her book *Restoring the Teenage Soul*. "A parent's role is to first understand this evolution and then aid the teen by teaching the broader concept of love as a feeling *and* a behavior."[2]

> **If it was going to be easy to raise kids, it never would have started with something called labor.**
> —Author Unknown

Teaching this broader concept is not something that can be accomplished in a "talk" or some type of class. So remove "program" concepts from your mind. Much more is required. Every day, you as parent are shaping them. It is by your actions, your hugs, your muffled conversations as you speak words of comfort, wisdom, and guidance into their neck that shape their feelings into outward behavior. Your teens are watching carefully how you respond—not only to them, but to those around you.

Flirting or Hurting?

Is it just me, or does the phrase *sexual harassment* strike fear into the hearts of men? Recently I spoke at a national sales meeting for a large and successful safety equipment company. Just before I addressed the sales teams, their HR department presented a required 45-minute sexual harassment seminar. This crazed crowd hardly let the presenter—who was a friend of theirs and an employee of the company—get the bulk of her message out. Only later did I learn that many of those attending the presentation not only made flirting in the workplace common, but some had experienced full-fledged intra-office affairs.

So which is it—flirting or hurting? If we as adults are to spend great amounts of time at work away from our spouse and children, then we need to know how to navigate this minefield of intentions. One peer of mine who speaks and researches has taught that flirting has absolutely no place outside of a married couple. She makes a strong case that flirting can do nothing but damage trust and lead to imminent pain.

But as a purity speaker and author, I enjoy fun, laughter, and teasing all the time. Anyone who knows me knows that speaking about sex full-time can probably cause brain damage, and I'm the poster child. But when I tease, I observe very clear boundaries. No one is more careful than I when in a public school setting around teenagers who long to meet me, shake my hand, give me a hug, and share stories of their sexual history. It's dicey work, indeed, especially with school principals watching you closely.

Listen carefully. It is better to err on the side of conservative respect and honor than to lead with unsolicited flattery, flirtation, or sexual comments. Sexual harassment has become serious fodder for our court systems, and rightly so. I know many who have been paralyzed by comments and even gazes from others in schools, churches, and corporate settings. They did not ask for it, and they shouldn't have to put up with it. However, sexual comments are easy to avoid. There's only one place for them—at home in your bedroom with your spouse.

What about Homosexuality?

If it's true that love is a feeling and a behavior, as Dr. Meeker says, then next comes a tough question, one I am asked frequently by parents, youth leaders, and teens: What about teens who are gay or lesbian? What if your teen is wondering about this or pursing such a lifestyle? What if your teen's friends are? The problem comes when a teen or his peers assume that feelings and behavior are one and the same thing.

Some years ago Steve, a friend of mine and a former homosexual, explained to me the difference between being gay and having homosexual feelings. Sometimes you can have strong feelings of intimacy toward someone of the same sex. In essence, those are *homosexual* (meaning "same sex") desires. And they're not wrong in themselves. Men longing for intimacy from other men is not a gay activity; it's the natural development for men to be connected. This may sound strange for a minute, but hear me out. Every man, for example, has a longing to be held, loved, and embraced by his father. Such "same sex" feelings are natural and wholesome.

When men watch movies like *Braveheart, The Patriot,* or *Gladiator,* they'll respond physically. Sometimes their eyes will water or the hair on their neck will bristle. Because they are passionately moved by the story line, they respond in force. Why is this? Because every man needs friends he can trust in battle. These are the guys he loves, the men he's bonded to. Again, it's the human need for intimate connection—the need to join our souls "until the death" for one another. Truly, it's "all for one, and one for all!"

Homosexuality at its core is a desire to have intimate encounters of a healthy nature with someone of the same sex. It is only when those feelings become sexualized and are acted upon with someone of the same sex that perversion enters the equation. Twisted mars our story when he calls to young people to find a pseudo-intimacy by sexualizing the longing for connection. Sadly, statistics reveal that these relationships are rarely long-term and fulfilling.

Helping our teens understand the longing for intimacy with others gives them the proper perspective when dealing with issues of homosexuality in our culture. In God's view, homosexual sex is wrong because it takes a natural longing and perverts it.[3] And the results are not only physically damaging but spiritually and physiologically damaging. That means in order to protect our teens and to help steer them toward a whole, healthy life, we have to be up-front about the dangers.

But more importantly, we need to teach teens about the soul and how God created it to be deeply connected to others without sexuality as an issue. It means, as Dr. Meeker says, being willing "to help teens struggle with hard emotional and intellectual issues and sort out how one impacts the other." It also means restoring to them a sense of "dignity that necessitates an ability to help teens feel, think, and then separate their feelings from their behavior. This concept . . . is vital to establishing healthy maturity and a sense of healthy empowerment in a teen's life."[4]

> **We need to help teens feel, think, and then separate their feelings from their behavior.**

And I believe it's is the key to restoring the soul of our teens.

Is a "No" Really a "Yes"?

I've met many young men who ask in all sincerity, "When she says no, does she really mean yes? At least that she wants me to keep trying?" Others have said, "We all know that saying no is just a way to get out of the responsibility. She wants it as bad as I do, but if she says no, then she can try to pin date rape on me later."

What's happening here? Is this the effect of relativism on our culture? No, it's clearly the effect of pornography and lust. Having been duped by the wiles of pornography, some men think women are attracted and turned on by the idea of being raped. Just this week some moron sent me an e-mail promoting rape sex on the Internet. Do women actually feel that way? Does rape—a woman's "no" against a man's "yes"—turn women on?

Because I'm not a woman, I had to ask women. So in some school assemblies, I have used a scenario I learned from my friend Pam Stenzel to find out how women feel about rape. I have asked student bodies as small as 50 and as large as 2,000 this question: "Girls, I have two scenarios that I want you to pick from: A or B. There is no other option. Here's scenario A. Let's say you are at the mall, and you return to the parking lot alone to get your purse. Just as you reach your car, a van pulls up. Two guys get out of the van and begin to knife you repeatedly. Then, when they see somebody coming, they jump back in the van and speed away. The other person sees you and takes you to the hospital. You'll survive, but it hurts.

"Now, scenario B. You are at the same mall, same parking lot, same car. A van pulls up. Two guys get out of the van. This time they don't stab you. Instead, they throw you into the van and take you to a remote area, where they rape you repeatedly. They bring you back to your car and throw you on the ground. Again, someone comes and they speed away. This person takes you to the hospital. You'll survive, but it hurts.

"Girls, these are two ugly scenarios. But if you had to choose, A or B, which would you choose?" Do you know what every high school girl in America and Australia has chosen? Scenario A! And loudly!

This may seem like an extreme example, but the fact that women would rather be knifed repeatedly than raped tells me several things. First, it shows that women are not "turned on" by the idea of some guy forcing sex on them. Most women see sex as an intimate act. They are not interested in connecting their soul with the dark soul of a soon-to-be felon. Second, it reveals that sex is not just a physical act.

A woman never wants someone to steal or take away something from her that is so personal, so private, so much a part of her like her virginity or her offering of sex. Never. Women know better than most men the vulnerability **Sex is not just a physical act.** of a woman's sexuality. They realize the physical difference between the sexes. They want to be an equal partner with equal respect and equal control. And that is well deserved.

The rules are pretty simple, I think. "Yes" means "Yes," and "No" means "Get your ugly, selfish, lust-driven hands off me before I head-butt your nose, poke you in the eyes, and crush your groin!" That's for my daughter, Brianna. And I'd also want her to add, "Or I'll tell my father everything you're trying to do." (After the talks I'll have with my daughter's dates before they leave my house, she'll have plenty of ammo.)

"No" doesn't mean she wants it. That's the initial lie of Twisted's from back when he was trying to mess up Eden. Remember when he said, "Did God really say . . . ?" Twisted is a perverter of what is right. Porn may portray women supposedly enjoying painful sex or rape. But that industry feeds on what is twisted and incorrect. Women do not enjoy that, and we must, we must, we *must* teach our young men how to respect and honor women. And we must teach our young women how to say no far earlier than 20 minutes into a heated kissing encounter in some secluded location. Date rape results too often not because the girl "changes her mind" but because she is unaware of how early sexual arousal occurs for the male and because he has heard that her "No" means "Let's make it rough." We must teach our young men and women self-control and honor. Otherwise, because we are all created with a longing to connect, we may be leading our teens right into trouble.

> **Build me a son . . . who will be strong enough to know when he is weak and brave enough to face himself when he is afraid.**
> —Douglas MacArthur

But Will Teens Really Believe and Practice This?

For the answer to this question, listen to what real teens are saying. Teens like Rayna:

You touched me so deeply that it's almost like your words haunt me. You knew the perfect angle to get to us. My boyfriend, Jim, who is my best friend, and I have been dating for about a year. We decided a long time ago that we wanted to abstain from sex until marriage. This has been the most comfortable, pressure-

free, worry-free, and simply fun relationship I could ever imagine. Your speech gave us so much hope and just warmed us inside. When you said that a girl came up to you and asked if anyone could ever love her for just what's inside, Jim reached over and took my hand. I believe you completely when you said that you loved your wife and that she was beautiful no matter what, and I pray that the world will be graced with the kind of love you felt.

Not only can teens *believe* in an intimate encounter that is based on character, they can—and many are—*live* it! Today's teens are more solid in their relationships than teens of our generations ever were (thank God!). No longer can we judge them based on our history and our own inabilities in self-discipline. Now teenagers are, on their own, choosing to postpone damaging activity in their relationships as they find the depth and hope that comes from intimate encounters without sexuality. So how can you help them stand firm?

Take a look at your own intimate encounters.

If you're a single parent, what perspective on romance, love, and sex are you portraying to your kids? Does your bitterness from the past flow to them? Do your actions now, in dating situations, match what you are telling your teens?

If you're married, you can have all the sex you want. But are those times really intimate encounters? Do your conversations have the depth and romance that you long for? Is it real in your heart first, before becoming routine in your bedroom? Oh, it can be. And then you can have the most fulfilling relationship on this earth that you can imagine.

So now's the time. Stand for what you know is right. Brave the cold, and open discussions again with your spouse or potential spouse about the deep issues of value, intimacy, and honor. Let your own relationship flow with the fruit of renewed connection. And then, from there, your influence will flood pure intimacy into your community, your home, and directly into your teens' lives.

pure **education**

okay, moms and dads, put your smirk away. Of course you've lived much longer than your children, and yes, you probably know much more about relationships than they do. But look again at the title of this chapter. It's not what teens wish you knew about *relationships*. First, it's what teens wish you knew about *sex*. *Then* they want you to know about love and how you can convey it to them.

In her handwritten letter to me, one sophomore girl from Kansas shares how she was the "good girl" in her family. With a sister and brother always in trouble and her parents' attention always turned to them, this sophomore felt very isolated and alone.

It seemed like I wasn't part of the family anymore. I basically had to raise myself. My parents probably figured I was smart enough to get by. But there was no more love for me in that house. It made me feel unworthy of love.

She wanted her parents to love her and talk with her about her feelings and the sexual choices before her. When she got involved with a guy, she still needed her mom and dad to fulfill the intimate needs she had.

But since they wouldn't, she gave up on them and tried to find that fulfillment in sex. She ended up telling a friend how awful she felt after having sex, and the friend betrayed her, telling everyone at school about it. The school counselor heard about it and reported it to the girl's parents. Her letter goes on:

My mom treated me like the dirt I thought I was. It was a nightmare, and I came very close to taking my own life. I thought no one cared, I was worth nothing. At least this new guy acted as though he cared. By now my parents and I were barely speaking. I had built a thick wall around myself because I was afraid if they got to know me too well [intimacy], they could hurt me terribly. Even more than they already had.

Obviously, if your children are biologically yours, you know enough about sex to guide them safely. But why you need to read this—and buy copies for your mothers' and parents' groups, your spouse, and your friends—is because of the "ammo" in this chapter, intended to bring you up to speed culturally and medically on the subject of sex. Most likely your children are receiving sex education in schools. If so, they are learning things that you may not realize. For instance, if you ask your son what he learned in school, he will probably give you a grunt. Can you blame him? If I learned from a teacher the physical dynamics of the female vulva, clitoris, and how eggs are fertilized, I'd grunt too!

> **Your children are learning things about sex that you may not realize.**

I've written this book, and especially this chapter, because I believe you need to be equally or more educated about sex than your teens are. In today's confusing, fragmented world, where Twisted runs rampant, it is even *more* imperative that parents are able to guide and direct their children.

> **The school can teach children how to think, but the home must teach them what to believe.** —Charles A. Wells

Look at it this way. Recently I tried to help my child with math homework. Help! What has happened to math? It's become so complicated that I couldn't help. It just goes to show me that my kids are being educated far beyond what I received growing up. The same applies with sexuality. Our kids are learning more from schools than the basic lessons on how the "human plumbing" is designed. They're learning a particular worldview too.

Are things the same as when we were teens? Certainly not. In fact, the times have changed several times over since we were teens. Oh sure, we all have sex drives, and in our teen years there were parties with alcohol and drugs too. But moms, do you remember being afraid to set your drink down because someone might slip a date-rape drug into it? Did you ever think of consequences such as AIDS, cervical or anal cancer, or permanent infertility? Probably not. So don't judge your teens by what you did or thought as a teen. This generation is far different from yours.

One of the easiest solutions to the issues of purity among teenagers is a parent's involvement. Why are some parents not involved? When I conduct parent seminars and evening events following my school assembly programs, I find the majority of the parents who attend are not aware of the choices, risks, and possible consequences of those risks that their teens face. "We had the same choices, and we turned out fine," seems to be their general attitude. Or even more poignant, "I made bad choices, so how can I ask my child to make the right choices? Who am I to be a role model?"

No matter what sexual experiences you've had in the past, you *do* have a right to teach your kids how to make better choices. Who else would you rather have talking to your kids about sex besides you? If you think you're going to get the old "eye roll" as you talk with your kids about this, okay, yeah, you might. But stick with it. Kids really *do* want to be educated about sex—they want to have discreet conversations. And, perhaps surprisingly, they want these conversations to be with *you*—the adult they trust the most (eye roll or not!). And if your sexual experience has impacted you negatively, you should be even *more* concerned about your teens staying sexually pure, and you should be even *more* up-front about the consequences of sexual experimentation.

> If I made bad choices, how can I ask my child to make the right choices?

I've discovered that the best way to prevent any "risk behavior" in teens is for parents to be connected to their teens—and to clearly communicate their position on these risk behaviors.[1] But how can you as a parent have an educated opinion without current information? This book and its resources provide exactly that. Once informed, parents and leaders of youth then have the tools to communicate adequately with the teens they love.

So, moms and dads, don't give up being the resource for your teens. No matter what your teens (or their body language) say, they *want* you to be informed. They want you to connect with

The best way to prevent risk behaviors in your teens is to stay involved in their lives.

them and have meaningful conversations. In chapter 9, "It Takes a Family First," I'll talk about how to build or rebuild that sense of connectedness with your teenager so the bridge of communication can be easily crossed and your message heard. Teens want you to know about (but not always invade!) their lives and their culture. Yes, they want you to care. This, then, is what they want you to know about sex and love.

Double Standards? Double Trouble!

In a series of national surveys, adults were asked what they believe about sex outside of marriage for teenagers. Why should we care about that? Because it's *adults* who direct programs and program funding. These adults represent the teachers in your schools, the clergy, politicians, plumbers, carpenters, trash men, and stay-at-home mothers.

So what does America believe today?

Two recent studies reveal that American adults strongly disapprove of young teens having premarital sex (72 percent in 1998) and that parents are concerned about raising their teens in a sexually permissive society (72 percent in 2000).[2] It is quite clear that adults are not only concerned about the sexual society in which we raise our children, but that these same adults want teenagers to abstain from sex.

> In 1998, 72 percent of adults surveyed said that it is always wrong for young teens to have premarital sex.[3]
>
> In 2000, 72 percent of parents of teens said they are very concerned about raising their teens in a sexually permissive society.[4]

But do teens see a double standard from adults? You bet they do. In 2001, the majority of Americans polled believed it's "not wrong for a man and a woman to have sex before marriage."[5] Yet 72 percent say teenagers should not! Clearly this is a huge double standard that treats teens like children instead of men and women.

When teens graduate from high school and move into the college years, the pressure only seems to increase. It's common to see Americans encouraging sexual activity among single college-age students. Nearly every commercial portrays women in their twenties as sexy models.

So the big question remains: At what point do you feel people are actually "ready" to handle sexual activity and all that comes with it? This is a question you must answer, especially if you are going to express an opinion that challenges and encourages teens to abstain from sex. Because if you only say "wait," they will ask, "Wait until when? Until what?" Some parents will answer, "Until you are ready for it and prepared."[6] But what does that mean? Does "ready" mean "in love"? Some teens think so. One girl said her parents wanted her to wait to have sex until she is 17 years old. But is there a magic occurrence she will experience moving from 16 to 17, or 19 to 20? This same girl writes:

> Mothers and fathers are granted a single decade in which to lay a foundation of values and attitudes that will help their children cope with the future pressures and problems of adulthood.
> —James C. Dobson

I am in a relationship and we talk about having sex and he asks me if I am ready and in a way I think I am and I love this kid so much and I have never felt this way about anyone and I really think he might be the one and I kind of want to sleep with him but I don't want people to think I am a bad person if I don't wait until I am married. My mom told me to wait until I am 17, but what if it happened before? What am I supposed to tell her? I don't want her to be mad and not let me see him anymore since we've been together for 11 months.

—Priscilla, WI

Whew! (Don't you love teens' e-mails?)

Because teens are in adult bodies, taking adult action, and bearing adult consequences, maybe we should treat them like adults. If you do that, which way are you going to go? Tell them not to have sex (which is reflected in the first two polls)? Or tell them it's okay to have sex (as the adults in the third survey said)? As the parent of your teenager, only you can decide that.

I find it interesting that in 2000 and 2001, a strong majority of adults polled about adultery (78 percent and 79 percent, respectively) believed it's always wrong to have sex outside of marriage.[7] Then what are we as a society saying to teens? That it's wrong to have sex before marriage and it's wrong to have sex outside of your marriage, but so long as you are over 19 years of age (not a teenager) and you chose not to marry, you can have all the sex and sexual partners you want? If you think I'm stating it strongly, just take a look at how this philosophy is played out in most TV sitcoms today. And since singleness seems to make it "okay," married people are willing to lose their marital "restraint" and go hog-wild. Others refuse to marry at all, saying it's an antiquated cultural concept.

What you believe about sexual behavior within and outside of marriage is vital to how you influence a teen's belief system. Of course, young teens don't learn to be responsible adults from their peers—none of them are adults! Instead, they learn to be responsible and mature by observing adults around them. So *you* are being watched and modeled, even if you think you're not or if your teen acts as if he wants to be as far away from you as the earth is from the outer reaches of the galaxy.

> If a child sees his parents day in and day out living without self-restraint or self-discipline, then he will come in the deepest fibers of his being to believe that that is the way to live.
>
> —M. Scott Peck

The teens I've talked with make another good point too. If you, as an adult, don't stay sexually faithful to your spouse, why should they strive to stay sexually pure? Why indeed? Especially when you as a parent are a role model to them for how feelings and behaviors interact. That means *before* you step into your teen's territory, make sure your own behavior, conversation, and beliefs are strongly secured. Does this mean you have to have a "clean" sexual record? No, because your teen can also learn volumes from your past mistakes. But it means that you have to choose *now* to follow God's plan for sex—keep it within the bounds of marriage only.

So the next time you see your teen, take a look at her with new eyes. Isn't it amazing how fast she grew up? Only yesterday she was crying because her freezer-pop fell onto the floor, and now you're reading a book about her becoming an adult! Changes happen much more quickly than we'd like to admit or we're ready

> Before you step into your teen's territory, make sure your own behavior, conversation, and beliefs are strongly secured.

for. But every day, your teen is maturing emotionally, intellectually, and sexually. So even if her maturity can be childlike in many ways, don't treat her as a child.

Even a quick look at her body says that she's becoming an adult. And it all starts with the scary *P* word—*puberty*.

Uh-Oh! Here Comes Puberty!

Have you ever noticed how easily children hug you and hold your hand? Then puberty approaches, and suddenly it's like pulling crocodile teeth to get them to show outward affection. My youngest son, Luc, is very much an individual. At five years of age, he really didn't care about his appearance or how he dressed. But I know things will change—physically and internally— when he becomes a teenager. Dr. Meeker explains why:

> Teens, being developmentally egocentric, believe that their actions and thoughts are constantly on public display. They have an imaginary audience that diligently critiques their every move, outfit, and conversation. Teens decide to believe what "others" are thinking about them, and their perceptions are filtered through opinions they believe others hold about them. Thus, their feelings regarding their identity and abilities are not always based in reality.[8]

Having moved from concrete thought processes to more abstract thinking, these young "adults-in-formation" are exploring concepts about who they are. As they shape those concepts (identity formation), they place great equity in what they perceive others think about them. That puts "wearing that certain pair of pants" in a different light, doesn't it? To put it bluntly, those pants are important to your daughter, so forget the sigh, and just put up with her having to constantly wash and wear them! She may feel judged negatively without them, and that impacts her self-value. Your son, too, looks at how his shirt fits his body and compares himself to what his "imaginary audience" may either approve of or disapprove of. That's why teens often move from one peer group to another, searching for someone who will embrace them in those moments of vulnerability. This acceptance is monumental in their identity formation process.

> As teens shape their concepts about themselves, they place great equity in what they perceive others think about them.

"Healthy parenting," continues Dr. Meeker, "involves teaching a process whereby a teen learns to recognize, embrace, and raise up the deepest truest sense of who he is. This is extremely important because the teen is then able to draw strength from that positive image of himself and move forward in life."[9]

Much more can be said about character development and identity formation. As we look at puberty and the physical changes in our children, we also have to understand this cognitive shift. Puberty may be seen as mostly physical, but the core of our children takes dramatic leaps at this time, forging belief systems and patterns of behavior that will affect their choices now and for a lifetime. That means we must be aware of the life changes they experience, and we must encourage and embrace our teens through those changes—whether physical, social, emotional, intellectual, or spiritual.

It's All Part of a Girl's Life

I'll admit it: I'm a guy. So what am I doing talking about important events for girls? Well, there are a lot of dads and doctors who are very educated about menstruation and ovulation, who can lecture quite professionally on the anatomy and reproductive system of a female. But then there are those fathers of daughters who, like me, need professional information presented in a clear, clean, and simple format.

Marilyn Morris, president of Aim for Success, Inc., does a great job explaining the menstruation process for young girls. This is important for many reasons. While many realize that ladies have a "period," few know why. Even my mother, who is in her sixties, wasn't aware of much of this information when we talked about it. And why should she be? She didn't need to discuss these anatomical functions with my sister because there wasn't a need to do so when we were growing up. Today there is.

If we are to discuss later how STDs and abortion can affect the reproductive system, then we need to understand this reproductive system created by God. If you are a single dad raising a daughter, just go ahead and fold this page corner down. While it would be best to share this information with your daughter in your own words, Marilyn Morris does a great job in detailing the information in a way you could practically read to a daughter who is at puberty's doorstep.

Here, in her words, is what you and your daughter need to know:

Girls typically begin sexual maturity around 11 to 12 years of age. During this time there will be a growth spurt. Estrogen, the female sex hormone, will cause the breasts to begin forming and hips to widen. Bodily hair will begin to grow, soon followed by menstruation and ovulation. At this time a girl will have the ability to have a baby.

The uterus, or womb, is located inside the lower abdomen of the female. This muscular organ resembles the shape and size of a small pear, but it is capable of growing much larger when a woman is pregnant. When a girl reaches the age of 11 to 14, her uterus will prepare for nurturing a fertilized egg. Every month the uterus will build a rich lining where the baby can grow for nine months. However, if the egg is not fertilized by a male sperm, the lining in the uterus is not needed and is discarded. This process is called menstruation, menstrual cycle or monthly period. This cycle occurs about every 28 days.

As the lining of the uterus is discarded, the woman

experiences a bloody discharge from her vagina for three to seven days. The vagina is a special opening between a woman's legs. It is also referred to as the birth canal, because this is where a baby passes at birth. When a woman experiences her menstrual cycle, she can use a variety of different products to keep her clothes from becoming soiled.

Once the lining of the uterus has been discarded, the process will start all over and continue every month. A woman will menstruate about 400 times during her life. Then typically when she is in her late 40s or early 50s, her monthly menstrual cycle will stop. This is called menopause. At this time she will no longer be fertile (capable of having a baby) and can no longer become pregnant.

The other important event which takes place each month inside the female body is called ovulation. During ovulation, one or both ovaries release a ripened egg (also called ovum) into the fallopian tube. Each egg contains the mother's genetic material necessary to produce a new life.

Women do not continue to produce new eggs. Unlike men, who produce sperm on a daily basis, women are born with eggs in their ovaries. In fact, a female has the most eggs when she is still inside her mother's womb. By the fifth month of pregnancy, an unborn baby girl will have about five million eggs in her ovaries. At birth the number will have dropped to about one or two million. By the early teenage years, she will have about 300,000 eggs. Of course, she will only need about 400 eggs since she will only ovulate about 400 times during her life. By the time a woman reaches menopause, there are no healthy eggs left in her ovaries and she is no longer capable of having a baby.

Ovulation occurs about 14 days before the woman's next menstrual cycle. Once the egg is released, she will be fertile, or capable of becoming pregnant, for approximately 24 hours. Some adult women are able to tell fairly accurately when they are ovulating. They often have a small discharge, slight cramping sensation, and even a slight change in their body temperature.

If a woman wants to get pregnant, she needs to have sexual intercourse at the time of ovulation or during the three to five days before ovulation.

Teenage girls and many women often have irregular cycles and are unable to tell when they are fertile. Because of this unpredictable cycle and not knowing exactly when she might ovulate, a girl needs to realize she might become pregnant almost any time she has sexual intercourse.

> **Because a menstrual cycle can be unpredictable, a girl can become pregnant almost any time she has sexual intercourse.**

When the egg is released from the ovary, it travels down the fallopian tube. It is inside this small, delicate tube where fertilization takes place. The egg must be fertilized by the sperm within 24 hours or the egg will disintegrate. Remember, a woman is only fertile when she ovulates. Usually, this is also when she is most easily aroused sexually.[10]

A Boy's Sexual System

It is equally important for parents of young men to know how the male reproductive system functions. Sometimes young boys have questions that they are too embarrassed to ask. For example, one junior high boy in New York wrote this to me:

> *I'm kinda worried. I get like these bumps on my penis and then a couple weeks later a hair will grow through. . . . is that common?*

This poor young man was concerned. He was growing hair in strange places and had no one to talk with other than me. But if the teen's relationship with a parent encourages open communication, the parent can greatly help him through such uncomfortable times and questions with informed answers.

Again, Ms. Morris lends us sage advice.

A boy usually begins sexual maturity around 12 to 13 years of age. At this time, the male sex hormone, testosterone, causes numerous changes. Growth spurts will cause boys to finally grow taller than most girls. Their voices begin to change. They develop hair on their face and body and their muscles become larger.

It is also during this time that a boy starts to produce sperm from his testicles. The testicles are attached to the body by a pouch of skin called the scrotum. To produce sperm normally, the testicles must be cooler than the rest of the body. Therefore, the scrotum is suspended away from the body to provide this lower temperature. The scrotum stays at 95°F or 35°C. . . .

A healthy young male will produce about 100,000,000 (one hundred million) sperm each day. That's more than one thousand sperm a second. . . .

Each sperm is so small that it can only be seen through a microscope. A sperm consists of a head and a tail. Within the head of each sperm is a selection of the father's genetic material to create a new, unique person. The sperm wiggles its tail back and forth, swimming with only one goal: to fertilize an egg. . . .

Sperm leaves the male body through a small tube inside the penis called the urethra. This is the same tube used to eliminate urine from a man's body. Sperm leaves the body in a milky looking fluid called semen. When the sperm leaves the male body, this is called ejaculation. Each ejaculation produces about one-half to one teaspoon of semen. That may not sound like much, but it contains up to 500 million sperm all striving to win the race to the female's egg.

A healthy young male produces more than one thousand sperm a second.

A man may ejaculate as a result of sexual excitement. He may also ejaculate during his sleep. Ejaculation during sleep is called nocturnal emission or a wet dream. This is normal and is caused by certain reflexes triggered during sleep.[11]

But *when* do we have these conversations with our children? So many loving parents ask that question. While we don't want our children to be ignorant, causing their choices to be uneducated and possibly dangerous later on, neither do we want to damage their innocence by discussing topics so graphic.

My wife and I live by this rule: *The level of information they need to know is determined by the questions they ask, and we answer in an age-appropriate way.*

If your child wants more information, he'll ask for it. All you have to do when he asks, "Where do babies come from?" for example, is to follow your response with, "Does that answer your question?" He will let you know **How much information do you share, and when? Hold to this rule: If they want more information, they'll ask for it.** whether or not you've satisfied his curiosity. If not, he'll take his question to the next step, and you can do likewise with your answer.

One conversation I had with my daughter Brianna when she was eight was on the topic of genital privacy. I explained that we wear swimsuits over our "private parts" for a reason. No one is to see or touch those areas other than mommies, daddies, and doctors. "God has made boys and girls different down there," I explained. "Have you noticed how Luc and you are different in the bathtub?" Both she and Luc, who was now listening to our conversation, giggled and nodded. I continued to make my answer age-appropriate for an eight-year-old and a five-year-old. "God made boys to have a penis, but girls don't. They have a vagina. When a girl and boy from different families grow up and become adults, they may fall in love and want to get married. Only after they are married can they see each others' private parts."

I had hoped to stop there. But Bri's wrinkled brow caused me to explain a tad more. "You see, inside a lady are eggs. And inside a man are seeds. When they are married and want to have a baby, the man makes his seeds go to the lady's eggs. One of those eggs becomes a baby and grows in the mommy's tummy until it comes out." The wrinkles were gone. "Do you understand that?" She responded "Yes," and Luc spun on his heels and headed out of the room. "I've got seeds!" I heard him say to himself.

When my oldest son was in the second grade, I was driving him to school when he asked where babies came from. I knew I had 10 minutes to answer him, and I figured that would be enough (this was going to be a very basic lesson). So I told him the basics of conception and birth. The entire time he was looking out the passenger window; I'm sure his eyes were wide. When I asked if that answered his question, he quickly said "Yes." I don't think the information was too much for him, since it was his curiosity that prompted it. Besides, if I hadn't answered him, he would have asked one of his friends. Then his education on birth and sexuality would be delivered to him by a peer, a second grader. My adequate response was vital. And it was obvious that he understood too.

Later that week his friend came to our house for a sleepover. "My mommy is going to have a baby," my son told his pal. My wife grinned from the next room as she overheard him. "And do you know what?" he continued. "They don't come out her belly button!" Half choking in a mix of laughter and panic, my wife hollered out to the boys, "It's time for bed, you two!"

> Many children are afraid to go to their parents for counsel. Often parents treat children as children when they need to be talked to like grown-ups.
>
> —Billy Graham

In other words, while there is much more we *could* say to our children, it isn't necessary to give all the answers at once. Let them be content with the knowledge they have gained for the day. Then as questions arise on occasion, give an accurate and medically sound answer, while trying to preserve their innocence. No matter what, frame every answer to show God's purpose and design. God has created us beautifully and wonderfully, and children should never be ashamed of how they are created. So don't make your explanation about sex a shameful experience.

To solidly cement God's love and purpose in your child's life, you can even use these words, directly from the Bible:

> *For you created my inmost being;*
> *you knit me together in my mother's womb.*
> *I praise you because I am fearfully and wonderfully made;*
> *your works are wonderful,*
> *I know that full well.*
> *My frame was not hidden from you*
> *when I was made in the secret place.*
> *When I was woven together in the depths of the earth,*

your eyes saw my unformed body.
All the days ordained for me
were written in your book
before one of them came to be.[12]

After hearing these words, what child wouldn't feel the warmth of God's love and your love wrapped around them?

And that type of assurance is what every child and teen will need to navigate the minefields of people who are offering them short-term and selfish love in the guise of sexual pleasure.

Chapter Six

To Be Sexually Active—or Not?
pure **choices**

do you remember good old Isaac Newton and the law of gravity, which he discovered when an apple fell on his head? Well, his third law of motion formally states, "For every action, there is an equal and opposite reaction."[1] Isaac Newton is right—you see, every choice we make *does* create a reaction, or consequence. It's absurd to think that we can do something and have zero consequences. Just as throwing a rock into a pond creates a ripple effect, so does every choice we make—including whether or not to have sex outside the bounds of marriage.

In the hundreds of public schools where I've spoken, I have to define what I mean when I say "having sex." You see, most teenagers believe that having sex only means "sexual intercourse." For the majority of these students, oral and anal sex are not considered sex. Also discounted as sex are fondling and mutual masturbation.

I'll say it as simply here as I do to teens internationally: High-risk sexual activity for two unmarried people is *any* genital contact of any kind. Even with the correct and proper use of a condom, any genital activity is a risk (to see more on why, consult the Contraceptive Protection Rates on pages 142–143). And, as with any other action, there will be an equal and opposite reaction.

The exciting news today is that more teens are choosing to abstain from sexual intercourse than ever before! For the first time in over three

decades, this generation has reduced the swelling statistics of teen sexual intercourse.[2] Their decisions are powerfully affecting their peers and creating a strong movement away from sexual activity. This is encouraging! No

With any risky action, there will be an equal and opposite reaction.

longer do our teens have to fall prey to the adage, "Everyone else is doing it." In fact, the majority is not.

Why is this? There are probably several factors. While contraceptive education wants to claim this as their success, it's hard to equate the many decades of their education, influence, and paralleled increases in teen pregnancy and STDs with only *recent* success in reducing teen sexual intercourse. More likely, the decrease in sexual contact is a combination of the prevalence of deadly STDs (namely HIV, which causes AIDS), the growing influence of abstinence education, and a generation of teens with a different mind-set than generations before.

However, there are still far too many who choose sexual activity—and the consequences are life-changing. In this chapter, we'll talk about three of the four consequences of teen sexual activity: pregnancy, relational changes, and character and future changes. The fourth consequence—the deadliest one—we'll address in the next chapter, "The Real Facts about STDs."

Consequence #1: Pregnancy

A few weeks ago my boyfriend and I had unprotected sex numerous times. One day I got out of the shower and felt really dizzy and sick to my stomach. He came and sat down by me and asked what was wrong, I told him that I was feeling really sick, like throwing up sick. He got real quiet and said I hope I didn't get you pregnant! I got really scared. So did he.

The first and obvious consequence results in a teen girl becoming pregnant, like the six girls I talked to near Van Wert, Ohio, at a home for pregnant teen moms. Although each one has to process her pregnancy and the choices following her pregnancy individually, each one said she "never thought it could happen to her." What teen girl does? It's called *unplanned pregnancy* for a reason! Yet every year nearly 900,000 teens get pregnant in America.

In our nation, if a girl is pregnant, she has three options: She can parent the baby, abort the little one, or place that child for adoption. Sadly, there are no other choices. Yes, she had a great choice before: "Should I have sex or not?" Now, after the fact, her choices are much different. And the choice she makes will affect her not only physically, but emotionally, for her lifetime.

> A pregnant teen only has three options—and the choice she makes will impact her for a lifetime.

We'll look at each of these choices—and their consequences. Since the best choice is always an informed choice, we need to know as much as we can before we guide teens and peers through this valley of decision.

CHOICE #1: PARENT THE BABY

This *can* be a good choice, but it's certainly not an easy one. If a teen girl chooses to parent the baby, she will need to have an incredible support network behind her. Ideally, this should include her family, church and youth group, school, and friends. But this ideal is rare.

A friend of mine shared how the daughter of a church's pastor became pregnant. As a result, her parents asked her to stand on the platform, share the news, and apologize to the entire congregation.

I was stunned. Now some of you may think that is appropriate, but I do not. This young girl had enough challenges before her, just facing the consequence of unplanned motherhood and the immediate loss of her own childhood. Then her parents added public shame and forced humiliation—only to better their own image. Shame on them! What this girl needed at that time was loving support and encouragement, not condemnation. A parent certainly shouldn't excuse her actions. However, I believe it is wrong to rub her nose in a decision she can't take back. That pastor's daughter certainly didn't need to tell her story and what she'd done wrong again and in such a public setting. Every day, the changes in her body as the child grew would be a constant reminder.

No parents like to hear that their daughter is pregnant, because it also means the end of many of their dreams for that child. And it means that life will change—drastically—no matter what decision is made about the growing baby. But pregnant teens should never be treated with degradation, shame, or embarrassment. Instead, they need adults, like you, to be compassionate and sympathetic. They need adults who will gently guide them through the tough choices before them. If you step out of their life, physically or emotionally, due to embarassment or anger, there will be others waiting in the wings to take your place . . . and many of those won't share your faith or values.

Teen parents find themselves facing many hurdles. Because of the heavy taxation on their time and the stress incurred from huge changes in their social lives, teen mothers find it very hard to complete their schooling. Only half finish high school while adolescents or young adults. As a result, nearly 80 percent of teen mothers live at or below the poverty line.[3] Teen mothers are also more likely to remain single for most of their children's early years. Why? Because few teen birth fathers stick around much past the words, "I'm pregnant." And for those who do stick around through the pregnancy and birth, their long-term "promises" often prove to be temporary.

Many teen girls have told me the lines that their boyfriends have used on them, including this one from a pregnant teen named Kathie: "He told me that he would be there for me and our baby if I was pregnant and that he loved me and would never leave me." I would love to believe this boyfriend—and, in fact, I have met some who have become wonderful fathers and husbands. But the reality is that only 20 to 30 percent of teen fathers actually marry their baby's mother.[4]

Only 20 to 30 percent of teen fathers actually marry their baby's mother.

That means most of these young girls raise their child without the help and support of a father. Most are still unmarried five years after having the baby, and "less than half of the teenagers who have children out of wedlock marry within ten years after giving birth."[5]

I would like to ask the guys what they believe "being there" for the girl really means. Yes, it's easy to be there during the pregnancy, baby showers, the birth, and the first months. But any parent knows how the glory runs out when the responsibility and the inevitable exhaustion kicks in. And all this at a time when a teen would normally "just" be involved in the world of junior high or high school. Instead of evening phone chats with friends, birthday parties, sports activities, the teen mother is changing diapers and feeding a baby.

Is this the only consequence of pregnancy—how it affects the mother's relationships? Sadly, it impacts the child as well. Studies show that children of teen mothers compare unfavorably to other children on a variety of measurements. These include having low math and reading scores, repeating a grade, having sex before age sixteen, fighting at school or work, or skipping school. They also are more likely to "not graduate from high school, to be abused or neglected or to have a child as an unmarried teenager."[6] Is this information derived from some small random sample? Not in the least. Concerning juvenile delinquency, "A 1997 study of more than 50,000 adolescents found that those born to teenage or unmarried mothers were at a greater risk of juvenile delinquency than were those born to married mothers. Males from these families were 1.7 times more likely to become chronic offenders, while the females were 1.8 times more likely to be offenders and 2.8 times more likely to be chronic offenders."[7]

Scary statistics indeed. Ones that show how immensely teen pregnancy and teen parenting affect the mother *and* the child—not to mention you and me, the taxpayers. "Teenage childbearing costs U.S. taxpayers an estimated $7 billion per year in social services and lost tax revenue due to government dependency."[8] This report went on to state that "the gross annual cost to society of adolescent childbearing and its negative social consequences is $29 billion." This is one of the driving factors of those promoting birth control to teens.

However, let's say that all teens suddenly use birth control. Would the problem then be solved? Only partially, because birth control cannot prevent infections (we'll cover that topic soon).

But there's also another reason—a big, compelling reason. What about a teen's emotions? As Lakita Garth, a national abstinence speaker, has said, "They don't make a condom big enough to cover the human heart." Sadly, I have seen the truth of that played out in hundreds of thousands of teens' lives across the country.

An eighth-grade girl once told me, "I *want* to have a baby." When I asked her why, she said, "Because I want the baby to love me." I ached for this girl because she was so lacking love in her life that she'd fallen for one of Twisted's lies.

> **They don't make a condom big enough to cover the human heart.** —Lakita Garth

Birthing a child is not the way to find love. Besides, babies don't automatically love you. They don't! No, they *learn* to love you. For the most part, babies are barbarians (just watch them scream, burp, eat, and fill their diapers!). You must love them, not expecting them to love you back. Love is all about self-sacrifice, not about warm feelings. Jesus himself said, "Greater love has no one than this, that he lay down his life for his friends."[9] In order to raise a child properly, you too must "lay down" your life. You must sacrifice your life—including your comfort, your commitments, your time, your sleep—for the life of that baby. Yes, you sacrifice due to pain during childbirth, but the sacrifice isn't over then; it isn't over until that child is a mature adult, able to function responsibly without you.

CHOICE #2: ABORTION

Some years ago I was of the opinion that abortion is wrong except in extreme cases of incest, rape, or if the unborn is somehow threatening the life of the mother. You may believe that too. I held that opinion for several decades, until I met Pam. And then my opinion changed radically.

Pam's mother was only 15 when she was raped. When she discovered she was pregnant, instead of choosing abortion, which was a legal choice for rape victims at that time, this brave young lady carried the baby to full term. After delivery, the baby was placed for adoption. When Mr. and Mrs. Wood encountered this child and learned of the story, they took the baby into their home and lives. They named this precious little girl Pamela Wood. Today this same girl—now married and known as Pam Stenzel—is an international speaker and author who impacts countless thousands with her life and her message.[10]

As I watched this beautiful and intelligent lady speak to teens in Minnesota, I was spellbound. No one seemed to breathe when she shared her story. Tears began to stream down my face when she eyed the 1,500 teens in the school and said bluntly, "My father is a rapist. I don't even know my nationality. Do you really think my life is worth less than yours because of how I was conceived?" She paused, and the silence in the gym was deafening. "I didn't deserve the death penalty for some crime my father committed." Because Pam's birth mother chose not to take the easy way out, Pam is alive today. Even more, her desire, like mine, is to better inform teens and their parents, helping both make wiser choices for the future.

So is abortion a *right* or a *choice?* I suppose to some degree it is your body, therefore your right. But if you believe the Bible, then you also believe that God knows us before we are conceived or formed in the womb.[11] So we exist before conception, meaning there is life before birth. And to end that life before a baby is born—is that your right?

Several years ago a dear friend of mine called me on the phone with deep concern in her voice. This beautiful, 28-year-old model was single and pregnant. She didn't love the father of her child enough to marry him, but she was torn. I shared with her about God and life, and the potential of that child she carried within her. Then I reassured her of my love for her as a friend. Weeks later she left me a voice mail; she had aborted her baby. Heartbroken, she tried hard to justify issues of personal health and personal choice. I tried to reach out to her in love and compassion—she was still my friend. But to this day she never returns my calls.

Is abortion a *right* or a *choice?*

Yes, it was her legal choice. But she deserved a better choice than that. And what choice did that child deserve?

Pam Stenzel, who could have been aborted, is a smart and attractive woman who makes wise choices every day. Thankfully, her mother, even when faced with the torturous situation of rape and a resulting pregnancy, gave Pam the right to exercise her choices as well. Yes, it all does come down to making a choice—and abortion is one choice readily available today. Many (perhaps even you, in your past) have chosen the route of abortion to get rid of an "unwanted pregnancy." Roughly 3,000 abortions occur every day in our nation.[12] When the Columbine school shootings occurred in my neighborhood, it rocked our nation. I sat with teens and adults who had lost their friends and their children. Their grief was heavy, all consuming. And while there is no way to measure loss of life numerically, compare the 13 deaths at Columbine to the 3,000 abortions that have taken place today—and every day. If the shooters at Columbine had bombed the entire school, 2,000 would have been killed. But just today, in one day alone, one and a half future high schools were eliminated through abortion! Just add 17 years to the current year, and imagine that year's graduating class reduced by 3,000 yesterday and by 21,000 in the next week.

3,000 abortions took place today . . . and every day.

Worse, abortion has become quite a business. Without going into great detail, I wonder if we are harvesting the lives of the young for the sake of the old? Look at any issue—whether it's stem-cell research to help those with Parkinson's, or partial-birth abortions, or standard abortions. All of this research is to extend or "enrich" the lives of adults. No self-sacrifice there. But what about the millions of babies who are dying in the process?

If you believe these unborn children are alive before birth or have rights before they exit the womb, then this research may bother you. If you believe that this is only birth tissue—a fetus—until fully delivered, then such research is not a big issue for you. But here's something interesting: The word *fetus* is actually derived from a Latin word meaning "act of bearing young, offspring" and is akin to "newly delivered, fruitful."[13] While *Webster's* definition postures away from the word's original meanings, its origin is sound in my mind. Others may call an unborn child a *fetus* to keep the spin away from *life, baby,* or *child*. But those people do not realize they're saying, according to the word's origin, that the unborn child is still someone's offspring, someone's fruit. Sadly, there are those who think harvest time for the fruit of human life is a choice available to prevent unplanned pregnancy or to improve quality of life for adults.

Pregnant women considering abortion must realize that they have already had their *easy* choice: "Should I have sex or not?" If only they could go back, maybe they would change their actions. But they can't. They've made that choice and are now living with the consequences. I want to be clear here. I am compassionate toward those who have had abortions—including dear friends of mine. But I also believe, with all my heart, in being honest. Just because someone doesn't like the consequence doesn't give him or her the right to eliminate another life. Especially when God says that every life is precious and that he sees and watches over the progress of every baby in the womb.[14]

Is there any good news? I think so! "Although the adoption rate has remained relatively steady, nationwide abortion rates have continued to decline since 1990."[15] That means this young generation is not increasing the use of abortion as a contraceptive! And it means that more are realizing regard for life *is* something to celebrate!

CHOICE #3: PLACE THE BABY FOR ADOPTION

One of my favorite moments when speaking before large audiences of teens is to address the topic of adoption. I invite teenagers who are adopted to come up to me later and shake my hand. I want to personally meet them. Why? "You are a chosen child," I say. "That makes you special to me." Faith, a ninth-grader from Texas, wrote me this letter afterwards:

> *I've never met my real parents, but I know my mother was a teenager when she got pregnant, so that's why I was put up for adoption. But I guess I am very fortunate because I was adopted by the best set of parents I could possibly ask for. The only thing I didn't like about being adopted is that I always felt kind of singled out, or different from everybody else. After you talked to us, I felt so much better about being adopted.*

Placing a baby for adoption is no simple or easy choice. A young girl has to decide to carry the baby full term, which means experiencing all the discomforts of a pregnant mom. She will also feel every movement of the child and experience a special bond. Then she has to birth the child, knowing she will not be there when that baby smiles, says "Momma," or graduates from high school. Placing a baby for adoption brings with it deep and immediate loss for a young mother. By any stretch of the imagination, this is not an easy choice for the birth mother—and it won't be easy for the child in later years.

Many students have told me sadly that they were "given away" by parents or families who must not have wanted them. So I simply share with them Rachel's story. She was 15 and seven-and-a-half-months pregnant when I met her in northwest Ohio, where she was staying in a home for pregnant teenagers. As girls around a circle shared stories, most talked about how they were going to keep their babies. Some talked of the baby's father, but most found the fathers were not as dependable as they'd initially thought. When we finally came to Rachel, she placed her hand on her enlarged tummy.

"Mr. Herman, you need to understand something," she began. Tears formed in her blue eyes as she explained. "I can't raise this baby. I don't have a family that supports me. And God knows, I don't have the money. I don't even know who the father is." Looking at the girls in the circle, tears began to race down her cheeks. Her long curly hair snagged in wet lines. "You may want to raise your child, and that's cool. But I can't. I really want this baby to have a happy family and a great future. But it won't find that with me. This baby deserves better."

> "I don't want to give this baby away—I want to give it a chance."—Rachel, pregnant at 15

Compassion glistened in her eyes. "I don't want this baby to ever think I gave it away. But I want it to have a family, a future, and a hope. Mr. Herman, I don't want to give this baby away—I want to give it a chance."

"You were not given away—you were given a chance." Teens who were adopted are silent and often teary-eyed when I tell them that. And they do come up to me later and shake my hand. Even when their adoption stories are much uglier—and many are—when those adopted teens realize that adoption is not an act of getting rid of a heavy burden, their hearts melt. They begin to see adoption as a wonderful act of sacrifice. To love a child as much as Rachel did is not selfish. Placing a child for adoption is a tough choice but a wonderful one as well. It is a lifelong gift to the child.

I wish more teens could make this difficult choice, and through my words and my story about Rachel, I hope they are encouraged to do so. But statistics show the reality: "When they become pregnant, very few teens choose to place their children for adoption. In a 1995 survey, 51% of teens that become pregnant give birth; 35% seek abortions; 14% miscarry. Less than 1% choose to place their children for adoption."[16]

Why is this? Experts say it may be because pregnant teen girls don't have higher educational and vocational goals for themselves. "Women who voluntarily place their children for adoption are likely to have greater educational and vocational goals for themselves than those who keep their children. Women making adoption plans often come from higher socioeconomic backgrounds. These women come from intact families which are supportive of the placement, and which have not experienced teenage pregnancies by other family members."[17]

Moms and dads, our teens need to value life—and that includes theirs and their unborn child's. Additionally, they need you to support them in this powerful choice, if that is the path they are going to take. It can be done. Keep at the front of your mind that the teen who chooses adoption is giving that child a chance rather than giving the baby away. Explaining adoption in such a way to a pregnant teen can make a life-changing impact on both the teen and the baby.

Another thing you can do is talk through the process with your teen. Make sure she's aware of all the emotions she will go through during and after the birth and that she understands how her heart will bond with her baby. If you support your teen through this difficult process, you should also assist in all the red tape of the adoption process. With open adoptions and the clause regarding a mother's last-minute "change of mind," families can be hesitant to adopt from a pregnant teen, especially since teens are known for being highly changeable and emotional. Supportive families can make all the difference—not only in the process of adoption itself, but in the subsequent emotional and physical health of the teen. We'll talk even more about how you can make a difference in chapter 9, "It Takes a Family First."

WHAT ABOUT MISCARRIAGE?

I'd had a wonderful evening event one night at a youth camp. The following morning I'd challenged students again, causing them to laugh through their tears and reexamine their lives. I was talking with several students when a girl came up behind me and slipped a note into my hand. I turned quickly to see who it was, but she was already headed out the door. I never did see her face.

But I heard her heart. In the note Kirsten shared how her boyfriend had taken her to a remote area and had asked her to sleep with him. If she didn't, he said, she'd lose him. Emotionally invested in the relationship, this 14-year-old had sex with her 18-year-old boyfriend. Her parents learned about the situation and forced a breakup. "Turns out the rumors are false. You can get pregnant the first time," she wrote in the letter. When she learned of the pregnancy, she couldn't tell her parents for fear of their reaction. So she suffered in silence. Soon she was three months along. One afternoon, alone at home, she had a miscarriage in the bathroom. Listen to her story, and weep. I certainly did.

The baby was no bigger than my hand. It had see-through skin, and I could see its tiny heart. Now I had truly lost everything. I clung to the toilet for the next three and a half hours, crying and asking God, WHY ME? I made one mistake in 14 years and now I had lost everything. My whole dream in life was to be a mother. That's all I ever wanted, and now I had to flush it down the toilet.

I told my mom a month or two later. She didn't want me to tell anyone, not even my own dad. She also told me that aborted and miscarried babies didn't have spirits so they couldn't go to heaven.

For the last three years I have felt the pain of losing my baby, never getting to hold it and say good-bye, and never having the hope of seeing it in heaven. I was able to forgive everyone involved except myself.

Is your heart as torn as mine? I weep as I read and re-read Kirsten's handwritten letter. She deserved so very much more. Trying to find love in sex, she fell into our culture's standard: Sex is fine as long as you both consent. Although she was pressured by her boyfriend, she did consent. But reality crashed into her dreams and fractured her family relationships. She will forever remember that short time with her boyfriend and the poignant moment in the bathroom. Yes, she deserved so much more.

Consequence #2: Relational and Emotional Pain

Each time I leave for a speaking engagement, what do you think the conversation with my wife at my front door is like? Do you think it goes something like this?

"Sweetheart, I'm leaving!" I shout to my wife, Stephanie.

Running up to me with one of the kids' half-folded shirts in hand, she offers me a kiss. "I love you, honey," she says. We hug long and hard. Although I love what I do professionally, it's always hard to leave my family.

"I need to go," I say, giving her another warm kiss.

As we separate, I grab my bags and open the door. Stephanie turns me to face her one last time and says, "Honey, remember, I'm your wife."

"Of course I'll remember. How can I forget?"

"I want you to be faithful to me."

Somewhat taken aback, I blink hard and say nothing for a moment. "Uh . . . of course I'll be faithful, honey."

"But just in case you aren't, take these," she says, handing me a box of condoms.

Now, that is definitely a fictional story! But ask yourself, why doesn't this happen in our marriages? Because, contrary to those who believe in "open" marriages and that it's okay to have multiple sexual partners even within marriage, marriage is intended to be a life of honor, respect, and commitment. Our faithfulness is based on our soul. It's a relational, an emotional, and a deeply internal issue. So to have a marriage where my spouse is more concerned about my contracting an STD than she is about me being unfaithful is ludicrous. The consequences of relational and emotional betrayal are immense—both in the short-term and in the long-term.

> Faithfulness isn't merely physical—it's relational, emotional, and deeply internal.

So why do we disrespect our teens and give them that scenario? And why is it less important to discuss these issues with our teens than the issues of pregnancy and STDs? Dating today is such an intense relationship that many experience the darkness of depression following a break-up. Many teen relationships today have all the factors of a marriage—without the vital component of commitment. But without commitment or self-sacrifice—the faithful expression of true love—there can be no lasting relationship.

So how can you help?

FRIENDS DON'T LET FRIENDS . . . GET HURT

What is a *friend* to you? Friends are extremely valuable to me. You see, I've found over the years that I'm extremely overtrusting. Well, like many of you, after repeatedly getting stabbed in the back by alleged friends, I've had to change. I still trust, albeit now with caution. But finding a true friend is a real challenge. What makes a friend true?

As a culture, Americans have learned to befriend people easily. Celebrities who appear on our TV screens or sing on our radios have prominent positions in our homes. It's as if they are a part of our families. For example, it seems like I know Val Kilmer personally after watching him perform in a variety of movies. But *is* Val Kilmer truly my friend?

To answer that question, think back to the definition of *love* as "self-sacrifice." For you to have a friend—a true friend—they have to love you unconditionally. And you have to love them unconditionally in return. We have to show some form of self-sacrifice to one another to show that we truly care. The truth about a relationship becomes clear if you look at it this way: If I got into a tough situation, would Val Kilmer be available to help me? The chances are highly unlikely. Because there is no self-sacrifice, there is no friendship.

Who would ever sacrifice themselves for a mere acquaintance? There are some, I guess. But true friends will lay down their lives for one another to some degree: "Though one may be overpowered, two can defend themselves. A cord of three strands is not quickly broken."[18] What does this mean practically? When I'm in pain, I'll call my friend and he'll take a brief moment from his very busy schedule to connect and let me vent. When my friend needs me but doesn't call because of his stubborn pride, it hurts me. I want to be able to sacrifice for my friends and show them my deepest care. In those times of need, true friends step up. And you know who they are.

Now, if that's how friends respond to each other, then what's wrong with our nation? People are getting hurt relationally, emotionally, and physically, and no one seems to care!

I meet hundreds upon hundreds of teens, adults, and parents who have been involved in various activities that have caused them harm. Some have had sexual trysts that were "fun" or "just a simple thing." When asked, they say, "It's not like either of us expects anything, Doug." In fact, one young boy in LaPorte, Indiana, said "She's just my [sex expletive] buddy. It's not like we're in love or anything." Sexual activity has become a sport to our nation. It sells nearly everything from shoes to cars to shampoo. Many see the practice of waiting for sex until you are in a faithful, monogamous marriage as an antiquated idea. More and more sexual deviance permeates our homes and schools.

If we care—if we really care—can we just stand by and watch?

Although you may have a political and medical agenda radically different than mine, I think most of you reading this book have compassion for others in harm's way. I truly believe you want people to avoid nasty diseases, death, and unfair restraint. That means we all want the same for our nation—health, freedom, and the pursuit of happiness. But can we get there from two different paths?

Let me start answering that question by telling you a story about something that happened recently. One afternoon I was returning from the post office in my truck. As I drove down the street to my house, I watched to make sure I was under the speed limit. In my neighborhood, signs say "Speed Limit: 19." *Stay under 20!* they instruct. Rounding the bend, I approached a home where some friends live. In the driveway were a gaggle of children—including two of mine—from ages three to eight. As I drove closer, suddenly one young boy on a three-wheeler turned and drove straight toward the street, directly into my

> I believe that unarmed truth and unconditional love will have the final word in changing this world's reality.
> —Martin Luther King, Jr.

path. Two mothers saw him and what would happen if he continued, and they began screaming, "D'Wayne!" I pressed on my brakes. The young boy turned a hard left and averted disaster as I rolled by slowly.

Looking at the faces of these two mothers, you would expect a sigh of relief and a smile. Oooh, no. There was anything but! In fact, they were both yelling at him as I continued to my home. Why? Because D'Wayne had done this repeatedly before. He would continually drive into the street without looking for any oncoming traffic. At seven years of age, he should have known better. He had been trained, instructed by his parents and by neighbors. But still he would race in front of cars, including many who did not obey the 19 miles-per-hour speed limit.

Now, think about it. D'wayne has a right to ride in the street, doesn't he? After all, it's in front of his home. He has also received instruction on how to ride in the street safely from driveway to driveway, with minimum risk. He's been told to *never* ride in the street when cars are coming. But still he puts himself in harm's way. Why?

If you say, "He's just too young," your argument fails. There are several in his peer group who are younger yet more responsible. Are we to ground him from his own three-wheeler, removing his right to play that way? Should we let him get hurt "just once" to learn his lesson, gambling that the one time it occurs won't be life-altering or fatal?

No. We as neighbors continue our exhausting cries to teach him not to drive into the street when cars are coming. The distorted faces of the two moms screaming "D'Wayne!" and the command "Stop!" are etched in my memory—and in his! They forced themselves past the lines of rights and risk reduction into the zone of deep concern. They are friends. We are neighbors. Regardless of where we come from, we join together on this path. And friends don't let friends get hurt. Regardless.

THE SCHOOL ZONE

Think radically for a minute. Let's say you had a sexual tryst with someone at the place where you work. Some employers have strict guidelines about this. Even so, if you were to have an affair with the person sitting in the cubicle across from you, how strange would it be once the affair ended? Have you ever paused to wonder how tense and personal any question or comment from them might become? Could you continue working together?

Now let's place this scenario in the already highly relationally and emotionally charged teen culture.

Teens *are* having sex today. Not all, mind you, and that's good news. In fact, 63.6 percent of teens have never had sex or are currently abstinent, which means they've started over. But 65 percent of teens will have lost their virginity by the time they graduate from high school.[19] And that doesn't account for those who are involved in other types of sexual activity, such as the oral sex clubs (more on this later), which are not typically deemed "sex" in their culture.

> 65 percent of teens will have lost their virginity by the time they graduate from high school.

If it's tough to imagine working with someone you've had sexual activity with, try to fathom sitting next to him or her in history class day after day! How hard would it be to concentrate on the "Gettysburg Address" when your ex-fling keeps stealing glances at you?

"I still blame myself somewhat for this happening," explains Savannah in Dayton, Ohio. She shared how hard it was to break free from her boyfriend. "It took me nine months to get out of that relationship, and I finally realize that even though he said he loved me, it wasn't for who I was."

The teen social structure is more turbulent than ever before. Caught in a whirlwind of emotion, teens are forced into one of two choices: Either they can disconnect with their emotions, so as not to feel anything, or they can view sex as something nonemotional. After all, they've been taught that sex is only a physical activity devoid of a deep inner connection. One Web site says, *"Love* can mean many different things to many different people. Sex, on the other hand, is a biological event."[20]

This is the state of teen emotions—and at a time in their lives when they are learning to categorize themselves. In public school they are taught that they are essentially animals at their core, only more complex. With such a view of evolution, morality and other higher ethics hold little value. Emotions, then, become a by-product of the human existence instead of something foundational to the sexual act, as God designed.

No wonder we see all around us the death of the teen spirit. Could it be that through this continued "logic" we are training students to disconnect emotion from the physical, thereby separating the soul (mind and spirit) from the body? How are we to begin developing men and women who will sacrifice themselves for one another and who truly know what love and friendship is? As these men and women later decide to marry, what foundation will they have to remain faithful to their spouse? Are we training our children for divorce?

Certainly, as we divide the human life into categories and try to keep those categories independent of one another, we crush the individual as a whole. We cannot divide the human emotion from the spirit or the body. They are whole only as all three components are fully interconnected. And when a man and a woman are linked through this powerful tri-connection, a marriage is healthy—it benefits both parties, physically, relationally, and emotionally.

Without the knowledge and experience of this powerful connection, today's teens are being divided—from the inside out. They are learning to separate morality from the sexual act. That means they bury or make light of the loss or grief they experience from broken relationships by demeaning the relationship or their "ex." When feelings do come to the surface, teens often drown those emotions with other risk activities (we'll read more about these in the next chapter).

> **"I like how it feels not to feel."**
> —Sally, a teenager who uses drugs to cover her pain

After a recent school assembly in Texas, Sally wrote me this letter:

I was the last one to leave the auditorium after your assembly. We talked for a while about my drug use. Which, frankly, surprised me immensely after I left. I never talk to anyone about things I consider personal, and I shocked myself by telling you about it. I really enjoyed speaking to you. That came as another surprise to me because I like how it feels not to feel. That is one of my reasons for using. It's easier to live that way, but I know (from experience) you are not really living.

People can only take so much pain. If they can't find healing, they will find an escape. Sally began using drugs at age 12 to cover her pain from sexual experiences. Since then she's tried heroin and Ecstasy; currently she's using prescription drugs, including Vicodin. Sally is trying to escape her pain, and she knows it. She's afraid to stop using drugs because she likes *how it feels not to feel.*

But there are those who are searching for and truly finding help. Who are responding to messages of truth and value. Many turn to their pastor, priest, or rabbi. Crisis pregnancy centers' doors ring as these teens enter their offices, seeking someone who can guide them through the entangled messes they are in. Some ask a doctor or therapist for guidance.

All of this reveals that as concerned adults, we cannot think of teen love today as the "puppy love" of our youth. Today's teens are bonding much more intensely. The consequences truly hurt—and they can hurt for a lifetime (for more on this, see the next chapter, "The Real Facts about STDs"). As a parent, you are in the best position to discuss issues of the heart. If you have been widowed or divorced, you have also experienced the death of a relationship. And that's even more reason for you to fight for the purity and health of your teenager's soul.

Consequence #3: The Impact on Your Teen's Character and Future

If you owned a business, what kind of employees would you like to hire? Would you want those who are concerned about themselves more than you and your business? Who live by their desires and have no ability to control themselves? I doubt it. If you did, your business wouldn't last very long. Instead, you place ads to find those who have a team spirit. You want to hire men and women who have developed self-control and self-discipline, because they will represent your company well. The best employee for your company is one who sacrifices selfish desires for the good of the business.

The application is pretty obvious. If character and future issues are important to us as parents, then we should begin working hard on these character developments in our children. Faithfulness, self-control, and goodness are all considered "fruits of the Spirit,"[21] and they are highly prized in every culture. In today's world it's even more important that we aggressively train our children and teens to develop these "heart" issues.

Many of us parents have enrolled our children in sports of some kind. As our children have grown up, they've found physical training essential for their development as athletes. They enter a weight room and lie down on a narrow bench as a teammate places weights on the bar above them. Though it may cause great pain, our children push against the heavy pressure. When they are successful, the team encourages them. But then the "team spirit" forces them back to the same bench to push up on an increased amount of weight. It's obvious: no pain, no gain!

How is that different from our struggles against sexual impurity today? Anyone can go with the flow and have sex. Big deal. But to become strong, our teens must encounter that pressure. Then, with the encouragement of others such as yourself and other trusted teens, they must force that pressure away. Gradually, the pressure increases as they mature, but with continued success in the "weight room," they find themselves stronger than ever before!

> To become strong, our teens must encounter the pressure—and learn how to resist it.

As parents, our natural inclination is to hide our children from all impurity. But that's not God's plan. If we are to be salt and light in this needy and dark world, our children need us to help them when they encounter the pressures to have sex. They need us to coach them and encourage them as they push away the powerful temptations. As they learn self-control, they will only get stronger and more confident. When the day comes that you are not beside them, it is my hope that your training will help them be more aware and powerful in their fight for purity and a healthy life. If they exhibit faithfulness and self-control, their future marriages and careers will produce only healthy fruit.

Isn't that the kind of life you want for your child?

pure **prevention**

have you ever watched the lips of a strong football player quiver as he shared the consequences resulting from a bad choice? Have you ever been moved inside by the dark black eyes of a 14-year-old filled with tears as she grabbed your hand in hopelessness? Have you ever listened to the heart of a student who was in great need of help?

In this chapter we'll not only talk about the real facts about STDs, but we'll also see the ways in which they've impacted real teens—teens I've met. Teens like those in your home, your community, and your church.

Recently there has been a change when we talk about this conse-quence that can possibly affect sexually active people. Rather than call these Sexually Transmitted Diseases (STDs), some are asking that we call them Sexually Transmitted Infections (STIs). But note what's *really* go-ing on behind this new spin. If these are called "infections," then they don't sound as serious. Calling these diseases "infections" implies that treatment is available. After all, an infection isn't permanent. But the re-ality is that many of these infections *are* permanent—I have two death certificates to remind me of that—and we have to understand the full dynamic of these infections and how they impact a person's future life and available choices.

The Medical Institute states, "The United States is experiencing a major epidemic of sexually transmitted disease (STD)."[1] Over 65 million Americans are currently infected with an STD. An additional "15 million people become infected with one or more STDs each year, roughly half of whom contract lifelong infections."[2] One quarter of these new STD infections occur in people between 15 and 19, and two-thirds occur in those under the age of 25.[3]

> **By age 24, at least one in three sexually active people will have contracted an STD.**

That means that "of the 15 million new cases every year, 10 million occur among people aged 15–24. Put another way—by age 24, at least one in three sexually active people will have contracted an STD."[4] With the average age of people getting married being around age 25, an STD infection will most likely impact their marital relationship and future family. And remember, over half of those infections are lifelong.

Our government believes that this is "one of the most under-recognized health problems in the country today."[5] What is driving this epidemic? Doctors believe it is "a combination of factors including the initiation of sexual activity occurring

> **Some STDs are curable. Others are not.**

at younger ages; a delay in the age of first marriage; and high divorce rates. These changing social norms have increased the number of lifetime sexual partners for many Americans."[6] One factor that increases risk of infection for STDs is the increased number of sexual partners.[7] Additionally, many of these infections are asymptomatic, meaning they have no noticeable symptoms, so the infected individuals do not get treatment and are unwarily still contagious. This makes them hard to track and diagnose. Therefore, the federal numbers we have may be somewhat conservative.[8]

What are STDs or STIs? First, sexually transmitted diseases can be classified into two general categories: bacterial infections and viral infections. One is curable; the other is not. For you who, like me, are years removed from your biology class, this will be a quick refresher course for you!

Bacterial Infections

Bacterial infections (caused by bacteria) are treatable and curable.[9] But all is not good news. The Medical Institute advises that, "Though effective antibiotic treatments for bacterial STDs exist, antibiotic resistance is increasing. Even treatments with antibiotics cannot guarantee that later complications will be avoided. Antiviral medications do exist, but are not uniformly effective and even in the best scenarios, not curative."[10]

What are the bacterial infections? Of these five bacterial STDs—chlamydia, gonorrhea, trichomoniasis, syphilis, and chancroid—we'll discuss only the first two because they are most common. You can access additional resources in the back of this book for further information on any of these topics.

The fact is that teens are at high risk for acquiring STDs. "Teenagers and young adults are more likely than other age groups to have multiple sex partners, to engage in unprotected sex, and, for younger women, to choose sexual partners older than themselves," says America's Centers for Disease Control and Prevention (CDC). "Moreover, young women are biologically more susceptible to chlamydia, gonorrhea and HIV."[11] The most common curable STDs among teens are chlamydia and gonorrhea.

Chlamydia

Not only is chlamydia the most commonly reported infectious disease in America, but the Centers for Disease Control (CDC) in Atlanta believes it may be one of the most dangerous STDs among women today:

> While the disease can be easily cured with antibiotics, millions of cases go unrecognized. If left untreated, chlamydia can have severe consequences, particularly for women. Up to 40 percent of women with untreated chlamydia will develop pelvic inflammatory disease (PID), and one in five women with PID becomes infertile. Chlamydia also can cause prematurity, eye disease, and pneumonia in infants. Moreover, women infected with chlamydia are three to five times more likely to become infected with HIV, if exposed.[12]

STD	SYMPTOMS MALE/FEMALE	COMPLICATIONS
SYPHILIS	Painless sores, rash, and fever.	Severe damage to the brain and body organs; heart disease; paralysis; insanity; death. Destructive skin, liver, and lung tumors.
GONORRHEA	Burning sensation during urination. **Males:** discharge from penis. **Females:** discharge from vagina. Many people have NO symptoms.	Sterility can occur in both sexes. **Males:** urethral damage and joint infections. **Females:** ectopic pregnancies, PID (pelvic inflammatory disease), death.
CHLAMYDIA	Pain during urination. **Males:** discharge from penis; inflammation of urinary tract. **Females:** discharge from vagina. Many people have NO symptoms.	**Males:** inflammation of male organs, which can lead to sterility. **Females:** tubal pregnancies, PID, infertility.

Source: Deborah D. Cole and Maureen Gallagher Duran, **Sex and Character** (Richardson, Tex.: Foundation for Thought and Ethics, 1998), 77.

sexually transmitted diseases
bacterial

COMPLICATIONS TO INFECTED BABIES*	TREATMENT	PREVENTION
Deafness; crippling from bone disease. 25% will die in the uterus.	Antibiotics: Penicillin Other	Sexual self-control before and after marriage.
Blindness	Antibiotics: Penicillin Ampicillin Doxycycline Other	Sexual self-control before and after marriage.
Eye, ear, and lung infections; pneumonia; conjunctivitis.	Antibiotics: Doxycycline Other	Sexual self-control before and after marriage.

*Babies can contract STDs from the mother during pregnancy or birth.

Three-quarters of chlamydia infections in women have no symptoms. Half of the men infected do not know they are. Therefore, this bacterium is continually spread, doing damage while the victims are unaware of it. The CDC reports that an estimated two million people are currently infected with chlamydia and are passing it on to an estimated three million new victims annually.

Gonorrhea

What about gonorrhea? Although syphilis and gonorrhea were the two prevalent STDs in the 1960s (called *VDs* then, for venereal disease), they were treatable with penicillin.[13] From then until the late 1990s, gonorrhea rates declined. Gonorrhea is a major cause of PID and subsequent infertility and tubal pregnancies in women. Men and women alike may experience infertility plus infection in their joints, heart valves, or brain.[14] They also run a greater risk of HIV infection if they are exposed, which may be why HIV transmission is spreading significantly in the south—a prominent area of gonorrhea infection.[15] Unborn and newborn babies may suffer blindness, meningitis (inflammation of the membranes that envelop the brain and the spinal cord), and septic arthritis (inflammation of joints caused by infection).[16]

Prevention and Cure

Is there a way to prevent these illnesses and infections? Of course! The safest prevention is sexual abstinence until marriage and remaining faithfully monogamous from then on. (Monogamy is only one sexual partner for life, not one after the other, which is known as *serial monogamy*.)

But many have not remained abstinent or monogamous. So please listen closely. No longer can we hide these issues under pious blankets of shame and embarrassment. If these teen girls and guys can be open with us about their past choices, then we need to step past our embarrassment to get them tested. These are bacterial infections; we can treat and cure them *if we know our teens are infected.* Here, ignorance is not bliss. In order to protect our kids' welfare, we need to get them tested before they have to suffer lifelong consequences that could have been avoided.

Adults, you are not exempt either. If you've place yourself at risk, get examined today.

Viral Infections

Viral infections (caused by a virus) are very different from bacterial infections. Viral infections may have treatable symptoms but are not curable. Will there ever be a cure for HIV or other viral STDs, you ask? Research doesn't look very promising. In fact, one source says, "New medical advances to prevent and/or treat viral STDs appear to be years away, and in fact, may never occur."[17]

Concerning viral infections, there are four that students are commonly educated about. Because they are so serious, and noncurable, we'll briefly touch on all four—genital herpes, hepatitis B, HIV, and HPV. Not only will you see the consequences, you'll meet real students with lives damaged as a result of these infections.

Genital Herpes—Shaniqua's Experience

Of the thousands of assemblies I've presented on the topic of sexual choices, few have impacted me like one at a high school in Texas. Following my final words, the principal came on stage. Typically I would hand the microphone to him and shake his hand. But instead this large ex-football player gave me a hug—a very strong, hard, *long* hug. The audience erupted in applause and a standing ovation quickly followed. I wept in response to this school's acceptance of the message of value and sexual abstinence.

After the principal hugged me, I walked down the steps to the auditorium floor as the principal made his closing remarks. A beautiful freshman girl came up to me, introduced herself as Shaniqua, and said, "Mr. Herman, do you think I will find someone who will love me . . . for me? Not for what I look like physically, but for who I am on the inside, as a person?" I began to reply quickly with my "Yes," but she cut me off. "Even . . . even if I have to tell him that I have herpes?"

I squeezed her hand. "Sweetheart, I believe there are men in this community—even in this school—who have enough character to love you for who you are. Even if you have to tell him you have herpes. Yes, I believe he's out there."

Her eyes began watering. "Thanks," she choked out. Then she added, "But I wish . . . I wish you'd been here . . . before."

"Me too," I whispered as I hugged her. My eyes burned with tears as she turned to walk up the auditorium aisle. Other students began to speak to me, but my heart was fully torn.

Shaniqua had contracted genital herpes (HSV2) while in junior high. *If only someone could have told her the consequences,* I thought. But then, maybe many people—like you and your teen—don't realize the consequences either.

Although HIV gets the most press, genital herpes is one of the most common sexually transmitted viruses in the United States. Infection with HSV2 may lead to painful and recurrent sores, blisters, or ulcers in or on the genital organs. HSV outbreaks may also appear in men and women on any location on the skin.[18]

The viruses that cause genital herpes (herpes simplex virus I and herpes simplex virus II—HSV1 and HSV2 respectively) are widespread. Researchers say that anywhere from 20 to 40 percent of whites and 30 to 60 percent of nonwhites may be infected with type II.[19] An estimated 45 million adults are currently infected (more than one in five Americans),[20] and there are an additional one million estimated new cases every year.[21]

But most people with herpes have no symptoms and are unaware of their infection. The CDC says that "with or without visible symptoms, the disease can be transmitted between sex partners, from mothers to newborns, and can increase a person's risk of becoming infected with HIV. Genital herpes can also make HIV-infected individuals more infectious and is believed to play a role in the heterosexual spread of HIV in the United States. Preventing the spread of herpes may help slow both epidemics."[22] In fact, if you watch TV, you'll begin to notice commercials that promote products that treat these painful sores. (And I was just getting over the tampon commercials!) Genital herpes has now helped to create big business.

Most people with herpes are unaware of their infection.

Although the ulcers can be treated, this is a virus that cannot be cured. In fact, in the whole history of human beings, we have yet to cure or eradicate a virus from the human body. Once you contract herpes, you have it for life.[23]

But Doug, herpes is not fatal, you might be thinking. *If 45 million Americans have herpes, what's the big deal? You need to relax.*

But what are statistics worth without looking into the lives and stories of those with the disease? You see, the ulcers are open lesions similar to HSV2's cousins, the cold sore and the chicken pox. Because they are open wounds, they make a person with herpes more susceptible to other infections when exposed. They heighten the risk of future infections of other diseases that can be more fatal, such as HIV leading to AIDS.

What kind of impact will herpes have on Shaniqua's life? Let's assume that she abstains from sexual activity throughout the rest of high school and even college. Perhaps she graduates from Harvard and meets the man of her dreams. Guess what she will give him, besides herself, on their wedding night? That's right. Most likely she'll transmit genital herpes to him. And they will both go to their graves with this disease.

They're only sores, and they can be treated, Doug. In the safe context of a marriage, it isn't that big a deal.

Correct! But let's look at that marriage. Let's say Shaniqua and her husband have been married for seven years. For the sake of imagination, let's pretend he's a successful businessman and a loving husband. But on a business trip, he cheats on her. He only does it once, though—I mean, it's not that big of a deal, right?

He returns home. Do you think he's going to tell her what he did right away? Probably not. And because he has herpes, was he more apt to contract another infection from the other woman? Of course. Will he give that new infection—that he doesn't realize he now has—to his bride? Probably so.

So the one choice that Shaniqua made in junior high will forever affect her future. How I wish that someone had taught her at a young age about the consequences of choice and had based that education on character.

You see, it comes down to character. If Shaniqua is ever to marry, she needs to find a man who is faithful—someone who can control his feelings and his actions. If we're going to teach couples how to be safe and faithful in marriage, why are we not teaching that before they say "I do"?

Hepatitis B (HBV)—Karyn's Experience

Karyn, an attractive and energetic redhead, is 17. But she'll never forget her sixteenth birthday. Some of her friends had decided to give her a great present—a visit to a body-piercing salon. And her then boyfriend, Ryan, had taken her out for pizza afterwards. Later, they'd parked at a romantic spot, and "The kissing got out of hand," she told me. The next day she felt ugly and used. She told him she'd never do that again, and he broke up with her on the spot.

Six months later she was in a doctor's office because she had chronic stomach pain. That's when she found out it wasn't her stomach that was hurting. It was her liver. And she had hepatitis B. She'll never know if she got it from a dirty needle at the body-piercing salon or from the "kissing" with Ryan. What's been worse than the physical pain, though, is her parents' anger, the way they treat her now that she's "broken their trust," and their insistence that she tell Ryan so he could be tested.

Hepatitis B (HBV) is rarely discussed as an STD, but its lack of popularity in sex education doesn't make it less dangerous. HBV is a serious viral disease that attacks the liver and can cause extreme illness and even death. HBV is transmitted through blood and blood products, semen and vaginal fluids, and saliva. You can contract HBV from an infected person by sharing IV needles with them or even from kissing, oral sex, or intercourse. In some people the infection resolves and the virus is cleared. However, many will remain chronically infected with the virus after the symptoms associated with their new infection have subsided. They still run the increased risk of liver disease, including cirrhosis (scarring) and liver cancer, and for transmitting HBV infection to others. Roughly 120,000 of the 200,000 HBV infections—mostly in young adults—that occur each year are acquired through sexual transmission.[24]

> **HBV is a serious viral disease that attacks the liver and can cause extreme illness and even death.**

The good news here is that a vaccination became available in 1981. Hepatitis B vaccinations have been recommended for people with risk factors for HBV. "However, many teens and young adults at risk through sexual or drug-related behavior have not been vaccinated for HBV."[25] With the increased interest in tattoos and body piercing among teens and young adults, it is very important that only clean, sterile needles and fresh inks are used. Regardless, anyone at risk should be vaccinated for HBV.

HIV—Laticia and Brandi's Experience

Dear Mr. Herman, I found out about two years ago that my big sister Brandi has had HIV for around 6 years. It has not gone into AIDS yet, but lately, her white blood cell count has been going down. She lost her virginity at 15, dropped out of school during 10th grade, and was pregnant around 19. She is the reason I wish to remain abstinent. I do not want to put myself at risk of contracting a disease. It is very important to me to be a virgin when I get married. I just hope the man I marry made the same choice.

And, Laticia, in the Texas panhandle, so do I! Because I would never want you or your family to go through what I and my family have been through.

The human immunodeficiency virus (HIV) is that widely known virus that causes a syndrome called acquired immunodeficiency syndrome, or AIDS. This syndrome powerfully thwarts the body's ability to fight off infections, thereby creating an immune deficiency. It is this virus that has ravaged the continent of Africa, orphaning millions of children. It is also this virus that took the lives of two people I loved dearly— Evon and Ashli—just because someone chose to lie about his sexual past when he donated blood.

There are a couple stages and classifications you should be aware of here, as they affect the statistics and information you receive. I'll explain these as I share the infection process of HIV.

When someone is infected with HIV, that person is contagious for life. The human body detects the virus and immediately begins defending itself against it. Antibodies are developed to fight off this viral infection but are unable to do so. The virus reproduces itself uniquely.

Although there is some treatment for the symptoms of HIV, and various drugs are available to retard or delay the growth processes of the virus, there is no cure for this infection. It is fatal. Technically, when someone dies, they don't really die from HIV. They usually die from an opportunistic infection or various cancers that the body could not destroy because of a compromised immune system.

There are an estimated 50,000 new cases of HIV infection reported in the United States each year.[26] CDC's Divisions of HIV/AIDS Prevention 2001 report lists 495,592 persons reported to be living with HIV and AIDS, bringing the cumulative total of AIDS cases in America to 816,149.[27]

The majority of HIV infections are diagnosed in men between the ages of 25 and 39 and in women between the ages of 25 and 34. Consequently, since the highest percentage of death rates for HIV infected individuals are ages 35–54, the average length of time between the diagnosis of the infection and death is from 10–15 to 29 years. It is the leading cause of death of people ages 25 to 44. This is a generalization, mind you, as individual life expectancy of an HIV-infected person varies greatly because of the personal and health conditions of that person. In 2001 there were 1,155 reported HIV cases among 13–19-year-olds and 3,402 cases among 20–24-year-olds. (This does not include those already living with AIDS.)

HIV is easily the sexually transmitted disease we are most educated about today. Various groups that have been devastated by its impact know only too well the nasty power of this infection and lobby our government for various changes. But it's also very important to understand that we look at this virus as a medical consequence of high-risk activity rather than concentrating on its many political or perceived spiritual implications.

Certainly we understand that choices bring consequences. If people are involved in high-risk behavior, such as sharing IV needles or engaging in sexual activity outside of a faithful, lifelong union, there are consequences that can occur. The HIV virus didn't start with people who are gay. But it is obvious from statistics that this virus spread rapidly in the 1980s and 1990s due to the homosexual lifestyle. In Africa, however, HIV and AIDS are spread largely through heterosexual behaviors. But it is the unfaithfulness (again, a high-risk activity) on that continent that is infecting unknowing mothers and unborn children.

Let me also say strongly that I believe AIDS is not "God's judgment" on anyone's sin or lifestyle. We live in a sinful world, and the fruit of sin is death—a consequence we must deal with. Those who have lost a child to a drunken driver would concur. AIDS has certainly affected our nation, and in doing so, has caused many and varied opinions. The purpose of these few pages is to give you a brief overview so your opinion will be based on quality medical information and not just hearsay.

HPV—Emily's Experience

I had just concluded my conversations with about a dozen junior-high students in a Nebraska school auditorium when the side exit door opened slightly. Peeking in to see if any other students were there, an eighth-grade girl with long, curly blonde hair opened the door fully and walked over to me. Her face was slightly swollen from crying; little puffy pillows framed her blue eyes.

"I just wanted to thank you for your message," she said. "Thank you for telling all my friends the truth."

"What about my presentation touched you so deeply?" I asked.

"Well, I've been sexually active. And . . . about six months ago I went to the doctor and discovered I had HPV." She was wringing her hands so I grabbed them in mine as she continued. "Well, a couple of months back we discovered that I have the beginnings of cervical cancer. I've already had a colposcopy and a biopsy."

"Oh, honey. I'm so sorry. I wish we could have talked before," I said.

"Me too," she replied. Then a courageous smile spread across her face. "It's not that I'm going to die. I just have to be careful and work with the doctors. . . . But you did get here *before* for my friends. And I just wanted to thank you for that."

"You are so welcome," I said as we hugged. Thirteen-year-old Emily turned and left through the same door she had entered. *A colposcopy?* At

STD	SYMPTOMS MALE/FEMALE	COMPLICATIONS
HPV VENEREAL WARTS	White or gray warts appearing on the penis, cervix, anus, vagina and vulva. Many people show NO symptoms.	Cancer of the cervix, vulva, penis, vagina, and anus. Warts may reappear for a lifetime.
GENITAL HERPES	Both Males & Females: blisters and sores, fever, headaches, pain while urinating. Females: vaginal discharge; painless sores on the cervix.	Sores may reappear for a lifetime.
HEPATITIS B	Headache, fever, nausea. Later symptoms: abdominal pain, yellowing of eyes.	Cancer of the liver.
HIV/AIDS	Weight loss, fever, tiredness, swollen glands, and diarrhea.	Destroys immune system.

Source: Deborah D. Cole and Maureen Gallagher Duran, **Sex and Character** (Richardson, Tex.: Foundation for Thought and Ethics, 1998), 83.

sexually transmitted diseases
viral

COMPLICATIONS TO INFECTED BABIES*	TREATMENT	PREVENTION
Warts on the larynx.	There is no cure. The warts can be removed by podophyllin, trichloracetic acid, or laser.	Sexual self-control before and after marriage.
Blindness, brain damage, nerve damage.	Oral acyclovir helps healing; no cure.	Sexual self-control before and after marriage.
Pass disease on to baby.	Vaccine	Sexual self-control before and after marriage.
30% of all babies born to mothers with AIDS will die.	No cure.	Sexual self-control before and after marriage.

*Babies can contract STDs from the mother during pregnancy or birth.

that time I didn't even know what the procedure was. So why should this teen girl have to know? After all, she lives in a rural American town. But at a young age she had made one choice that would affect her for a lifetime. That choice had the consequence of HPV.

Human papillomavirus (HPV) is the fastest spreading virus, with 5.5 million contractions annually and an estimated 20 million people currently infected. That makes it the most common sexually transmitted disease in our nation.[28] It can cause genital warts, but most infected people don't have noticeable symptoms.

HPV has approximately 100 different types (or viral strains). It has been determined that over 30 of these types infect the human genitals. HPV16 accounts for more than 50 percent of cervical cancers and high-grade dysplasia (abnormal cell growth). Along with types 18, 31, and 45, these viruses account for 80 percent of cervical cancers,[29] with the HPV virus in general found in 99.7 percent of *all* cervical cancers, certainly a common denominator.[30] With "improved testing technology, researchers have been able to get a much clearer picture of the true extent of HPV in certain groups in recent years, and the infection is even more common than originally believed."[31] With over 5,000 women dying annually from cervical cancer in our nation, that makes HPV (the leading cause of cervical cancer) a more common killer for women than AIDS (3,596 in 2000).[32] Did you know that?

And did you also know that the leading malignancy in a woman's body today is breast cancer? Of course you did. We have little pink pins to remind us of the "race for the cure." We also have red pins for HIV/AIDS—a virus I personally hate, since it killed my late wife and daughter.

HPV may be the leading cause of cervical cancer.

But we don't have a little pin for HPV. Why? Because it is a sexually transmitted disease, and the only way to stop the spread of infection is to stop sexual activity outside of a mutually faithful (read *wholly monogamous*) marriage.

Recent news about an "HPV vaccine" to prevent women from getting cervical cancer created an exciting stir. This wonderful vaccine however, is only for type 16. They have not announced inoculations for the other types of HPV. About 30 of these types are sexually transmitted and cause genital HPV,[33] which cannot be entirely prevented by a condom. This is because this virus is not limited to blood, semen, or mucus membranes. Any genital area around the anus, scrotum, penis, or vagina is highly contagious. Since a condom cannot cover those areas, HPV can be transmitted with skin-to-skin contact by any part of the hands, genitals, face, or body.

This is why I define high-risk sexual activity as *any genital contact of any kind.* Moms and dads, would you agree that things have changed? When I was a young teen and my

> **High-risk sexual activity is genital contact of any kind.**

friends joked about getting to "third base" on their date, it implied touching or caressing a girl's vaginal area. Today even such touching is high-risk.

Sadly, Emily was never told the truth. But now she knows. In fact, she knows the details of biopsy and colposcopy procedures. And she may even get the chance to experience cryotherapy as well.

Other Infections

There are certainly more infections than those discussed here. Some infections that are also risks include: "vaginitis (inflammation of the vagina), pubic lice (crabs), [Sarcoptes scabei] scabies, moluscum contagiosum, chancroid, lymphogranuloma venereum, granuloma inguinale, cytomegalovirus infections, amebiasis, mycoplasma infections, and streptococcal infections. The list of germs that can be passed through sexual contact continues to grow."[34]

For a great book that balances physical consequences and issues of character, I suggest you examine the book *Sex and Character,* listed in the Resources section at the end of this book.

The Myth of Safe Sex

Obviously, as you learn about all these diseases, you may be taken aback. If you are still *reading* this chapter, I applaud you! The consequences of sexual activity can be difficult to read about, not to mention incredibly

Method	Protection Rate For	
	PREGNANCY	HIV
Withdrawal	76%	None
Condom	84%	57 to 90%
Birth Control Pills	94%	None
Depo-Provera	99%	None
Norplant	99%	None
Abstinence	100%	100%

contraceptive protection rates[36]

HPV	EMOTIONAL SCARS
None	None
Almost None	None
None	None
None	None
None	None
100%	100%

far-reaching. Not only do they affect the person who chose that activity, but they create waves for you and me.

These diseases affect me too? Even if I have a sexually pure past?

If you are an American, you are affected by STDs more than you know. Back in 1994 it was estimated that "the direct and indirect costs of the major STDs and their complications were estimated to total almost $17 billion annually."[35] That's a lot of cash we could save if we . . . if we did what? Revolted against the sexual revolution and chose *not* to be involved in high-risk behavior! Again, if adults—not just teens—would postpone any sexual activity until marriage and then remain wholly faithful and monogamous in that marriage, the problem of STDs would largely disappear in a few generations. Yet today unfaithful adults continue to infect unassuming spouses. Even recent reports from retirement areas in Florida reveal high rates of STD transmission among the elderly. All this can come to a halt!

Is that a pipe dream? Perhaps. But there's no better place to start than with you and your family, and there's no better time to start than now.

In order to prevent unwanted pregnancies and contraction of diseases, one solution has been to produce and distribute contraceptives. But look at the Contraceptive Protection Rates chart on pages 142 and 143 to see the *real* reliability of the various methods of contraception in protecting against STDs. Would you want to trust your own or your teen's future to to these statistics?

You see, there may be some protection from an unplanned pregnancy using various contraceptives, but the percentage rate for protection against HIV and HPV is highly reduced. Sure, contraceptives are better than nothing. But does promoting condoms give a false hope to those who use them? Do they think they are getting full protection—when really all they're getting is risk reduction? The risk reduction of devices such as condoms depends greatly on a variety of factors, including correct use, consistent use, no breakage, areas not covered, drug or alcohol use, and awareness of hidden STDs.

Birth control does not mean "safe sex."

So those who want to provide birth-control methods for their teens to "keep them safe" need to rethink their position. There's no such thing as "safe sex"—it's purely a myth. Even the proponents of safe sex changed their slogan to "safer sex" some years back. No wonder. The reality is this: Birth control focuses on preventing the fertilization and development of an unborn child. It does not, however effectively protect from all forms of sexual disease. Today's parents and teens need to know that.

Chapter Eight When Is Enough, Enough?
pure revolution

Mr. Herman?"

I turned to see a very pretty junior girl from the Tulsa, Oklahoma, school I was speaking at standing with a friend. Tears had streaked her mascara down to her chin except where she'd wiped it to the side, blurring the path of black with rosy blush on her cheeks.

"Yes, sweetheart," I replied. "Can I help you?"

"Well . . ." She paused for a moment, as if to gather her strength and composure. Her friend placed an arm around her, rubbing her shoulder. "I was wondering," she stammered. "Can you get HIV if . . . if you've been . . . raped?"

Her friend squeezed her closer as I grabbed her hand. "It's possible. Have you?"

"Three times!" she choked out, then burst into tears again.

I continued to counsel her and offer her hope. Through the contact person who had invited me to that campus, I connected her with a couple who could help and guide her for the long haul.

As I drove away from Tulsa and began my trek toward my home in Littleton, Colorado, I thought of that girl again. *Three times,* I thought to myself. *She's only 16 years old, and she's terrified of some fatal infection like HIV, and she's emotionally scarred. This was never her choice.*

How can these infections and this emotional pain be prevented? Should the rapists have used a condom? But even if they had, latex possesses no protection from the emotional pain.

There's got to be a better way to bring change! I agonized. *Who will befriend this girl? As an educator, motivator, and adult concerned for teens across our nation, how can I best help her?*

Imagine if you saw a sign like this for a new national campaign aimed at teenagers: "Don't drink and drive . . . but if you do, or if you ride in a car with a drunk driver, be sure to buckle up!" That would be ludicrous, wouldn't it? You probably have never heard, "Smoking cigarettes causes lung cancer and shortens your life. But if you can't stop, use multiple filters to smoke safely." Binge drinking, now pandemic in colleges and universities, is not deterred by messages saying, "Cut consumption—in half." No; the fact is, it's *illegal* to drink under the age of 21. School violence cannot be stopped by themes promoting, "Violence is your right . . . so fight carefully." No; instead we have metal detectors in some schools to prevent teens from carrying weapons! Why? To instruct those who are determined to fire off weapons about the safest way to do so? Certainly not. It's to keep weapons *out* of schools. In that case, everyone agrees that *risk elimination* is the best. Why then do we settle only for *risk reduction* when it comes to sex outside of marriage?

If you care for our nation and its teen population, you don't want them to get hurt. And that includes challenging them to stop their high-risk behavior before it kills them or someone else.

But Doug, come on, you might be thinking, *this is an entirely different situation. We're not talking about assault rifles in schools or situations of rape or lung cancer. We're talking about sex between two consenting people. Isn't sexual expression everyone's right?*

To engage in a choice is to automatically assume the ownership and responsibility of that choice.

If that is true, then why are we so predisposed to fight against the disease and unplanned pregnancies resulting from these sexual actions? Are these not also the natural results from those actions? I believe that to engage in a choice is to automatically assume the ownership and responsibility of that choice. Pregnancy and disease are certainly possible consequences, as we've seen in the last few chapters. If the sexual activities are "only natural," then why is our nation so poised to fight off the consequences? And why are relationship counselors booked solid by teens with emotional damage stemming from torn relationships?

> There are people who want every right and freedom but are hell-bent on destroying every self-limiting consequence that naturally flows from those actions.

I'll tell you why. There are people who want every right and freedom but are hell-bent on destroying every self-limiting consequence that *naturally flows* from those actions. They have been successful in their work to free the *promotion* of sex outside marriage without any consequence because the nation as a whole seems oblivious to the many consequences that occur. Just take a look at the following snapshot of sex and today's kids.

Just a Normal Day?

The school hallway is vacant except for the stray papers with varied red marks and letter grades emblazoned across the tops. A folder lies crumpled in a corner, a victim of some seventh-grade boy's awkward rush to the final period of the day.

Suddenly a bell rings, and the silence is shattered by loud cheers and the rush of hurried bodies. School is out for the day, and these junior-high students run to their lockers to deposit their books before heading out the doors to go home.

This is a normal day. It's similar to most days you and I had as seventh- and eighth-grade students. But . . . watch.

On the way to the buses, some of the popular kids gather in a circle. They giggle as they plan a party. A few of the girls smack one of the boys on the shoulder and he grins widely. "What? What did I do?" He laughs. "You know it's true!"

A girl rolls her eyes at him and turns back to the group. Another girl looks at him a bit longer, her eyes narrowing, and a grin shapes her lips. Then they join in the group discussion again. It turns out this "party" is more of a get-together than an actual party. They'll have music, watch some videos, and hook up. That's the plan. It will be at Devin's home, since her parents are gone until 6:00 P.M.

Later at the house the music roars from the large-screen television as the videos show sexy girls and men with hardened abs bumping and grinding. The smell of fresh-popped popcorn fills the basement. Over at the bar, red plastic cups are filled with Coke. Devin shows Jana where the hard liquor is kept and Jana removes several bottles. They mark the levels with a pencil, then pour about a third of the contents into the cups. Jana refills the bottles with water, bringing the level in each bottle back to the pencil mark. Wiping the mark off with her finger, she puts the bottles back. *What they don't know won't hurt them,* she whispers to herself.

The afternoon continues with these students laughing and drinking. They start to play a game of truth-or-dare but abort it. It's just too childlike for some of the more experienced students in the room. They wanted to come over to have a good time and hook up. This isn't their first experience, so there's no need to waste time. Jana and Mark have been "buddies" before, so they offer to go first. The game will be "follow the leader," so every girl has to do what Jana does.

Mark pulls his shirt off and drops his pants and underwear. Jana then kneels down and begins giving him oral sex. After a few minutes, she looks up to Jason and says, "You're next." Jason does as Mark did and Jana gives him oral sex while Devin follows Jana's lead on Mark. Girl after girl performs oral sex for the guys. Later, some girls give each other oral sex. One guy and girl go to a more private corner of the room and have intercourse. "They think they're having feelings for each other," explains Jana to a new girl. "Making love is very different from sport sex, like we have here."[1]

The Full Truth

While the above story is fictional, these "assembly line parties" or "oral sex clubs" are not a figment of some adult's imagination. They happen every week in schools, homes, and communities of all kinds. That story was based upon *actual* reports shared by junior-highers.

Why do I include such a brash story in this book? Because to bury such happenings is to live in denial of what's really going on in our kids' world. And that's not helping our kids. Such stories are why we need extraordinary wisdom. Such stories are why we need to choose to act—and to act *now*—to protect the purity of our kids.

On May 27, 2002, *U.S. News and World Report* had this title emblazoned on its cover: "Teens & Sex." The bullet points listed were

- They're starting earlier
- The growing health risks
- Is abstinence the answer?
- How to talk to your kids

On the May 7, 2002, *Oprah* show, Dr. Phil discussed the oral sex clubs I just depicted above. Why? Because whether we are aware of it or not, these clubs are really happening. Dear friends, not only must we be aware, but we must engage in a Pure Revolution to keep our kids safe from a lifetime of pain.

And the problem is, these "clubs" are reaching younger and younger kids. While I was speaking in a rural northwest Pennsylvania area, a local crisis pregnancy center revealed to me the discovery of these oral sex clubs involving students as young as third grade! Obviously, the children have learned this behavior from older friends and siblings. And they're encouraged to do more and more in the club, because the more they do, the more power and the higher rank of authority they get in the club.

> The more they do in oral sex "clubs," the more power they have. And all kids are hungry for peer acceptance.

In my own neighborhood in southwest Denver, middle-school students were bragging to their peers about "assembly line" sex parties they have after school. So parents asked a local middle-school principal to allow us to present to the student body a program about character, abstinence, and the consequences of sexual activity. His response? "This is a conservative community. We don't have that kind of problem here."

No. We have a bigger problem. We have students involved in activities with serious consequences—and they don't even know any of these ramifications! Worse yet, we have adults who are focused only on themselves and their careers, oblivious to the cultural conditions of students in their own care. In some cases, even when adults do know about these cultural conditions, they're nervous about "rocking the boat" and making parents angry. Thankfully, I've found that youth pastors in our community are eager to help. But convincing school principals and senior pastors to present this information from a pulpit on Sunday morning worship is difficult indeed. It seems so often that we adults are caught in the whirlwind of our own world—and no one wants to break free, even for a minute, to see what's really going on with our kids!

> Oh, what a tangled web do parents weave
> When they think that their children are naive.
>
> —Ogden Nash

Okay, Doug, you might be thinking, *obviously this is your soapbox. And I can see why. But don't you think you are overexaggerating just a bit?*

Just listen to this source about why we need to pay attention:

"Why is attendance to our teens' sexuality so important? Because sexuality is intertwined to their emotions, psychological maturity, physical health, and spirituality. When sexuality is confused, then all aspects of teen identity are confused as well. At the heart of restoring the teenage soul, therefore, is the restoration of teen sexuality. Teens can't do it alone—they need adult help."[2]

Every week that I travel I look into the eyes of students who had never been told the full truth about sexuality and the consequences of sexual activity—of any kind—before marriage. I hear their stories and I cry with them. It exhausts me. My only hope comes from a source who fuels me enough to go to another school. Someone who cares as deeply about these teens and their futures as I do. My hope lies in God's leading and in the hard work of teachers, counselors, crisis pregnancy centers, and parents who are educated and culturally relevant in their work with students.

When I leave those students, I need to know they will have someone to guide them through the myriad of questions and choices they will have to make. Working with others who are passionate about getting the message of sexual purity across refuels me for the journey ahead and for my time with the teens at the next church, the next school. Teens who've already been sexually active and need help, healing, and hope.

Teens who are teetering on the verge of sexual experience and are wondering if that's what they really want to do.

And teens who are still sexually pure and need strong encouragement to stay that way.

Join the Fight!

The great news is that because the younger generation is now hearing this information about sexual choices and STDs, they are beginning to integrate it into their relationships. In fact, some are embracing sexual purity and abstinence. How different their stories are, and how encouraging to those of us in the fight to keep our kids sexually pure!

Adults, listen to my heart. Perhaps no one has ever told you this information about sexual choices and STDs. You didn't know, so you couldn't act. But now you know—and it's time to act. For the sake of your kids and the sake of this nation.

Pastors, please read this carefully and hear the tenderness of my heart. You have been called by God to *pastor*. What a wonderful calling! It is *not* your job to build a large church for some sort of expanded ministry or to erect some monument portraying success to your peers. No. You are a pastor. It is your call to nurture the flock. And that includes discussing morality and its value in life based on Scripture. But such discussions must also be relevant to our current culture in order to make an impact. If you had never heard of these choices and consequences, I'm thrilled to empower you. However, you need more equipping. In your position and role, you are perhaps the best person to empower families in helping their teens. So don't take this lightly! Grab the Sword of Truth and defend the flock in your care.

Is anyone else tired of Twisted stealing from young couples their choice to have children due to scars resulting from STD infections? Is there a leader holding this book ready to find vengeance for the slain of this globe, lost from disease or sexual violence? Have we had enough of the destruction of morality and healthy relationships in our nation? The enemy has come to steal, kill, and destroy.³ We are to proclaim God's offer of life to the fullest!

But *when?* I ask you—when is enough, enough? At what point are you pushed over the edge to finally respond? When you finish reading this book, will you simply place it on a shelf and grab another? Can you truly go back to life as it was before you read *Time for a Pure Revolution?* Will you remain unchanged?

No. I don't think so. You selected this book for a reason—because you care about today's teens. And because you needed the information to empower you to act. So now you must ask yourself this question, my friend: When is enough, enough?

Pure Revolution!

The time is now to revolt against the sexual revolution that has deeply warped our country. So let's join efforts together—without concern for fame, territory, or power—and work for a common goal! It's time to create this new revolution, a Pure Revolution. Are you ready? Teens certainly are. Just listen to Linda.

> *I haven't always made the best decisions in the past, but today, after I heard your story, I decided to practice abstinence from now on. I say from now on because I'm not a virgin. But you said we can make the change whenever we want, and I want this to be a new beginning for me. It's my 18th birthday, and I think that's as good a time as any to begin my second chance. It's hard sometimes when I tell my friends that I'm going to change and be different, when they look at me and say, "Oh yeah, good one, Lin." But it's true. I've realized that sex isn't worth it at all, and I'm going to prove it to all of them. Thank you again for talking to us because I really believe that my life is going to change from now on. Sex is just not worth all the pain and the risk.*

And so the sexual counter-revolution—the Pure Revolution—begins, one teen at a time, one adult at a time. It is not limited solely to

American teens and families, either. News reports from the United Kingdom and Australia are encouraging. One reporter from Sydney reported recently on this revolution "down under" and her observations in Europe.

> If ever there was a hint that a sexual counter-revolution may be afoot among the young who have grown up in an age of unprecedented sexual openness, then it is to be found among a British group of "New Puritans"; young Catholics who are eagerly practicing what they preach, including a strict ban on sex before marriage.
>
> "Chastity is fundamental to our lives," says Paul Bray, 21. "For us, it means real freedom and it's far more radical than anything else on offer. There's a feeling of renewal among young people. We are no longer under false illusions about the world and we are no longer slaves to the notion that anything goes."[4]

This reporter stated that in the United States, chastity is the fastest growing movement! Indeed it is. And that's exciting! When our generation could not stand for purity decades ago, this new generation is turning away from our choice and fighting for purity. Good for them!

But with teens stepping into the stream and standing firm against the flow of sexual activity outside of marriage, who will be there to empower and encourage them? Remember Shaniqua? Someone needs to guide her as she struggles to bring her past into a new relationship with a great guy. Emily could use a strong leader to pray with her as she makes her doctor visits every six months for the rest of her life. Linda too needs someone to embrace her decision and treat her as a strong and responsible adult, not belittling her for her choice. All of these teens needed to know—*before*. Each one needs empowerment today.

This new generation is fighting for purity. Who will empower and encourage them?

As for Kirsten, who miscarried her baby, what does she need? She needs to forgive herself. In fact, you too may be struggling with this entire topic because of choices you have made in the past. With your own array of failed decisions, do you wonder if you could ever join a Pure Revolution? After all, if you made such bad choices yourself, how could you hope to influence teens in the right direction?

Well, I'm here to shout this loudly to your soul: You are not only worthy to lead, but *because of your history* you are more fully qualified![5] But you must begin by forgiving yourself and taking that first step.

> **Only YOU can do what God has planned for you.**
> —Max Lucado

This time, let's learn from Kirsten. Here's the concluding page of her four-page letter to me.

> *When I felt hopeless, I remembered the Scripture about God knowing us in the womb and realized he can't know us if we don't have spirits. Then you talked about seeing your little girl in heaven and having her run into your arms and call you "Daddy." That's when I realized my baby did go to heaven and I would see it some day and get to hold it. I asked Jesus to come into my life and finally have forgiven myself.*
>
> *I wanted to thank you for being my door to realization and forgiveness. I will eternally be grateful to you. I pray God continues to bless your life and your family. You taught me so much last night and if it touched no one else but me, then I thank you for flying out to talk to me.*
>
> *Your sister in Christ, Kirsten*

A revolution of purity has begun! All you need to do is step in. Will you?

Chapter Nine It Takes a Family First
pure connection

---

my *parents are divorced and I've only met my dad once and that was probably about 4 years ago,"* writes a high school girl from Texas. *"I don't remember that much. But I think God meant for that to happen because my mom and I have the closest relationship. It's just me and her, and that's all we need. Every weekend we work with horses together. And every Sunday, Sunday night, and Wednesday night we go to church. She used to be a singles' minister but she had to pull away from that job because there were some difficulties at our church."*

How is your relationship with your teenagers? Do you spend much time with them? If a ripping such as divorce tore their hearts, would they consider it a "great relationship" to spend time with you?

The young girl who wrote the paragraph above touched my heart. Her mom has obviously spent time investing in her daughter, despite some troubled times in her marriage and her church. And it looks like she's not lost faith! Good for them both.

When a marriage disintegrates, is there that great of an impact on the entire family? I believe so.

When this young girl looks back at her parents' divorce, she assumes, "God meant for that to happen." You may agree. Sometimes divorce may be God's will, especially in situations where the marriage is abusive and threatens the lives and safety of those in the home. However, the loss of any relationship hurts because, per God's original design, we are created to live in community. I don't believe God "means" or "plans" for the painful moments to happen; these moments are a result of our own or others' sinful choices. But when these choices cause pain, God has this wonderful ability to take the broken shards of fractured relationships and create a beautiful mosaic from them—like the mother-daughter relationship described in this letter. Through this close and encouraging relationship, both mother and daughter are seeing the handiwork of the Creator as he rebuilds their family.

> The loss of any relationship hurts because we are created to live in community.

What Is a Family Anyway?

What is a family to you? In the many decades that I've been working with teens and families, I've seen many combinations and definitions of a family. The "look" of a family has certainly changed over the years. When working with teens attracted to gang life, I discovered these "tough kids" were hungering for a "family" feel. In my children's school, there are kids who come from families with same-sex parents. Single parents reading this book have no less of a family than those with both a mom and dad. Those who adopt children are just as much of a family as those who bring children into their family by birth. I myself have been widowed, and later I provided my son, who is now 18, with a stepmother. Now he even has a half brother and half sister. We are certainly a family.

A family is important to every growing teen. Just ask a teen who has no family. When I was meeting teens after a school assembly in New York State, several students who had been adopted came up to introduce themselves. As I asked a sophomore boy my standard question, "How young were you when you were adopted?" his eyes twinkled in delighted anticipation.

> There are many combinations and definitions of *family*. But every kid longs for the "family feel."

"Probably 16!" he replied.

When I raised my eyebrows in surprise, he explained, "I'm only 15 now, but it looks like I'll get a family in a few months."

Then he turned on his heels and left. Was a family important to him? You bet your life.

"Adlerian psychology teaches that humans need to experience a sense of belonging," writes Dr. Meeker. Then she goes on: "We are a part of a whole, and a teen's sense of value comes from being integrated into a larger unit—family, friends, and society. While each teen has individuality, he has a need to fit his uniqueness into a higher order. Naturally he learns this in the family structure. Family, after all, is the place of his most intense needs, dependency, and connectedness."[1]

Clearly God has wired within each of us a desire to belong, and that belonging comes from a family—ultimately the family of God. So it's vital that we as adults provide a sense of belonging for teens and children. In fact, I believe this is our *primary* calling as parents and adults! When we revoke that sense of belonging or deny our children access to it, a deep wound is cut into that child's identity development. Dr. Meeker explains: "If he perceives that he doesn't fit in, he becomes anxious, frustrated, and angry. When he does so, he often takes out his frustrations on his parents and siblings. Parents often take this anger personally, which can be a painful mistake."[2]

> Our primary calling as parents is to provide a sense of belonging for our children.

Remember, though, that developing a sense of belonging does not imply rolling over and lazily giving in to your child's every whim. No; it goes much deeper, as we will discover.

Poor America?

In our nation there is a poverty greater than any of the financial woes I've seen. It's called *moral poverty,* and it runs rampant all over the United States:

> Moral poverty is the poverty of being without loving, capable,
> responsible adults who teach you right from wrong; the poverty of

being without parents and other authorities who habituate you to feel joy at others' joy, pain at others' pain, satisfaction when you do right, remorse when you do wrong; the poverty of growing up in the virtual absence of people who teach morality by their own everyday example and who insist that you follow suit. . . . And moral poverty, not economic poverty, is what marks some disadvantaged youngsters for a life of crime while passing over others in equal or greater material distress.[3]

"If anyone has material possessions and sees his brother in need but has no pity on him, how can the love of God be in him?" writes the apostle John.[4] I believe we can view this accurately in the context of moral need as well. If you who are morally rich see those who are morally bankrupt and do nothing to help them, can the love of God be in you?

If you are a Christian, it is your calling and mandate to reach those who have been robbed morally and find themselves facing a foreclosure on belief. We must rise up and bring the power of absolute truth, ethical integrity, and spiritual purity back into the lives of our young! But who can do such a task? Shall we look to celebrities, speakers and authors, or famed religious leaders to solve the problem? No; even if they tried, they could not accomplish this on their own. But there is a person who's more qualified—and that's you! It's you, my friend, who can change your child's world. And maybe you can even change the world of another!

> We must rise up and bring the power of absolute truth, ethical integrity, and spiritual purity back into the lives of our young!

For those children who have grown up in moral poverty and who feel alone, let's do our best to create a place for them to belong, a place where others laugh when they laugh and cry when they cry, a place where others rejoice in their accomplishments and encourage them in their failures. Let's create again a family for those who are poor and alone—a place where they can belong, where they can feel validated, loved, and cared for—the kind of home and family that every child longs to have!

But how can we go about that? Isn't it

> Every word and deed of a parent is a fibre woven into the character of a child that ultimately determines how that child fits into the fabric of society. —David Wilkerson

impossible in today's world, a world where a large number of marriages entered into today end in divorce?

The Benefits of a Parent's Influence

In this chapter I'll share some information about the power of a family and its impact on a child's life. Understand, though, that the information is just that. The numbers and statistics are not meant to judge your current marital state or family makeup. But they will reveal the truth—that divorce does hurt. They'll also reveal how having a "blended family" (even like mine) is less than the ideal of living with a biological mother and father.

> **Children will invariably talk, eat, walk, think, respond, and act like their parents. Give them a target to shoot at. Give them a goal to work toward. Give them a pattern that they can see clearly, and you give them something that gold and silver cannot buy.**
> —Billy Graham

The information may sting on occasion, but let the research speak for itself. We cannot undo our histories. But perhaps we *can* help our teens and children see the power of a unified family and the reasons we fight for healthy marriages, quality relationships, and this Pure Revolution! Marriages *can* be for life, and they *can* be filled with wonderful contentment. But in order to teach that to our children, we need to know and model it ourselves.

So what benefits do children have whose parents stay married and involved in their lives?

Less Violence and Delinquency

It's not a hard argument to win to state that teen violence is prevalent today. Whether we examine newspaper headlines, TV news, current music, movies, or computer games, we will see an abundance of angst. A survey taken in 1998 revealed that 72 percent of Americans agreed that married parents are less likely to have children who are violent and commit crimes.[5] And when those surveyed were asked to compare other strategies to prevent teen violence, the largest percentage believed that the best strategy to prevent violence is for married parents to stay together and stay involved in their children's lives.[6]

The Best Solution to Youth Violence: What Americans Think

- Parents who commit to marriage and stay involved—45 percent
- Teach moral principles—24 percent
- Positive role models participate in kid's lives—23 percent
- Less violence on TV/movies/music—6 percent

It's true. Lack of parental involvement and adult supervision seems to correlate directly with youth criminal activity.[7] And here are a few of the studies and stats to back this statement up.

A 1994 study notes that juvenile homicide rates and robbery rates are higher in communities with large proportions of single-parent families. As a result, the study concludes that two-parent families are better able to prevent adolescents from engaging in activities that lead to delinquency.[8]

The 1997 National Longitudinal Study of Adolescent Health Study (known as the AD Health Study), which surveyed 90,000 teens and specifically interviewed 12,000 youth, found that those who felt connected to their parents and family and experienced greater parental supervision were less likely to use alcohol and marijuana frequently.[9]

A 1999 study found that teenagers from single-parent homes were more likely to use illicit drugs or alcohol. The author linked these findings to the lower level of supervision in single-parent families.

A 1999 study of sixth and seventh graders found that those from intact families were more likely to be home with a parent or other adult after school than were students from single-parent families, who were more likely to be with friends during after-school hours. Students who experienced little parental supervision showed more aggression, delinquency, substance abuse, and vulnerability to peer pressure.[10]

Clearly, parental involvement is a key to healthier children and teens. Additionally, 52 percent of adults believe that poor upbringing by parents is the underlying cause behind young people committing acts of violence—even eclipsing those who believe peer pressure, violence in TV/

movies, or availability of guns (17, 17, and 8 percent respectively), is the largest cause.[11] Nearly all respondents in two separate polls believe students' home lives and their relationship with their parents, as well as parental supervision, are major factors in teen violence.[12]

Is it true, America? Do we really believe in the power of a parent's influence on the lives of our children? If so, then perhaps children and teens are not where we should focus our attention. Maybe we first need to look at the values, standards, beliefs, and lifestyles of parents. That begins with you and me. It requires us to take an honest look at the home life we bring our children up in. We must reevaluate the time we spend with them and what we do with it, such as dialoging about issues of importance, reading appropriate books, and encouraging a growing personal relationship with God. We must also let our children see us battle with moral and ethical issues and find pure resolve in the struggle. We must let them see us remaining faithful in marriage.

> **If we believe in the power of a parent's influence, we need to take an honest look at ourselves first.**

Overall, statistics prove that a healthy marriage and a healthy family structure produces healthier children. So in order to create a Pure Revolution that transforms a nation of teens and children, we adults must allow our own thoughts, beliefs, and actions to be transformed *first*.

Intact Families Impact Risk-Taking Behaviors

When both of the biological parents raise their children, research has revealed that these children are much less likely to act out various risk behaviors. The National Campaign to Prevent Teen Pregnancy released this information: "Teens who are raised by both parents from birth have lower probabilities of having sex . . . than teens who grew up in any other family situation."[13] To offer a Pure Revolution, we need to fully examine not only the validity of intact families but the power of them as well.

I don't know of any sane parents who want their children to begin using drugs. But when 4,000 teens were interviewed in 1999, it was discovered that those who had experienced one or more changes in family structure during adolescence were at a greater risk for drug abuse. Fifth and sixth graders were also examined. Children of divorced parents reported more substance abuse than did kids with married parents. Specifically noting the family structure, one study found that adolescents from intact families were less likely to drink alcohol than were those from single-parent families or stepfamilies.[14]

As I said, I'm not reporting this to condemn those of us who are single parents or stepparents. What we can learn from such studies, however, is that how intact a family is—whether or not both biological parents are present in the home, married to each other, and modeling a healthy relationship—has some impact on teen behavior. And that means if we are truly concerned about the teens of our nation, then the health and strength of marriages should be a priority.

> **If we're truly concerned about the teens of our nation, then the health and strength of marriages should be a priority.**

So where should we start? A great place to begin is the church. Since 1981, I have been involved in ministry, mostly to teens. While I've only served in five churches professionally as an associate and youth pastor, I've also visited hundreds as a guest speaker. The churches that I've visited and served have been quite healthy, and it was a treat to be there. But I am concerned about the church in general.

From what I'm seeing, it seems that the church in general is more concerned with its attendance than it is with who attends. There are those who so want to become great preachers and authors that they use their parishioners as a marketplace for their works. But what about our nation of broken marriages? What about people who enter church services on the verge of moral poverty and instead of finding help and challenge are greeted with polished slogans for the next building campaign? As a minister of the church today, it is my calling to place my ear to the ground and listen for changes and movements. As a communicator who blows the trumpet for a pure cause, I want to sound it clearly for marriages that are dying and taking children with them.

The church is the most amazing and powerful force at work on this planet. But if she doesn't awaken and embrace broken marriages and families today, she can expect a nasty backhand from those scar-laden lives who later are invited to darken her doors. So now is the time for the church to point the way to sexual and marital wholeness, to admonish sin, to help "morally poor" souls, and to challenge her members to a new lifestyle of Pure Revolution.

Will you help?

Wisdom from the Past

"Can I be candid with you, Mr. Herman?" one mom of a teen shyly asked me. "Well, the truth is . . . when I was a young teen girl I was sexually active—with alcohol use, drugs, and the works. I grew up in the seventies and eighties! How am I supposed to be honest with my teen about my history and still talk to them about their choices?"

Do you feel that way? Is your history laden with various land-mine choices you made? Well, the reality is that many of us have embarrassing stories. Do we tell our teens or not? And if we choose to do so, how much do we say, and how can we be authentic and not hypocritical by telling them to act in a way we did not?

I'll cut to the chase here: The truth is, tell the truth. As I've spoken to many teens nationally and internationally, what they say they want most is for you to *be honest.* They want honest answers and reasons. For example, why did **The truth is, tell the truth.** you race your car at 120 miles per hour with the lights off, and now you say they can't? Because you were stupid, that's why. And because you love them and don't want them to die.

Why did you have sex and they cannot? Same reason! But there's so much more. Today teen sexual activity is worse than it's ever been, thanks in large part to our generation and the attitudes we had about sex and free love. For those of you who were teens in the fifties and sixties, you only had a handful of STDs to contend with. Pregnancy was your main concern. For you parents who remember the seventies and eighties, more STDs reared their heads, but condoms reduced many risks, and various birth control options helped prevent pregnancy. Now into the 2000s, there are diseases and cancers that latex cannot stop. People *die* from sex and STDs now.

Not only do people die physically from sex and STDs, they die emotionally as well. Didn't you just say that you had regrets? If you want your child to grow up healthy, you need to influence them. So start by being honest about yourself and your history. If you were sexually active before you were married, it was wrong. As an author and abstinence speaker, I have had to look deep into the mirror myself and face my own history. No, it's not easy. But doing so makes you authentic—someone kids want to talk to. And it makes you stronger and more determined in your fight to keep today's kids pure.

And, my friend, we are not alone. "For the first time in American history," writes Dr. Margaret Meeker, "parents are faced with the difficulty of teaching their teens that they [the teens] cannot embrace a freedom that their parents had. We have to reverse a liberty for the safety of the kids, which evokes indecision and guilt in the minds of parents."[15] But even if your pride takes a hit or you feel embarrassed, don't stop. Establish this "safety" at all costs. You and your kids will be thankful down the road!

I know one mother who had a very wild life as a teenager and in college. "I'll never share what I did," she told my wife and me. "They don't need to know that." Although every person has a different comfort level regarding talking about the specifics of their past experiences, it's important to at least be honest with yourself. Privately examine the choices you made. Then ask yourself *Would I or wouldn't I make those same choices now, and why?* Use that reasoning as the foundation upon which to build your discussions with your child.

In other words, I'm not advising you to spill *all* the dark secrets of your life. You may not need to share all of your history, and it may not be currently age-appropriate for your child to hear. But you need to understand that what our teens face today is *much different* than what we faced as teens. The consequences are much different. Therefore, our attitudes and how we parent might require a different approach.

But this is where society lashes back at us. Those baby boomers who today are of the opinion that free sex is not only beneficial but acceptable need the theories of "safe sex" to work. Why? "We need them to be reasonable because it keeps us off the hook. If we could find a way to preserve a freedom 'enjoyed' by our generation, then we wouldn't have to (1) admit that what we had was wrong (at least harmful), or (2) struggle with urging our teens not to do something that we did."[16]

So is it guilt that makes so many of us not talk with our children and teens about high-risk sexual behaviors? Dr. Meeker explains: "That's why baby boomer parents are often indecisive regarding our teens' sexual activity. We are frightened for what could happen to them, but we don't feel we have the tools to instruct and teach them. We feel helpless because being sexually active has taken center stage in teen culture. Baby boomer parents find themselves saying to themselves, 'I had it, but they can't,' leading them to do nothing."[17]

The cultural permissiveness of our past creeps into our family room and slithers around our feet, binding us.

But can we simply do nothing? The cultural permissiveness of our past creeps into our family room and slithers around our feet, binding us. "We feel impotent in a culture screaming, 'Yes, you can have it all, including sexual freedom.'"[18]

Oh, dear friends, what we need is a Pure Revolution! There *is* something you can do. In fact, no one else can create a more powerful change for teens and children than you can. Just check out these statistics for some additional encouragement!

What the Polls Say Teens Say about Teen Sex[19]

- Teens say parents, friends, and religious/moral values most strongly influence their decisions about whether or not to have sex outside of marriage.

- In 2001, 49 percent of teenagers said their parents influenced their decisions about sex most strongly; 16 percent said their friends; 11 percent said media; 6 percent said minister/rabbi or religious leader; 6 percent said siblings. Only 5 percent said romantic partner!

- In 1995, 44 percent of girls age 15–19 who said they had never had premarital sex cited religious or moral values as their main reason for abstaining; 20 percent said it was to avoid pregnancy; 20 percent said they hadn't met the right partner; 13 percent said it was to avoid STDs.

This Pure Revolution begins with you and your family. The focal point is what I call your *connectedness* to your teens and children. But with this, your child's abstinence won't be passive. It will change the world!

The Power of Connectedness

"Fine! I don't need you anyway!"

The door makes a resounding *slam!* as Anthony stomps into his room. Audra, Anthony's mother, is brokenhearted. After all, she's a good mom and really cares about her son. But the teen years can be so difficult. She walks back to the living room, sighs, and sits down on the couch. Picking up the book she was reading about a Pure Revolution, she opens to the marked page.

Connectedness? she wonders. *I'm about as far from being connected with Anthony as I can get.*

Okay, let's face it. Teens aren't always easy. Who of us hasn't felt disconnected from them at times?

But here's a fact about children: They need adults. Without adults, they could hardly survive, much less mature into responsible adults themselves.

And here's an intriguing fact about teenagers: They too need adults. Even when the door slams. Even after they give us the eye roll—or worse, the vehement glare. Even when we wonder, *Is that a demon in my child?*

In his wonderful seminar for parents called "Understanding Your Teenager," youth specialist Wayne Rice states that 15- to 17-year-olds are "adults in need of experience."[20] They are adults! Admit it—as much as you might hate to because of the way they act at times. But where do these "adults" get experience? From other adults. Even when they don't want to admit it themselves, they need us.

That's why it's important to act like an adult yourself! For example, Wayne straight-talks parents: "Don't try to look like a teen. They will have to dress more extreme to be different than you." Your teens need you to be an adult. I'll never forget one girl I dated when I was a teenager. She took me to the swimming pool with her family. And I will never forget the horrendous feeling I had when her mother walked out of the locker room in a red string bikini and her hair in pigtails! Why was I horrified and confused? It didn't seem adult-like at all.

Your children need you as you are, adult-like. Listen to this pediatrician who has spent countless hours talking with teens about their lives and their needs.

They need clear direction in a confusing world that has discouraged many young adults to the point of submissive paralysis. These young people need help from those of us who can come alongside and help them progress to emotional, physical, and spiritual health. The adults in their lives— parents, teachers and health professionals such as me—have failed them because we are confused and frightened. We have transferred our fears of the emotional and physical health issues facing them (drug and alcohol use, teen pregnancy, depression) into fear of teens themselves. Many of us are parenting on the heels of the sexual revolution of the sixties and seventies, which has our moral compasses all aflutter.[21]

> **Your teens need you to be an adult—their parent—not their friend.**

Why is this? Baby boomers and baby busters learned from their parents that sex before marriage was wrong. It was on the basis of morality that they were educated—if anything was said at all. But they found the sexual freedom of the late sixties and early seventies enrapturing. They used condoms and integrated the birth-control pill into their lives. Morality was pushed aside as "their parents' religion," and they enjoyed the freedoms of sexual expression. Consequences were there, but their impact was barely noticeable. The ripple effect had only just begun.

Today, the ripple effect is in full swing. And we cannot afford to look the other way and allow our kids to get caught in it.

So don't be afraid to be the adult. Don't be afraid to be the parent.

> **You only have a few years to parent. Use them to your utmost advantage—and your child's!** —Ann Kiemel Anderson

Wherever possible, the adult in a teen's life should be his mom and dad. But for those who don't have parents or an intact family structure, the adult in their life could be someone else. Dr. Meeker mentions that groups of adults are needed in these situations. These groups may include an aunt or uncle, a teacher, a family friend, or some other significant adult. "We need adults to come 'under' teens, willing to understand their needs and help direct the choices they will make. We need adults to help them grow into emotionally, physically, and spiritually sound young adults."[22] Let's face it: It's our calling as adults. This is why God has entrusted you with children, has placed you in the service of children and teen ministry, or has simply put a burden on your heart for them. It's time to get armed with quality information, to be filled with pure compassion, and to take the lead. Our kids need us!

And although the structure of a family does influence a child, "other characteristics are clearly much more important," Robert Blum, a doctor and professor of pediatrics at the University of Minnesota, said in a report to Congress. "Connectedness with parents, highest among them, [and] a sense of caring and concern."[23]

So choose to be the adult who is connected to the teens in your life, and show them the utmost caring and concern.

A Surprising Start

In 1994 Dr. Udry from North Carolina convinced the National Institute of Child Health and Human Development (NICHD) that it would be good to do a large study of teens and risk behaviors. Upon their agreement, Congress funded this 25-million-dollar research project. Titled *The National Longitudinal Study on Adolescent Health* (known as *AD Health* today), the data is based on surveys of 90,000 students and interviews with 12,000 students. There were roughly 20,000 parent interviews as well. It's the most comprehensive information we have on youth and their behaviors today.[24] In fact, the information in this study was paramount to my motivation to write this book.

As parents, of course we realize that we need to raise healthy children. Parents who are Christians have the backing of the Bible, which instructs and commands us to remember the deeds the Lord has done for us and "teach them to your children and to their children after them."[25] The Bible encourages us to "choose life, so that you and your children may live"![26]

But when government studies unearth the *reasons* we need to raise healthy kids, even unchurched Americans take note. This study also mentions the means to reverse the high-risk choices teens make. From this we can de-

> Government organizations are backing up what Christians have believed and promoted all along—and they're asking for help to prevent damaging choices!

velop a balanced plan for everyone—including Christians—to use in public, business, and education settings, as well as faith-related and political settings.

What are the top reasons for teens to choose *not* to engage in sexual activity? Here's what one government study says:

1. They felt emotionally connected to their parents.
2. Their parents clearly disapproved of them being sexually involved or using contraceptives.[27]

That's it! These factors supercede *all others.* Yes, it's important to pray for our teens, and certainly we long for them to share our faith. But

> Why do teens choose *not* to engage in sexual activity? They're emotionally connected to their parents. Their parents clearly disapprove of them being sexually involved.

my experience with teens nationally and internationally reveals that a teen's faith in Christ can be undermined by parents, even Christian parents, who have no sense of connectedness with their children. Without a doubt, you love your children and would die for them. But if that relationship is not developed and nurtured, you are allowing their chances of engaging in risk behavior to skyrocket.

For instance, a 1994 study of adolescents whose parents had divorced in the previous two years found that the mothers' dating behavior directly correlated to early sexual behavior in their sons. Also, the study revealed that mothers with permissive sexual attitudes influenced their daughters to develop sexually permissive attitudes and behaviors.[28]

But here's the good news: A 1996 study of 14- to 17-year-old black adolescents revealed that those who perceived their mothers disapproved of adolescent sexual behavior either abstained from sex or had sexual intercourse less frequently. The authors of the study emphasized that "parents need to be firm in their emphasis on abstinence if they wish to discourage their teenage son or daughter from engaging in sexual intercourse."[29]

> **Providing emotional safety. . . doesn't require a psychology degree: it just takes one willing parent.**
> —Dr. Margaret Meeker

That means it's crucial that parents engage with their teens and build or rebuild relationships. No, this is not an easy task. It's "not for the feeble-hearted, but it is one that can literally give life to teens, and amazingly enough, life to parents as well."[30] So don't give up! As Dr. Meeker says, "Many emotional tangles parents have with teens are so frustrating and painful that parents often give up. But providing emotional safety in a home doesn't require a psychology degree: it just takes one willing parent."[31]

> **Sometimes what teens say and how they really feel inside can be vastly different.**

If you are willing, it's time to reconnect with your teen. But just how do you go about that, when a teen's emotions are like a roller coaster and life is becoming increasingly complicated?

It's All about Being There

What exactly does it mean to be connected with your teen? Does it mean you relate to her? That you understand each other? And whose perspective do you measure this from, yours or your teen's?

If I were to interview you about your relationship with the teenagers in your life, the majority of you would probably say that you are connected to them. Hopefully, your teens would say the same! But sometimes what they say and how they really feel inside can be different.

Just listen to Constance, a tenth grader from New York:

> *Teens need a lot of guidance, and I think that teens would rather take advice from a person outside their life instead of people like*

their parents. Some teens around here, however, don't have that in their parents. My dad tries, but to be honest, he doesn't know how to raise a child, especially a teenage girl. But I have it in my mom. You probably won't find too many teenagers that will say this, but I'm very grateful for the way my parents decided to raise me . . . and I can't say thank you enough!

Did you see the turnabout in her letter? She began by saying that teens want to hear advice from someone *other* than their parents, perhaps from someone like a youth speaker such as me. But as she typed, she processed *the truth*. She does have a good relationship with her mom and probably takes advice from her. Yeah, her dad is kinda "lost" for the most part—most of us men are when raising teen girls—but she ends up writing in plural when she says she is very grateful for the way her parents decided to raise her.

I wrote her back, saying, "You warmed my heart. You do sound blessed to have a great family, even though your dad doesn't know how to raise a teen daughter. But neither do I! See, ya'll didn't come with an owner's manual—as if guys would read one anyways."

What teens need are adults. But *how* do they need them? In a connected sense. This connectedness must be the primary goal of any parenting class. It has to be the foremost goal for any youth ministry, or all other goals will be in vain. This connectedness is foundational for the family's health. It's a theme that runs throughout the Bible, too, showing that the family is God's design.

That teens feel connectedness is extremely important in today's fragmented society. But what exactly is this connectedness? How do we define it?

In his report to Congress on the *AD Health Study,* Dr. Blum explained:

We actually went out and asked groups of kids, "What is this sense of connectedness?" There was this clear understanding on their part of what it is. It isn't that, "My mother or father is always there, is available, is sitting at home." But it's that "she or he is available when I need them." It's that "my mother remembers that I had a test last Thursday and asks, 'How did it go?'" It's that "my father remembers that I had a date, not only that I had a date, but it was with Johnny and not Sam or Harry or Larry, and asks how my date with Johnny was." "It's that my mother has a message on the refrigerator door, 'I'll be home at 6:00, but there's a snack in the refrigerator for you.'" "It's concrete things that say: 'You matter. I care, even when I'm not home.'" It's the neighbor who stops by who says, "Your mom asked me to come by after school and see how things are going." Connectedness.[32]

Read that again. Memorize it. For these are the things that really matter to *your* kids too. All of us could use the reminder, even me. I'm a professional communicator. But there are times when I ramble like an idiot trying to share my thoughts and feelings with my children! I can stand on stage and communicate dynamic truths to thousands, so why is it when I try to explain to my own kids that I love them but still have to ground them I lose my expertise?

Sometimes communicating to our teens is tough. I know many parents who want to parent differently than their parents did. But they go about it the wrong way. They dress like a teen, act like a teen, and talk like a teen. *Look at them, they relate so well,* they imagine people thinking to themselves. However, acting like a teen and relating to one are entirely different matters. And relating to a teen and really communicating with one is altogether different as well.

> **Acting like a teen and relating to one are entirely different matters.**

Since communicating our feelings and beliefs about sexual postponement until marriage is vital to our teens' ability to reject sexual activity, we must be able to communicate. But how can you do that effectively?

The best way is to get quality information first. Just the facts. Then you can use this information to plan and develop a bridge of connectedness. Only after the bridge is built can you cross it and actually talk with your teens. Will the gap between parents and teens ever be entirely removed? It's highly doubtful, because of the difference between maturity and experience. But this doesn't mean that you can't bridge the chasm between your two different worlds.

However, the way in which you build the bridge can make all the difference.

When I trained my hunting dog, I was taught to first pour love and praise on him as a puppy. This created a certain atmosphere and a standard. Later, when training him to sit, for example, all I needed was a harsh sound or harsh command. That removal of affection would sting, and the dog would do whatever I ordered to get my affection back.

No, teens and children aren't like dogs. They're a lot more complicated! But some of the same principles can carry over. To simply communicate our disapproval of our teens' actions or behaviors is not enough. It may sting them at first, but they'll develop immunity to that very quickly. So communication is not enough. What *does* work? At the Capitol Hill briefing concerning the *AD Health Study,* Dr. Clea Sucoff said:

> We found two things. Communication doesn't seem to be very effective at conveying disapproval. What seems to matter much more is that when there's a context of connectedness, kids accurately perceive the disapproval, whether or not there's verbal communication going on. Second, when mothers are religious, kids are more likely to perceive their disapproval and act on it.[33]

"I don't want to disappoint my dad," one girl told me when I asked why she didn't want to have sex even when given the opportunity to do so. "It would break his heart." Kudos to that father, for he has been successful at developing a sense of connectedness with his daughter. Since they are deeply connected, and were before any other "boys" entered the picture, she knows what her dad values and the dreams he has for her life. When moments of sexual temptation did arrive, her feelings for that boy had to compete with her feelings for her father. Connectedness won.

How to Really Connect with Your Kids

If you want to build or rebuild the bridge to the heart of your teenager, I have three simple words for you: *Enter their world.*

For you to connect with teens, you need to realize that they live in a different world than you do. Most teens—and I realize the huge stereotype here, so forgive this generalization—have three common factors in their world: their zone, their time, and their interests. You, as a parent, are usually concerned with these three common factors: their responsibilities, their performance, and their future. Not bad concerns, but if you don't major on the three factors in their world, you will rarely find them successful in the factors in your world.

Enter Their Zone

I've entered many teenagers' rooms and have had to be detoxed later! But it's their zone—their physical space. It represents them. Oh, how you wish they were more responsible and were great at keeping it clean, like their older sibling. However, is it possible that by forcing them to clean daily you're not really shaping them to be more responsible? That instead you're forcing their world to look like yours? I understand issues of responsibility, so save the e-mail. But if you develop connectedness first, your teen's compliance out of respect will come much easier.

> **What parents are interested in: a teen's responsibilities, performance, and future. What teens are interested in: their zone, their time, and their interests.**

Entering their zone can mean their room, their car, the youth group room, or other places where they like to hang out. So, with their permission, walk into their room and just enjoy it. Really! Learn to see their world through their eyes, not yours. Spend more than five minutes there. Forget analyzing the mess. Push the crumpled clothes you folded three days ago aside for a place to sit and talk. Don't blow a gasket when you see the grease from his paintball gun on the carpet. You can teach him how to remove grease stains later. Right now focus on the bridge. And let their zone be *their* zone, not yours.

> **Let a teen's zone be his, not yours.**

Remember too, the difference between a visit and an invasion. It's nice to have foreign nations visit America. It would be much different to have them invade our country. So put your own nukes back in the crates before you enter your teen's zone.

Get on Their Time

Is your teenager a morning person or a night person? If both, you have a future overachiever on your hands. If neither, they might be going through a growing spurt or might be depressed . . . or just plain grumpy! But typically you will find that your child enjoys a certain time of day best—it's a time when she is the sharpest, socially and mentally. Don't expect all your kids to all be in the same time zone, either. My three children are of very diverse ages, and naturally, all have different times of the day that are "theirs."

During that time zone is when you need to spend most of your quality time with your teen. And I'll tell you this: that time is usually *not* your time. My oldest son loved to come home minutes, no, *seconds* before his curfew. He'd walk into our home and right up to our bedroom where we were sleeping. Do you know what time that was? *His time!*

But my son was doing what we required him to do—come to our room and let us know when he arrived so we could talk to him. It wasn't just for accountability that we wanted to see his eyes, hear his speech, and smell his clothes and breath—although the accountability is beneficial—it was to let him know we cared and wanted to talk with him. Whether it roused us from REM sleep or interrupted a marital "conversation," we would still talk. Some of the time he was exhausted and wanted to go to bed. Most of the time, however, Stephanie would ask great questions as I fought to find my glasses. And then we'd engage with him. We would enter his favorite time of day and enter his world. You could tell how much he enjoyed and appreciated it. There were many nights when he *needed* it, even if it was just a brief connection.

It's never convenient to raise children. It's a sacrifice. And part of that sacrifice will be your time and energy—or sleep. So find *their* time and sacrifice yours for it. The long-term rewards are well worth the short-term sleep loss.

Share Their Interests

Are you good at video games? I stink. How about rock climbing? Chess? Paintball wars? Fixing up a sports car? For me, it's stink, stink, stink, and clueless.

But it's important to get to know your teens and their interests. And that means engaging in those as well.

Note: This does not mean taking over their interest or letting your skill or dominance nudge them away from something they like!

For instance, when my child learned to play chess very well, I got interested in playing with him. Because he beat me constantly, I began to study to get better—hey, no one likes to lose consistently, particularly males. Just as I was increasing my skills in that area, however, his interest changed—again. Even now it seems I can't keep up with his morphing interests, and that's probably just as well. It's not my job to compete with him or to be better than him. It's my job to engage in his world.

Some of the things our teens are interested in may stun us at first, especially if the bridge to their heart has eroded over time or been blown up during previous parent-child wars. But take your time, pray for guidance, and focus on the bridge. Show how you care about them and want to understand, for instance, the words to that song they play over and over again. I know some of the things you'll discover may be frightening and perhaps downright evil. But listen very closely here: If you reject and begin blasting at an interest they have embraced, teens will perceive that as an assassination attempt on their soul.

Focus on rebuilding the bridge first. As you work to develop the relationship, you will gain some clout in their lives. In future conversations you can discuss the music, games, magazines, etc. Many times teens engage in such activities to provoke reactions from parents, so be careful. Make sure your reactions are thoughtful and prayerful.

Many times teens engage in activities to provoke reactions from parents.

As you engage with their world, they will begin to perceive your love for them. It doesn't mean things will automatically be easy. Time and consistency will be a test of your sincerity as well. But you can only build this bridge as you walk on it. There is no simple blueprint, and you, as the adult, must place that first plank down. Hopefully, down the road your teen will assist you with other planks. Until then, it's up to you.

"While adults cannot force their love onto their teens, it is crucial that they communicate love to them," says Dr. Meeker. Notice that *communication* is not the standard here but *love*. She goes on to say: "Consistent communication of sincere love eventually breaks through to teens. The more he has been wounded (even by other adults), the longer he will take to receive love. But since his need to receive love is deep and real, eventually he will take it—provided he recognizes the safe character qualities and trustworthiness in the adult."[34]

Date Your Teen (and Children)!

Do you remember when you first dated? Some of us may have to go back a ways to remember! But it's worth the journey. Remember what it was like to get to know someone? Often you went to locations that had either food or an activity. Together you enjoyed your time and began to talk. You talked about life and beliefs. You discussed your families and school. You shared dreams of the future and began to realize that your heart had connected to the heart of another.

When I suggest you "date" your child or teenager, I'm not proposing anything strange. Instead, I'm asking you to pull from your past a skill you once used successfully. Now implement it with your family: your spouse, your teenager, and your child. Spend time specifically focused on them. Do a special activity or go out for food. Find fun things to talk about. Discuss their views on government, and respect their opinions, even if they differ from yours. Talk about the future, and laugh about the past. Get to know what they like and dislike all over again. There are many surprises waiting for you!

A while back I took my daughter Brianna, who just turned eight years old, on a date. My philosophy is simple: If I set the standard for what a "date" is like, anyone she dates later will be measured by my standard! When we arrived at Simms Street Bistro, I told her not to

> My philosophy is simple: If I set the standard for what a "date" is like, anyone my daughter dates later will be measured by my standard!

touch the car door. "Why?" she asked, a bit confused. I explained that when a man respects a woman, he treats her like a lady and opens doors for her. "Oh!" she replied with surprise, placing her hands in her lap waiting for me. As I opened the door she said cutely, "Thank you!"

When I opened the restaurant door, I heard "Thank you!" again. Clearly, Brianna was loving the experience. Before we reached the table, I told her not to touch her chair and explained why. "Thank you!" she said as I slid her gently up to the table. We had a great date coloring, talking, and giggling. Yes, I'm setting the bar high for her future boyfriends. But she deserves it. Those who are worth their salt will not only strive to reach that bar, but they won't cry when I routinely break their fingers before each date!

The Four Foundations of Teen Health

By "dating" Brianna early and establishing our connectedness, I am working to foster in her a sense of healthy intimacy, love, a sense of value, and safety—the foundation of complete health for all teens, whether male or female. I'm also trying to establish for her the appropriate boundaries and expectations for her dates when she's older.

THE FOUR FOUNDATIONS OF TEEN HEALTH
Healthy intimacy
Love
A sense of value
Safety

It's a different bird altogether for our six-year-old. Not only do we enjoy going out on "dates" to a restaurant or to the ice cream shop like I do with his older sister, but we schedule play dates. One of those play dates was Luc's idea—laser tag! We'll go to this place that is several floors high, and we wear gear and shoot at each other and chase each other for an hour. He loves chasing me as I "panic" and he's thrilled to get the printout that shows his scores doubling mine and the number of times he "hit" me. We plan several dates like these, in addition to riding bikes and watching movies together. It's more structured for the littler ones.

With my older teen son my times are less formal, much more spontaneous, and certainly not called a "date." But they are specific efforts to connect our hearts. When I tried to schedule events together, something always threw us off. But I discovered once that while he was changing the wheels on his Honda, he needed my help. That was a good time to talk and work together. When I needed help on my truck, we shared time then too. And since he likes movies, I've sometimes taken him to a show and out to eat afterwards. I've watched him compete in paintball tournaments and have even built a game table in our basement for us to play when his friends arrive. These "dates" are worth more to me than you can imagine.

Are there times when our teens don't want to connect? Sure, but they don't deter Stephanie and me from reaching out to them, wrapping our arms around them, and getting the eye roll. Why do we keep doing it, in spite of the outward groans? Because when they walk down the hall afterward, you can invariably sense a hidden smile.

Again, Dr. Meeker states it well:

> Physical safety, providing protection for the physical self and for basic physical needs, invests a sense that they are worth caring for and worth loving. Emotional safety teaches teens to accurately recognize their feelings and their perceptions of the environment around them. We must allow teens to resolve their feelings and finally to make healthy decisions regarding whether or not they should act upon what they are feeling inside.[35]

Sometimes as parents it's tough for us to see our teens going through so many multiple emotions—and so quickly. Yet there are times when we must sit on the sidelines cheering while they are in the game. For one of our roles as a parent is to prepare our teens to enter the adult world capable of making decisions on their own.

> The teen years are a critical time when teens learn healthy separation from parents. This occurs on physical, intellectual, and emotional levels as teens learn to recognize their own capabilities. They take responsibility for certain actions and the consequences regarding themselves. This choice, or control, is central to healthy teen separation. Learning control over oneself and

accepting responsibility for one's behavior is the very foundation for healthy psychological maturity into adulthood.[36]

That means we must allow our teens to exercise age-appropriate choices—and also allow them to wallow in the consequences sometimes. However, a parent needs to step in and take action when any of the four foundations for healthy life is being compromised.

But most of all we adults need to look at ourselves, for what we do is reflected in our teens. In 1992, researcher Victor Strasburger wrote, "Children learn by imitating adults. According to Bandura's social learning theory, children learn new behaviors by observing others, directly in real life and vicariously through the media, and they are more likely to imitate a behavior if they see an adult rewarded for it."[37]

Perhaps this is why sexual postponement is hard to teach. For where can kids see healthy, connected adults who model sexual postponement? In today's world—especially in the blitz of the media and the plethora of broken relationships—it's easy to find adults who model the opposite! That's why it's even more crucial that we parents step up to the plate. Single parents need to model sexual postponement in their own lives, without making themselves the point. Those of us who are married or remarried need to model the benefits of healthy sexuality in marriage in an appropriate and clear manner. And that means we need to model it whether we're at home, in the office, or on the road.

Parents, the jury is in. You are still the number-one influence in your teen's life today!

Parents, the jury is in. You are still the number-one influence in your teen's life today! So take that to heart, and let your confidence grow! Rebuild the bridge of connectedness to her heart, and then begin communicating the values that are important to your family.

The "village" surrounding your child—church, school, and friends—has great levels of impact on your child's life. But family community is vital.

It does take a family first. *Your* family.

pure **resolve**

i'll never forget one woman or the sadness I saw in her eyes as I spoke to a group of parents in North Dakota. After the crowd thinned, she approached me, and exhaustion and concern began to flow from her heart. "When I was a teenager, I was fairly good. I mean, no one's perfect. I did do several things I'd like to forget. But how? Now that I'm an adult, I find myself occasionally battling issues of impurity. Is this just the way we're wired, or is something wrong with me? Some of my friends say I worry too much about it. But if God calls us to be pure and holy, how is that possible? There are times I just want to give up. Can you tell me, how do I remain pure?"

Good questions, every one of them. Teens too ask similar questions. And they are the ones we'll address in this chapter.

The week after I met this woman, a young college graduate approached me and shared his heart. I could tell from the tenseness of his face that opening up about his struggle was very difficult for him.

"Doug, I want to be pure! I want to start over, too, but how? I haven't lost my virginity yet . . . although I've been very close. We've done almost everything else. But when I go to church I don't feel right about it. Am I a bad person? Someone said that once you've had sex, it's very hard to stop.

I haven't even had sex yet and it's hard to stop the things I'm doing now! I know I'm not perfect, but how do I stop and how do I stay pure?"

The battle is heated and fierce. You grimace in agreement as I do when you read the apostle Paul's words: "I do not understand what I do. For what I want to do I do not do, but what I hate I do. . . . I have the desire to do what is good, but I cannot carry it out. . . . the evil I do not want to do—this I keep on doing."[1]

Many times I think how easy it would be to just give in. If we didn't have to battle against what is impure and instead just lived by our feelings, wouldn't that be better? Wouldn't that be easier? My thoughts glide along that fantasy almost seductively until the dream turns the page. The next page is not ease or bliss. It's filled with basic laws such as "reap what you sow" and "choice brings consequence." But so many adults today have accepted the lie, and the resulting consequences have ripped at the fabric of our nation. It is now time for the harvest, and we are reaping the easy and free sex choices of generations before us: STDs, unwed pregnancy, lifelong emotional pain.

It's time that we fight for purity instead! Why? Because it's in keeping with our moral makeup and because the King, the Creator of the world and our bodies, has called us to this battle. Is there any question it's what God wants for us? "It is God's will that you should be sanctified; that you should avoid sexual immorality; that each of you should learn to control his own body in a way that is holy and honorable, not in passionate lust like the heathen, who do not know God; and that in this matter no one should wrong his brother or take advantage of him. . . . For God did not call us to be impure, but to live a holy life."[2]

Will the road be easy? No, but God has called us to remain bold and faithful: "For God did not give us a spirit of timidity, but a spirit of power, of love and of self-discipline."[3] For it is only by doing so that we can protect the next generation, and the generations after that from such horrible consequences. The battle is not for the fainthearted. But it *is* for those who care, who believe in the laws of reaping and sowing. For if we sow purity and perseverance in this battle now, we shall surely reap good fruit in the long-term.

But how? How do we who are mere humans and sinners become perfect? It seems impossible. And do you know what? Achieving moral perfection this side of immortality is impossible. That's why this book is called

Time for a Pure Revolution, not *Perfect Revolution*. We must acknowledge the difference between becoming *pure* and becoming *perfect*.

Pure—or Perfect?

When something is considered *pure*, that item is "unmixed with any other matter."[4] That's how the sister word *purge* came to mean the removal of other matter. When an item is clean, it is purified, or pure.

When something is considered *perfect*, then it is "complete" or "completely made."[5] For example, when God formed man and said this creation was "good," that implied it was perfect, completely made. Another example would be someone who takes a test and scores all the answers correctly, or perfectly.

But too often in dealing with our lifestyles and choices, we confuse these two words and their meanings. *Pure* is not *perfect* any more than *clean* is *complete*. Spiritually speaking, we as humans are sinners and are inherently impure and imperfect.[6] It requires God himself to forgive our sins (failures and imperfections) to make us pure. But the work is not yet complete. We can still have pure hearts spiritually and continue living a less-than-perfect life. Perfection comes when we are taken into heaven by Christ himself and there glorified. At that point, any earthly struggles will end and we will be like Christ, perfect! In our eternal home, we will be both pure and perfect.

Until then, however, we must continue on in an imperfect world that is overrun with impurity. Our lifestyles can be seduced by the darkness and we can mix sin into our soul. But there is a way to be purified today!

First, turn to the Creator and ask him to clean your mind and your heart. In this process, when you ask Jesus to become your God and you submit to his leadership, he will remove those impurities from within you. As he purges you from sin, you will become clean. He will claim you as his child. But that doesn't mean you are perfect.

Every day remains a challenge because our internal nature, which is inherently impure, battles with the standards of perfection set by God. That's why we can never become like God on our own ability. But we can make that our goal, something to strive for. And we can do this with pure hearts.

A *Pure Revolution,* then, is one that battles the impurity in our minds, our actions, and society in general. It means that we choose to turn from impurity and grab hold of purity afresh. Is this attainable? Yes! And the rewards are immense. But it's not an easy project.

For Teens Only?

So is all this talk about purity for our teens only? Uh, how about no. Faithfulness and honesty are honorable qualities that shape integrity in every person, whether child, teen, or adult. As adults, we cannot expect our teens and children to stand up for a Pure Revolution without our involvement as well. But does that mean you have to be perfect? No. As we just talked about, no one can be perfect on this earth. But you do have to turn away from your own impurity and allow God to purge those impurities from your life.

A dear friend of mine is a very successful businessman. He owns a sales company that he built with years of hard work, excruciatingly long hours on the road, and countless phone calls. In the eight years it took to build this company, he was not a Christian. He had no problem taking his clients to topless bars and clubs. In fact, he had a reputation throughout his industry as one of the craziest people on a wild night; large groups loved to party with him. A muscular, handsome man, he easily became a popular figure.

Faithfulness and honesty shape integrity in every person.

One Easter while sitting in church (something he'd promised his Christian wife he'd do, years earlier), he heard the gospel message. Suddenly everything became clear. "It was like somebody just turned a light on," he explained to me. After this life change occurred—when he accepted Christ as his Savior—he had some tough decisions to make. How would he change his business practices? What impact would these changes have on his income and those of his employees? He was wrestling with a Pure Revolution in his lifestyle and business practices.

Later, while on an important business trip to a conference in New Orleans, my friend was walking with his multimillion-dollar clients when they came to a topless bar. They all wanted to go inside, but he chose not to. Still a very young Christian, he explained that this was a choice he was making for his wife. He said he wanted to honor her and not go to such places anymore. They scoffed at him, called him names, promised not to tell his wife, and tried to persuade him to go in. But he held fast to his conviction.

Confused and becoming a bit upset, the clients pressed harder. It was typical for my friend to pay everyone's way and offer them a good time. It was how he'd done business for years. Some of the men were already removing their wedding rings in preparation for a wild night. Not only was my friend messing up their plan, he was acting as the group's conscience . . . and they didn't like it. Three of them even tried to pick up this 200-pound man and physically carry him into the club!

"I didn't know what to do!" he shared with me later. "I mean, God would forgive me later, right? And these were my top clients! But I knew it was wrong. So I took my elbow and slammed it into this guy who was a million-dollar-a-year client! I literally had to hit these guys to keep from going into the club."

I reacted to my friend's story as you probably are now. My heart swelled with pride for him, and my eyes watered as a smile creased my face. No, these men didn't enter the club. Instead they walked on and had an entirely different kind of night.

That New Orleans event was just three years ago. Recently I spoke at a conference that some of those same men attended. I watched my friend interact with these men that he'd "elbowed" in New Orleans some time ago. They treated him differently now. They talked about their families, their children, which church he attended, and the difference God has made in his life. One of the men shared how he recently had been baptized, along with his whole family. And that same man, who'd tried to drag my friend into the topless club three years earlier, had recommitted his life and heart to his wife! *Now that's a Pure Revolution indeed!*

As these businessman found out, living a life of purity is not child's play. Neither is it some slogan that we can preach to teens and ignore once we go to work. We adults, too, must grasp this Pure Revolution. Will it be easy? No! It's harder to live a life of purity than one of impurity. But it can be—and should be—done. Not only for your sake but for the sake of our kids and our nation.

It's harder to live a life of purity than one of impurity.

How to Remain Pure

What feelings grab the center of your chest when you watch that soap opera, visit the chat room, or view those photos and movies? Is it a feeling of pride and purity? When you get together with your friends and begin talking about others, do you walk away with a clean sensation? Or are you second-guessing the conversation, hoping you didn't say something you shouldn't have?

Even if you have placed your faith in God and have experienced the wonderful change in your heart as Jesus forgave your sins and purified your soul, all of us struggle with other issues.

In our world today, how can we remain pure? Here are four simple steps.

Step #1: Ask for forgiveness.
First, ask God to forgive you for your failures. He not only can—*regardless* of what they are—but he wants to. Accepting his forgiveness won't mean you suddenly become a perfect person or that your struggles will go away—*poof!*—like magic. But God can make you pure.

Step #2: Be honest with yourself and others.
Second, you need to be honest with yourself. *Really* honest. Sometimes that requires a deep look into those dark, hidden corners of your heart. There are areas in each of our lives that we don't usually want to venture

into because we are afraid of who or what we might find there. But to be a revolutionary and to live a pure life, you must be honest.

Some time ago I was working on my life with the help of a psychotherapist and "executive coach." He asked me to examine the dark corners of my soul, and I began the process. But then I refused to recognize what was there. Instead, I wanted to work on my "outer" person—the person I projected, the person everyone knew.

"But that person is only an image," he explained. "The real you is that deeply hidden, wounded, and perverted person inside." I was mortified! But I also knew every word he said rang true. This psychotherapist acted as a true friend—he didn't let up. In fact, he increased the pressure. "We need to kill the public image and bring healing to that person inside. That is *you*, Doug . . . not the image. That twisted, sinful being that you want to keep buried is really you. It's time to bring him to the Light and let Jesus touch him."

Did it feel great? *No!* The process was horrifying. But as I worked through my issues, I experienced a wonderful cleansing. As I tasted drops of God's pure mercy, I began to thirst for more. My choice to truly examine who I was and bring my wounded soul to God was a turning point in my life.

I can honestly say that if it wasn't for that dear friend, I probably would not be married today. And I certainly would not be teaching teens how to stand for sexual purity—or writing this book!

Now I can easily say, "I'm a sinner saved by grace."

Oh, wait. I think *cliché* just kicked on in your mind and you missed what I just said.

I did *not* say, "I *was* a sinner, saved by grace," presuming that I am no longer a sinner. Nope. I *am* a sinner. And today I *am* saved by grace. That's what makes grace so amazing! I am both, and fully accepting that has made my love and appreciation for God's touch all the more special.

> Be honest with yourself. Let God expose the real you.

So be honest with yourself and let God expose the real you. If you are a cheat, be honest. If you are a liar, for once tell yourself the truth and come clean. If you are a sexual addict, a gossip, a drunk, a user, a manipulator, or simply unkind at your core, realize that God already knows, and ask him to step into that sinful zone with you. Don't try to clean yourself up before you talk with God, because it's impossible to do that by yourself. Instead, invite the one who conquered all sin to step into your sin and meet you there. Jesus removes sin in the same way light dispels darkness. In that honest encounter with yourself and God, you will become clean.

If you're married, you also need to be honest with your spouse. You see, true intimacy, as we said earlier, is a complete vulnerability between two people. So speak with your spouse, and be

True intimacy is a complete vulnerability between two people.

completely honest. Don't fall into the lie of "what they don't know won't hurt them." That's baloney. What they don't know drives a wedge between you and them, severing your level of intimacy. So be honest, even when it hurts. Let your spouse choose to touch you and embrace you in your confession.

It may not always be easy, mind you. If you have hidden dark passions and you share those with your spouse, don't expect her to be thrilled. My wife sure wasn't! But we did work through the hurt and disappointment. I watched her embrace me while still hating the sin. She shared her opinion and why that ugliness within me hurt her so. And that explanation from her is one tool that I use to reject those old temptations. Am I perfect now? Hardly. But I'm pure, and my honesty with my bride has caused our relationship to be more valid, loving, and stronger than ever before.

Now is the time for you to be honest with a trusted friend or family member. If you don't have such a person in your life, you desperately need to go to your church and ask your pastor or priest to help you find one. Then meet with that person regularly. In those meetings, be honest. Share the struggles you have with impurity in your life. That person, if a real friend, won't judge you or look down on you. In fact, he or she may also confess such a struggle.

In this meeting, then, find a way to communicate regularly and check up on each other. Personally I don't like the sound of "accountability groups." The idea of "accounting" just grates on me, probably because previous groups have only used the accounting to rake me over the coals.

So instead I propose a checkup that's uplifting and encouraging, even fun, if you can. My friend (the successful businessman) and I call each other periodically and just say a phrase that we both understand. It's a type of code that surfaced in discussions years back, and we both know what it means. And when that code crops up again in my life, I know that I have a friend who will not reject me, will not judge me, who battles as I do, and for whom I would easily take a bullet. See, he's my friend. After building a bridge of trust, I can share my soul, knowing he'll pray for me and encourage me. He won't rake me over the coals, but he *will* speak truth to me—gently—when I need to hear it.

Step #3: Change your lifestyle.

I *hate, hate, hate* diets. I think they're ridiculous and lazy. For those of you who've had the experience of seeing me in person, you'll scoff here. My body-fat percentage is about 16 percent with little effort. I don't look overweight, and I'm really not. So when I share my opinion about dieting, my friends who struggle with their weight tend to roll their eyes and discount me.

But there's a reason I hate diets: They're temporary. Just because someone needs to lose 50 pounds, for example, doesn't mean going on a diet guarantees success. Even if the diet does work, when they go off the diet, the weight usually returns. Do you know why? It's really very simple. They returned to the lifestyle that made them overweight in the first place! Rather than go on, off, on, off a diet, how about this concept: *Change your lifestyle.*

The same applies for living a pure life. Instead of trying to dip in and out of the pure life, change your lifestyle. If you have no self-discipline and find yourself on erotic Web sites every time you turn your computer on, then you need to find a new way to change. Move your computer screen in such a way that others can see what you're working on. Change your e-mail address so you can start fresh with no erotic spam. Have someone else open your e-mail for you. Do whatever it takes to change, but *change.*

For some of you, maybe it's the television and its sexy sitcoms. Or maybe sleazy romance novels are a wonderful escape from normal life;

you enjoy getting lost in the heated stories. Chat rooms offer the same escape with the additional "danger" that these are real people. Change, change, change!

You cannot expect to teach your teens purity if you live in filth. Neither can you expect your spouse to trust you if you refuse to change your behavior. Twisted drives his talons deep into your mind as your addictions and experiences fight to keep you captive to this past. But you can break free if you want to. And that's the key.

Sometimes it's very tough to find freedom. Just ask Nick and Charlene. They'd been married for 12 years, were both in their early thirties, and had a toddler when Charlene discovered some pornographic material in her husband's study. Not only that, when she checked the Web sites her husband had visited, she realized that he was habitually visiting numerous pornographic sites. Since both Nick and Charlene were "regular church-goers," Charlene was in shock. She also felt betrayed. No wonder their love life had seemed so empty of late. She'd had the feeling that Nick was no longer pleased with her, and she'd secretly believed that it was because she hadn't lost the pounds she'd gained before she had the baby.

You can break free if you want to. And that's the key.

When Charlene confronted Nick with her discovery, it was ugly. He refused to admit there was anything wrong with him or the pornographic material. So, in tremendous shame, she asked a psychologist who was from their church to get involved. Through weeks of counseling, which Charlene insisted upon, Nick realized not only that he was addicted to pornography, but that it had done tremendous damage to his relationships for the past 19 years. He'd been only 13 when he'd happened upon his father's pornographic magazines, and Twisted had hooked him with those perverted images.

The fallout nearly destroyed Nick and Charlene's marriage. But Charlene had taken their vows "for better or for worse" seriously, and she refused to give up. Today, six years later, Nick's life has changed radically. He even drives a different way to work so he doesn't pass adult bookstores. And Charlene now is the only one who knows their computer password to get on to the Internet. Now, through their church, Nick and

Charlene privately counsel other couples who are faced with similar situations.

For the past five and a half years, Nick has not seen any pornography. And God has done amazing things—he's worked purity into Nick's mind again, given him the resolve to stand strong against the sexual temptations of Twisted, and increased his faith. God has accomplished a miracle in his life. When you meet Nick and Charlene, you immediately sense their hard-won humility and see the strength of their reconciled relationship that is impacting countless couples around them.

> A happy home is not one without problems or heartache, but one that handles them with patience, understanding, and love.
> —Author Unknown

Yes, God forgives sins and sets us free. But, unlike Nick, some of us accept this forgiveness and yet secretly hold on to the tail end of our addiction. We want to let go . . . but we don't want to let go.

Do you really want help? Then do this: *Fast*. Why a fast? The purpose of any fast is to cleanse your mind and body and to shape your thoughts and will. When you fast, you deprive your body of daily feedings and force your will to take control over your hunger drives. No, it's not easy. Who likes a growling stomach? But what I've learned during my own times of fasting is that such a step really empowers my will and self-discipline. So try it, and you'll be amazed at the results. Not only will you conquer your hunger drive but your sex drive as well. The longings and lust will come with a vengeance, but the hunger pangs will remind you of your battle. Do not be defeated!

Do you secretly hold on to the tail end of an addiction?

During this fast, I also suggest physical exercise. Since your self-discipline is becoming stronger, discipline your physical body as well. Drive yourself to a daily exercise routine. It doesn't need to be anything drastic—perhaps even a walk to enjoy God's creation. But while you are overcoming your hunger and sexual drives, you are also empowering your will. You are producing fruit now, spiritual fruit—self-discipline![7]

When the fast is complete (the length of a fast can vary, according to your metabolism and medical history, but the average fast lasts about three to seven days), you will find that you have turned a corner.

Is it time for a permanent change in your life?

This revolution can be a life change for you. How exciting! But you'll also end that fast with another serious question: Will you return to the lifestyle from which you came, or is it time for a permanent change?

Step #4: Guard yourself.

If you were Twisted, how would you attack yourself to try to destroy you?

This is a question I've asked many teens and adults. I believe we all know our weaknesses. That's why I believe none of us *fall* into sin; we step into it. And since you know your weaknesses, you know how the enemy will probably attack you.

> None of us fall into sin; we step into it.

Look at it this way, and you'll be prepared. When watching a boxing match, you'll find that the two fighters go at each other in a methodical way. Since the punches take so much energy, at the beginning of a fight each punch is strategically placed to cause injury and discover a weakness. A right lands on the rib cage. Then there's a left cross to the head. An uppercut seeks out the strength of the chin. When a weakness is discovered, then the fighter's strategy is to focus great energy on that weakness to exploit it. Many fights are stopped when, for example, a cut occurs over an eye and the aggressor pounds on that wound until the referee blows his whistle.

Even in J. R. R. Tolkien's *Lord of the Rings: The Two Towers* movie, we see the same strategies. As the Orc army approaches Helms Deep, Legolas advises his fellow elfs and the defending humans, "Their armor is weak near the neck and under the arm."

Where is your armor weak? Certainly you are not perfect, so if you just whispered that you have no weakness, perhaps your weakness is your overconfidence! We all have a weakness. Twisted knows it too, and if he hasn't hit it soon, he will. You can be assured of that.

How can you remain pure? This fourth step is crucial: Guard yourself. If you are not able to control your alcohol consumption, then you should employ your family and friends to support you as you abstain from it. If your mind is constantly spinning lustful thoughts, then you will need to gain control there with the help of a spiritual mentor.

If you do not guard yourself in the area of weakness, then you are basically dropping your arms and waiting for the blade to sever your head. My friend, do not lose hope, and do not give up! The battle is not over; God still has a purpose for you. How do I know? *You are still breathing.* Since there is life in you, there is divine purpose for your life.

So stand to your feet today. Accept God's cleansing forgiveness and become purified. Be honest with yourself, your spouse, or a trusted friend. Realize your weaknesses and guard yourself from attack in those areas. Change your lifestyle *today.* Don't wait! You *can* remain pure!

The "Love Brothers"

Some time ago I enjoyed a trip to Australia to speak in schools (or *colleges,* as Aussies call them) and in several churches. While there, my friend Jim Lyons got me hooked on the NRL (National Rugby League). So when a newspaper from Sydney published this article about the "Love Brothers," I took notice.

> Jason Stevens, the Cronulla Sharks rugby league player, . . . and his brother Paul, a former Shark, were notorious playboys. "It was so bad that my brother and I were nicknamed The Love Brothers," he says.
>
> But his older brother says he was going to hand his life over to Christ—and that meant waiting until marriage. Stevens followed his brother's example.
>
> "It was weird at first. To be totally honest with you, I really struggled. Sex had really consumed my life and I found it hard to adjust," he says on [the True Love Waits] website.
>
> "When you have sex with all these different girls, you can send back all the photos and you can send back the ring when you've broken up. But you can't send back the memories that are fixed in your mind. Those memories take away from your next relationship.
>
> "Basically, what I'm saying is, I want to respect my future wife. I don't know her yet and I haven't met her. But I am going to save myself for her."[8]

Australian rugby players with horrendous pasts have chosen to stop their sexual lifestyles and start over. The highly decorated NBA player A. C. Green sent the same message on a *Donahue* show that aired January 9, 2003—only he was a virgin until age 38 when he married. More than ever before, people are believing in themselves or their futures; they're not wasting energy on impure actions. Many are turning from a history of sexual activity toward renewed virginity. Some singles are finding ways to believe in their future spouse—even before they meet that person— and to refuse sexual advances and opportunities. Others who are married have committed themselves to a life of purity within that marriage.

I hope, my friend, that a sense of hope is rising within you. For it's true: You too can join the countless millions who are revolting against sexual impurity. Maybe you can link shields with my friend who battled to stay out of the topless bar, risking reputation and business. Perhaps you can join in with the friend who walked away from a flirt at work and back into the arms of his wife. Or the friend who decided he'd only check his e-mail when another person was in the room.

The revolution is here. And it's easy to join. Will you?

The revolution is here! And it's easy to join. But some of you may still ask: Why should I?

Why, Oh Why, Indeed!

In her book *Choices That Lead to Lifelong Success,* Marilyn Morris writes about some friends of hers who chose purity in their relationships. Listen to how it played out in their lives.

> They had a serious relationship for three years before they got married. During that time Mark never attempted to touch Pat. Oh sure, he kissed her, held her hand and put his arm around her, but he never touched her intimately. Now, keep in mind, Mark is no geek. He is a good-looking body builder who loves rock climbing.
>
> Stop and think a moment about their honeymoon. No

pregnancy. No STDs. No past memories of former lovers. For three years the passion has built. And now, after public vows and promises, they privately give themselves to each other for the first time. WOW! That's romantic . . . and a lot of fun!

By the way, Pat has shared with me that Mark's muscles and good looks were not what impressed her the most when they were dating. It was his strong character, self-discipline and self-control that really impressed her.

Pat and Mark have now been married for several years. Mark is still a good-looking body builder. He is also a very successful businessman who travels regularly throughout the United States and Europe. But Pat never worries about her husband being unfaithful while he is out of town. She knows the strong character which controlled his sexual appetite during their three years of dating will continue to provide the discipline to wait a week or two when he is away from home.[9]

I *love* that story! You see, when I challenge teenagers to wait until marriage to have sex, the primary reasons aren't to prevent them from unintended pregnancy or to keep them from contracting a sexually transmitted infection. Those are good reasons, but what they really need, even more, is the ability and strength to choose to abstain. Why?

This power to choose is the self-discipline we all must develop. If we teach teenagers the strengths in not choosing sexual activity before marriage—with someone they really want to have sex with—then later when they are married and on a business trip or stranded at an airport, we have built into them the self-discipline and strength to be faithful in a marriage. In essence, it's "faithfulness training."

> **Great souls have wills, feeble ones have only wishes.**
> —Chinese Proverb

Anyone who marries has a choice—to be faithful or not. When nearly a third of all couples (in first-time marriages) end up divorcing, and one of the top reasons for divorce is sexual infidelity, America is desperate for this strength. How can we develop it? We can begin by teaching self-discipline to our children when they are young. When they are teens, we can guide them through the benefits of delayed gratification in decision making. And we can do all this by modeling purity, delayed gratification, and self-discipline in our own lives.

But What If It's Too Late?

Listen carefully to what I'm going to say next. It's *never* too late for something good to happen! Regardless of the choices you've made, you can begin your fight to remain pure today. The teenagers and children you love and live or work with can also start afresh.

Mrs. Morris shares another story, about visiting a drill team camp. While she was there, an instructor told her:

> "Marilyn, you spoke at my school four years ago when I was in the ninth grade. The day I heard this program I was dying inside. You see, I had already had sex with three different guys. As you spoke that day, I realized I had made a real mess of my life. I kept thinking, 'It's too late!' Then you began to talk about how it's never too late to choose the best for your life. I listened carefully to what you were saying, and I made a decision that day to never have sex again until my wedding night."
>
> She then smiled at me and said, "I just want you to know I am now in a committed relationship with a wonderful man, but we are also committed to abstinence. I'm really proud to tell you, I haven't had sex since the day I heard you speak four years ago."[10]

What a wonderful story. This young lady had truly started over! Yes, there is such a thing as renewed virginity, and this instructor is a living example.

Recently I received an e-mail from a teen girl in Belfast, New York, that made me laugh *and* cry as I read it. You see, in my presentation I also talk briefly about perseverance. Specifically, I challenge those who are going through some pretty rough stuff. I help them realize that drugs, alcohol,

> **Great works are performed not by strength, but perseverance.**
> —Samuel Johnson

or suicide will not solve their problems. Then I quote the phrase, "When you're going through hell, don't stop." Here's the girl's e-mail response.

On Christmas Eve my mom and I took a whole van load of food, blankets, clothes, and other misc. items to a poor man. He lives in our town in this old ramshackle garage with a dirt floor and no running water or electricity. So, as you can imagine, his whole life has been kinda in the dumps. As we stood in his freezing little shack that he calls home, he told us all the bad things that had been happening to him. Then he said, "My life is pretty much hell right now and I'm not sure how to change it. I might as well give up." So I told him your words—"When you're going through hell don't stop." After that we decided it was time to leave.

Well I saw that man yesterday (two weeks later). He said he'd been thinking about what I'd told him. He'd even found an old piece of paper and a marker and wrote "When you're going through hell don't stop" on it and hung it in his house. He looks at it every day and thinks about those who care about him. Right there, in the middle of the store, I started crying. It was soo amazing. Just thought I'd let you know that you are still touching the lives of people in this little town of Belfast even though you're not here.

God Bless and keep rockin' the house, Roxie

How glad I am that Roxie looked at the garbage in *her* life and decided the fight to keep going was worth it. That has created a ripple affect as well, reaching even an old man living in a garage. You never know how far your choice will reach!

What do you want to do? We began this chapter asking some pretty honest and deep questions. There are many good answers and quotes for you. But here's the deal: No one can choose your action but you. The fight to remain pure is simple, but it's not easy. The benefits for adults, teens, and children are obvious. However, now it's up to you. As you finish this chapter and get ready to put this book down, what will you chose?

Why not take this opportunity to start over? Let God do his work. Take the steps to remain pure and join the many who are doing the same. Then watch as your choice creates a ripple effect that reaches thousands beyond your life!

Chapter Eleven Drawing Lines in the Sand
pure **strategies**

it was all fun and games at first. The children playing on the beach were enjoying the cool breeze as they built their sandcastles. Moving on from that activity, they ran to the water's edge and frolicked in the shallows as waves slapped them in sporadic regularity.

All was bliss until Joe and Sam crashed into each other playing tag. They got up and kept playing, but kept a wary eye on one another. As the competition increased, so did the animosity. The boys bumped into one another again, and this time it wasn't so accidental. The world stopped as they squared off; a battle was about to begin.

"Oh yeah? Well, I dare you to do that again!" shouted Joe.

Sam wasn't fazed. "Are you daring me?" he challenged.

"Yes I am," defied Joe. He reached out with his foot and drew a line in the sand between them. "Here's the line. You cross it, and I'll cream ya."

Everyone turned to look at Sam, whose face had solidified with an iron resolve. What would he do? Joe had defined the limit. Would Sam back down? If Sam did step across, would Joe really back up his challenge? Kids gathered from all over the beach area to see. Some began siding with Joe, others with Sam. A line had been drawn in the sand; what would happen next?

Where Do You Stand?

We've all been on playgrounds when some child screamed "Fight!" Running to the sound of the voice, we have added to the group to watch the brawl. "Who is it?" many would inquire, trying to peek over those in front.

Today there's definitely another fight in America's playground. And it's not child's play. In the fight over purity versus impurity, the crowds are parting and taking sides. "That's not fair! You can't call that impurity . . . it's a choice!" some scream. Do you agree with them? As you look at the issues in our families, our teens, our schools, and government, where do you stand on the issues? Lines are being drawn in the sand, and crowds are gathering to watch.

This book has given only a glimpse of the revolution occurring in America. Millions are revolting against sexual impurity, standing for a Pure Revolution. Now that you know of the "brawl on the beach," you can no longer claim ignorance. You must make a choice about what you will do.

Millennia ago, a great war hero named Joshua had a similar choice, and he chose to challenge his nation. "Choose for yourselves this day whom you will serve. . . . As for me and my household, we will serve the Lord."[1] But after Joshua, the leader, had laid out the challenge, the people still had to make a choice. They knew their history and had seen the power of their God. They also had seen the juicy seduction offered by the other gods and lifestyles. What would they choose? Could they sit quietly and simply not commit?

Choosing not to act is still a choice.

I personally don't think that's possible. You see, even choosing not to act is still a choice. Now that you have the information, you are responsible. And you are either on one side or the other.

There are plenty of people who would like wisdom to be ascribed to them. Wisdom is that which combines education and understanding. Now *you* have the information, and you have been educated on this issue. You have read stories of adults and teens, heard life experiences, and have a good grasp of the context of our battle. This understanding folds itself into your education. And now it's time for you to make a choice based on that education.

Where do you stand? The line is drawn. Do you believe we should sit back and do nothing, allowing this impure, sex-saturated society to go on in uncontrolled abandon? Or do you believe something should be done to curb the painful consequences gnawing away at the lives of teens, parents, and families? Twisted has his talons lodged deeply into our nation's soul. Certainly, we must pray. But prayer alone is not enough. How do I know that? Because some of us, including myself, have been praying for God to send revival into our schools and nation since the midseventies, and things have gotten worse!

Am I being irreverent? No. I certainly believe God can do amazing supernatural events without us and as a response to our prayers. But the very fact that Christ ascended into heaven and established his church on earth is testimony that God wants to work *through his people.* This is not the Old Testament, friends. When you pray for revival and ask God to purify the nation we live in, it's not time for you to simply sit back and wait for the news reports. Revival will never happen that way. There is no mystical power that suddenly changes people. God has a different design.

Here's the problem. People pray and ask God to cleanse the nation. Then they sit back and wait to see if it worked. It hasn't! So they return to prayer, adding fasting and more repentance. Some have even asked others to join them and hold events in our nation's capital, declaring revival and change. But then, once again, they return home and wait . . . in a void. Sadly, God is giving answers as to why, but no one is listening.

"God, cleanse our nation!" we plead.

"Okay," he answers. "Turn from your sin yourself."

"No, God. That's not what we mean. See how corrupt the school system is? Bring revival there!"

What's God's likely response? To look at us with a stunned expression and to wait for us to be silent. Then he whispers, *I gave you the powerful gift of salvation through Christ. Go share it with them.*

Undaunted, we continue our desperation for his presence in our government, rebuking the evil powers in spiritual realms. Again God nudges our souls: *My Spirit abides within you. Wherever you go, you take my presence with you. Place yourself in government and lead by the Spirit.*

Enmeshed in the busyness of our own lives, we shrug off that directive. "God, send leaders into our church. Send us someone who can truly lead us into revival!"

Then God brings Jesus' name to our remembrance. *I gave you the name above all names; every knee in creation bows to it. What other name do you need?*

Nearly exhausted, broken, we ask God to guide us. "Show us what you want us to do. Where you want us to go. Speak to us, Father," we pray. Waiting for some word, we hear silence. Finally, we get up from our position of prayer. Although we won't confess it, we're a bit confused. We take a deep breath and go about our daily business again. As we do, we walk by the Bible—God's Word to us today. His response to our prayer lies beside us every day, but we can barely hear it because of the dust.

Change will come only as you move.

Do you see my point yet? *God will never simply "send revival."* Never! Why? Because *you* are revival! God has given you his blood for protection, his name for power, his Spirit for guidance, and his Word as life for others. That means revival will come only when you move. Only when you speak at your church, when you take action in your schools, when you get involved in government, and when you lead your family in prayers of repentance and resolve. You see, revival sits in *your* chair, waiting.

Choose to Be a Change Maker!

Am I over the top here? You bet. Probably because I, too, have spent countless hours praying for change, only to return to my routine life unchanged. The change that's needed is in each of us. The influence we long to see in our world must be created by our own action. There can never be a ripple effect until someone throws a stone.

You heard it earlier; every choice creates a consequence. The choices we make to enlist ourselves in this Pure Revolution determine the consequences we will experience later. When you think of your alternatives, think deeply about the waves you would like to see years later. Imagine your children and grandchildren experiencing a society that has been influenced by tens of thousands of people actively choosing purity.

It's time to revolt against the lethargy of sitting on the fence and not choosing. If you care and want to take action, I'll share some ideas in a moment. But if you are thinking at this point, *This is simply another soapbox of a young author,* and you're getting ready to shelve this book, please, friend, think again. You are not impotent; you *can* get involved and make a difference—for yourself, your friends, your family. Each of us has a sphere of influence where we can be heard and respected. Will you speak up and act? Can you do something in your church or in your local schools? What about assisting in the political arena?

If you choose to get involved, things will not be the same. Perhaps a fruit of your effort will be changes in school education to promote character development and teach concepts such as self-discipline, self-control, value of life, and respect for others. Maybe statistics will reveal that marriages are stronger than ever before and that, as a result, our children are becoming more emotionally healthy. We might even see pastors and reli-

> **Each of us has a sphere of influence. Will you speak up and act there?**

gious leaders focus more of their energies on issues of the family and less on building projects. What a wonderful consequence it would be to have the whole church rise up from her slumber and work together for pure health, pure minds, pure education, and pure hearts!

If you're ready to draw a line in the sand, here's how you can do it.

Developing a Strategy

Vision without strategy is fantasy. Memorize that line and place it on your screen saver. Anyone can dream. But without a way to implement the dream, it remains only that.

First you must have a vision. Dream about what you'd like to see

> **Vision without strategy is fantasy.**

happen, then begin developing a strategy. Talk to as many people as you can about the problem that touches you deepest. Share your dream and tentative strategies. Find those who will lock their shield of faith with yours.

Then *implement* your strategy. Do it. Call that list today. E-mail those influential people today. Buy a case of these books and mail them to everyone on your contact list, if you'd like. But don't put off what you can do; do it today. Every schoolboard member, teacher, pastor, youth worker, and politician is in need of this information. They need you so they can make healthy decisions for our kids and our future. So do something! And do it today.

But what can I really do by myself? you ask.

Here are six simple strategies you can use and adjust for your own personal involvement.

Six Strategies for Action

I want to be clear up front: This is not a "blueprint" for you. Each person who understands this Pure Revolution has a different area of passion. That is God-given. So within these strategies, find your area of passion and take a realistic look at your strengths and weaknesses. As you share your concerns, dreams, and ideas, others will unite with you. From there you can network with others whose passions and gifts balance yours. Now you have a team. As a team, get together and pray for wisdom and direction. Then start talking, sharing, educating, planning, and implementing those plans.

STRATEGY #1: START WITH YOU AND YOUR FAMILY.

The very best place to start is with your own family. Each of us needs to change our hearts and minds. So ask God to do an overhaul within you and purify your soul. This vital process begins with individuals like you and me.

Now, look at your family. What dreams do you have for each individual and for your family as a group? Don't rely on someone else to take the lead. Instead, step out in faith, and trust God to multiply your efforts. What can you do to bring purity back into your home?

First, spend a great amount of time building bridges. If your relationship with your spouse has deteriorated, spend time reconnecting. If you have children and teenagers, work hard to build (or rebuild, depending on your situation) the bridge to their heart (see chapter 9, "It Takes a Family First").

Once your relationships are stronger and you gain credibility, then share your passion. Lead with your heart, not just your head. That means you need to suggest change in a nonjudgmental way. Talk about your own failures in an age-appropriate manner. If you have truly built or rebuilt your bridges, then as you express your concerns and why they are important to you, those you love will listen.

When you do all this humbly, without pointing any fingers (except at yourself!), and pray, asking for God's help, I believe God *will* begin a new revolution in your own life and your family's life. But it won't happen unless you try.

STRATEGY #2: REACH OUT TO FRIENDS AND NEIGHBORS.

This is your home place. It is where your children and grandchildren will grow and laugh. You have vested interest here. Do you long as I do for innocence in your children? Can we have them imitate musicians and artists without them having to dress scantily? I want to fight for the day when oral sex clubs do not threaten our kids with unpopularity. These are our neighbors and our children.

American adults strongly disapprove of young teens having premarital sex, and parents are concerned about raising their teens in a sexually permissive society.[2] Since this is the case, you can feel empowered as you leverage that opinion. Meet with your friends and neighbors, and again lead with your heart. Share your concerns and your dreams, and ask them their opinions. See where they stand, and educate them as best you can. Explain how times have changed and that teens today cannot enjoy free love and free sex as we may have in our own growing-up years.

Many will not join you in this revolution. But you may be surprised at those who will passionately stand with you. And remember, with every friend or neighbor who agrees to link arms with you, you can impact their sphere of influence of roughly 6 to 10 people. Can you do this? It's simple—just get together with them and talk.

STRATEGY #3: GET INVOLVED AT SCHOOL.

What does a pediatrician have to say about our schools and the sex education systems they offer?

Our culture at large agrees that something must be done to help teens live healthier lives, which most agree means reducing sexual activity. When professionals discuss how extensively teen sexual activity must be reduced, controversy erupts. Parents disagree, teachers disagree, feminists disagree, but most physicians who are up to date regarding the physical health risks disagree very little. I have never met a physician in adolescent or gynecological medicine who could, in all good conscience, state that teens who engage in sexual activity is medically acceptable or healthy. To encourage teens to be sexually active verges on malpractice.[3]

Doctors agree that abstinence until marriage is the absolute best way not to get STDs, unplanned pregnancy, or emotional damage. But in order for teens to make such a wise choice, we must teach them self-discipline and self-control—we must develop their character. And that means we *must* get involved in our school systems.

In the 150–200 schools I enter every year, I get a very comprehensive look at entire student bodies. And I have a great empathy for educators. The schools have a tough job; they have to educate to specific standards, they must teach against drug and alcohol abuse, they must create school spirit and have great extracurricular activities, and now they must teach issues of intimacy and sexuality. In essence, they've been forced to be the parents of America's children and teens. Then when parents don't like how schools mold their kids, they blame the schools. And that's faulty thinking.

> Because parents have abdicated their role, schools have been forced to be the parents of America's children and teens. But do we want them to be?

The first thing we can do to help schools is to *parent our own children.* PTA organizations, which are highly diminished today, need to become something more than a special interest. We need to empower parents of our teens to become better parents. That alone will help the schools immensely.

Additionally, we need to be involved in deciding what is taught to our teens. Do you know the curriculum used by your school district? If not, my point above is well made. Regardless, call your school district and ask for a copy of the materials. They should make it available or accessible to you. Then spend a weekend reading the materials. If you see things that concern you, you have every right as a parent of a child in the school to share your concerns and ask for the curriculum to be assessed. You can even help by presenting your own notes. Discussions with your new parent network will give added clout and guidance. Involve others—with your network of family, friends, and neighbors you can create great change.

This is especially important to me, as an assembly speaker who has the joy of presenting a one-hour presentation to entire student bodies. Why? Because I know these assemblies are not ends in themselves. Although they are very good for creating 100 percent awareness on campus for that day, they must be followed up by classroom education, teen peer-to-peer mentoring clubs, parent seminars, and other programs. So if you schedule an assembly speaker for your school district, do your homework first. Watch a live presentation yourself before you book that speaker. Used with these other programs, you can be an incredible influence in your schools, creating a ripple effect that lasts for some time!

There are those who say school assemblies are a waste of time for this issue. Perhaps, depending on the speaker and the encompassing programs they use. But this e-mail I received says it all for me:

> *You came to my school the week before prom and it was incredible. I was so touched by what you had to say. . . . I just wanted you to know that your assembly is the number one reason I am a virgin today. Thank you so very much.*

This was written from a female college freshman at Colorado State University eight months after my assembly program at her high school. It was certainly effective for her.

Recently I conducted an assembly at the charter school where my two younger children attend. I addressed the seventh through twelfth grades. Days before I presented, I learned from the principal that some teachers were upset with my program. They hadn't chosen to view the video I'd made available, so the principal discounted their opinions. But regardless, those opinions had been voiced to administration and students alike. What was their argument? That teens today are sexually active, so promoting abstinence is unrealistic.

If you look around you at media and advertisements, you'll see the basis for their opinion. Teens are expected to act on their sexual urges. As one source says: "Public schools approach sex education with the same foundational assumption—teens will be sexually active, so treatment should center on damage control. Have you any doubts? Look at many high school curriculums. Most are more heavily weighted on contraception *(you will be sexually active)* than on abstinence *(you have the ability to choose)*."[4]

But statistics show that more teens than ever are choosing to postpone sexual intercourse. When educated about the facts, even more are willing to abstain from any sexual activity. The main reason my assembly presentation communicates so well to teens is because I make it crystal clear: I respect teens, and I believe they have the ability to control their urges.

So get involved in your school's activities. Read the curriculum and influence what is taught and how it is taught. Be a force in booking speakers and classroom teachers for abstinence education. Help initiate character development projects. Get students involved in service projects where they assist others in need. Perhaps, like a school in Peoria, Illinois, did, you can choose to help link individual schools with sponsoring corporations that provide counsel, guidance, and avenues of internship and mentorship for the students.

If you respect teens, you'll believe they have the ability to control their urges.

Additionally, help the school develop an atmosphere where teens feel valued and cared for. This "school connectedness" is also a vital factor in preventing the various teen risk behaviors.[5]

Adolescents' connections to family and school make a difference to their health and well-being. The AD Health findings show that parents and family are still central in the lives of both younger and older teenagers. However, workplace pressures are putting the squeeze on families. Since the 1960s, American young people, on average, have lost 10 to 12 hours per week of parental time. Despite this, parents are making a difference in the lives of their adolescent children: by being home at key points of the day, by conveying high expectations for school success and behavior, by restricting access to guns, alcohol, cigarettes, and drugs, and, *more than anything else, by instilling in their children a sense of belonging.*[6]

STRATEGY #4: REACH YOUR CHURCH.

Why does this impact the church? Because her strength as a spiritual mother can be flexed best when she nurtures those families that come under her wings. Your participation in the church cannot be overstated here. It's crucial that you speak to other parents about issues of purity. This applies to entire families—not only teens—lest you be swept off to the youth director's office. A Pure Revolution is for moms and dads and church leaders as well. Faithfulness exemplified is abstinence personified. We as a church must teach faithfulness and commitment to everyone we embrace in our ministry.

This is not hard to teach to teenagers. In fact, the ground is fertile for this message. Public opinion polls revealed that teens' approval of premarital sex declined in the 1990s.[7] All you need to do is develop a strategy, recruit leaders and teens who want to take action themselves, and begin.

STRATEGY #5: REACH YOUR BUSINESS AND PROFESSIONAL COMMUNITY.

When I talk about local communities engaging in a Pure Revolution, I refuse to let it slip into a religious concept only. Nor do I want it to be a school education issue. Instead, I challenge you to look at your local community as a whole.

If we can create the mind-set of purity as a community, we can develop strategies and plans of action for our local businesses and the professional communities. For example, what kind of employee does an HR department want to hire: one who exhibits self-discipline and respect for others, or one who reveals self-indulgence and disrespect? The answer is obvious. Therefore we must help these professionals see how our ideas and programs benefit the community by the level of education and quality of future employees coming out of high school. When a community is more cohesive and families are involved, it creates a stronger climate for continued business. I'm certain the Chamber of Commerce would be interested in this.

There are many ways you can work together with these businesses. "Lunch and Learn" programs can be initiated, where employees bring a sack lunch and get a free parenting seminar. You can dream up other fun ideas to integrate local businesses for the betterment of your community. With each of these, find ways to promote purity and family health.

STRATEGY #6: REACH YOUR GOVERNMENTAL LEADERS.

Do we as Christians have the mandate to get involved in the political arena? Some are worried about the concept of separation of church and state. This concept is merely that, though—a concept, not a policy. And at its core, the concept is hamstrung. This is because as an American citizen, you know that the United States is a nation "of, by, and for the people." Therefore, you are the state. And since the church is the body of Christ, made up of Christian believers, you are the church as well. That means you are the church *and* you are the state; they cannot separate you from you!

Yes, I understand policy and institutional issues. But these exist for the purpose and betterment of the individual. It's all about the *person,* not the policy. Therefore, our government exists for each person. And as Christians we must get involved in politics so our nation can better serve each individual.

In *Why You Can't Stay Silent* Tom Minnery shares about a pastor who urged a parishioner into

> a political protest movement that was an act of righteousness
> consistent with Scripture. He takes direction from Paul's writing

in 2 Corinthians 10:3-4a, which starts by saying: "For though we live in the world, we do not wage war as the world does. The weapons we fight with are not the weapons of the world."

"That," Pastor Laybourne says, "is where a lot of people stop and say we shouldn't stand for righteousness in the public square. But then you read in verse five: 'We demolish arguments and every pretension that sets itself up against the knowledge of God, and we take captive every thought to make it obedient to Christ.'

"The church must be a public voice for the eternal truths of God," Laybourne says, and he believes pastors should show the way.[8]

We must get involved in governmental work today. Especially since a landmark poll (the CASH Zogby poll) was released in February 2003 that shows that American parents overwhelmingly support abstinence education for their children and overwhelmingly oppose comprehensive sex education. With funding for abstinence education hanging in the balance in the U.S. Congress, the results of this poll are critical.

The fact is, those who oppose abstinence education continually use unsubstantiated data to lobby Congress in opposition of abstinence funding. For example, groups such as Planned Parenthood, Kaiser, and SIECUS have released past polls that indicate parents want comprehensive sex education and oppose abstinence education. However, those surveys have been internally acquired, are not representative in their samples, and/or are intentionally vague and misleading. The CASH Zogby poll, on the other hand, is unbiased, quotes verbatim statements from sex ed guidelines and textbooks, and is representative of America in all demographic aspects.[9]

So begin by contacting your representatives and finding out their positions on sexual abstinence until marriage. Examine their views on various issues of purity. There may be others in your community whom God is moving to begin taking a lead in your government. Only by talking with others, networking with these politicians, and educating them of the facts can you find out what God is doing. You can create an intense ripple effect here as well. Our government representatives need to know that teens today value sexual abstinence.[10] They need to see how a Pure Revolution creates better families and healthier communities. Let them hear your passion and desire to shape character education that strongly implements self-control and respect for others. Our government is not some concept far removed from you and me. It *is* you and me! But there can be no change unless you take action.

The Pure Revolution Project: An Example

Following are some practical ideas to get the juices flowing for you. Begin with yourself and your family, and work out from there. Get as educated as you can and learn what is going on in your schools, churches, and community. Then create change!

> Far better it is to dare mighty things, to win glorious triumphs even though checkered by failures, than to rank with those poor spirits who neither enjoy much nor suffer much because they live in the gray twilight that knows not victory or defeat.
> —Theodore Roosevelt

Is it really that easy? I'll tell you, it takes a lot of work. In the introduction I shared how several of the parents in my neighborhood had heard of the rampant sexuality among our local teens and created "The Pure Revolution Project" to address it. You may want to read those few pages again for a reminder. But here are some thoughts about that project.

First, we had no plan to follow or blueprints to go by. The parents who got together wept as we shared the stories. Our hearts were truly broken for the teenagers who were hurting themselves and had no idea of the consequences that could await them. After the initial brokenness, we became stronger and found a point of resolve. I was the spearhead of this, realizing that of all the neighborhoods across the country that I would love to impact, my own was most important to me. I challenged my friends to do something with me.

But what could we do? There were several business people, a youth minister, a media producer, and a youth speaker. With our wives' help, we began to brainstorm using our strengths and passions. Our goal was 100 per-

> Press on! Nothing in the world can take the place of perseverance. Talent will not. Genius will not. Education will not. —Calvin Coolidge

cent saturation; we wanted every teen to hear this message. Thus "The Pure Revolution Project" was launched. In four days we communicated the message of pure health and pure relationships to 13,143 teens—and all in the week before prom! (Parents *loved* it!) Additionally, 50 physicians attended a breakfast, 250 adults responded to a parents' event, and 384 teens and youth workers enjoyed a community concert and message of salvation. A gifted producer among our group created a 60-second commercial that we aired on MTV. He bought air time in areas where we would be doing our school presentations and aired this during prime viewing times for two weeks prior to our week. When we opened the assemblies, we opened with his commercial. This linked the assembly concept with the commercial and allowed us to use that same commercial the following year prior to homecoming, holidays, Valentine's Day, and other special events.

Our event cost 50,000 dollars, so we raised half the funds through a network of concerned adults who went to every family and business they knew. The other half of our costs was donated by various vendors. Not one church carried the weight alone; this was a community effort that linked the various networks in the community. It was created by and produced by parents who had passion and skills. While this was not a religious event, it was a community project that offered expression for every network.

To learn more about how to plan such an event in your community, visit www.PureRevolution.com and order our Pure Revolution community manual.

Two additional projects in Nebraska also created similar events with incredible success. What was the key for these events? Concerned adults came together and utilized each other's strengths. They networked with various community organizations. Teens were addressed with respect; the truth was communicated. Thousands were impacted and deeply changed. All because a few adult men heard about a teen party with sexual activity—and they cried over it.

A Work That Has a Price

Nothing in life worth having comes easy. If this were an easy revolution, it would have occurred years before. It hasn't. But now we offer a new plan, and we need to link arms with you. I, too, love the "True Love Waits" concept. But rather than only focus on *waiting,* I want a Pure Revolution that will empower teens to *go forward.* They need a cause and a vision. And they need leaders.

Waiting also does not necessarily apply to you as a married adult. (Although, I must say, I enjoy giving abstinence T-shirts to parents. Many wives say they'll use them as pajamas . . . sorry guys!) But while waiting may not apply to you, a Pure Revolution does. Who doesn't want a pure relationship, a pure marriage, a pure mind, pure faithfulness, and even pure sex! Yes, God can purify all these if we let him. But we must open our lives to this revolution of purity.

Nothing in life worth having comes easy.

The problems we fight are both within and without.

First, our human nature within us opposes a turn toward purity. This is why weak-willed leaders say, "It is natural to have sex before marriage." They are slaves to their urges and have not learned to master them. Nor are some of them willing to try. We cannot underestimate this problem we fight within us. But you must know—*it is conquerable.* Thousands have done it, and many more are in the process of doing it!

On the other hand, one of the problems we fight outside of us comes in human form. There are many well-funded organizations that hate the message of sexual and holistic purity. They don't want to acknowledge the consequences to the sexual behavior they support and promote, and they fight those who make known the negative consequences, or fruit, of those choices. But try as they may to hide or deny it, pregnancies still arrive, STDs still infect and kill, and emotions still become scarred, no matter how calloused an individual may seem. So what can we do to counter organizations such as these? We must pray for the individuals within them and ask God to reveal himself, in his purest form, to them.

Another problem we fight outside of us occurs in the *spiritual* realm. The apostle Paul, who clearly faced many struggles, states, "For our struggle is not against flesh and blood, but against the rulers, against the authorities, against the powers of this dark world and against the spiritual forces of evil in the heavenly realms."[11] It is here that we experience a war against our souls as Twisted continues his destructive seduction. If you want to stand for purity, be assured you will be targeted for spiritual attack. Leaders always are.

But there is no need for fear because of this. Paul also states that the weapons we fight with are not the weapons of the world. On the contrary, they have divine power to demolish strongholds.[12] Since we are covered by the blood of Christ and are therefore protected from Twisted's arrows, we cannot lose. The only

> Evil's rage can only hurt you to the extent that you choose to entertain evil.

road to failure lies in our own hearts; what we choose to believe and how we manage our souls. Evil's rage can only hurt you to the extent that you choose to entertain evil.

This is not an easy task. But it is a revolution worth fighting! You have probably heard all the terrifying news coming from AIDS-devastated Africa. How does a continent like that begin a Pure Revolution? Should we simply teach them how to use condoms properly?

While I was standing in line at the grocery store, a story in *Vogue* magazine about people ministering to those dying with AIDS caught my eye. "Men really need to be reeducated," says Lindi, a young woman from an African AIDS-relief organization. "They lie, they don't want to be faithful. They don't want to use condoms. We do have that problem, of stubborn men. They say, 'I don't want to use this plastic.' And they have to learn how to love."[13]

They have to learn how to love! That's it! That is truly the answer for those torn countries. Teaching them that it's okay to indulge in their desires, in sexual activity, will never work. And that is the condom program: indulgence with reduced risk. But the continent of Africa will never find relief that way—and neither will any other continent or nation. Lindi said it best in that *Vogue* article. They have to teach the men how to love. And what is love? Self-sacrifice. When communities learn the power of sacrificial love, they will find self-control, patience, kindness, and gentleness. Yes, the fruit of the Spirit—not latex—is what is needed on the tables of these African nations.

It is no different in America. The only exception is that we have more money to fund our indulgences. We need to teach American men how to love, how to exhibit self-sacrifice. And who is better equipped to teach this than those who have experienced such a love themselves? The church is the most powerful force in the world—but it is also the most passive. She must arise from her sleep and become the "schoolmarm" she once was.

Nothing in life worth having comes easily. But if it's worth having, it's worth the pain and effort it takes to get it. Humanity needs this Pure Revolution, and the church can empower it!

Keeping in Mind Why We Revolt

So you don't ever forget the purpose of a Pure Revolution, remember to "future-cast"! Take moments and dream about the future and what it can look like. Think back to the famous "I Have a Dream" speech by Martin Luther King, Jr. With those words, he was "future-casting"—he was sharing his dream and getting the black community to dream with him.

Why don't you do the same thing? Dream aloud about the imagined results of the Pure Revolution you are helping to start. Let those around you hear your dreams and dream with you. That will help solidify your vision and will also give you a target to aim at. Then you can build your strategy.

Along the way be careful that you don't get caught up in useless debates about theology or politics. Yes, there will be times when you must argue your case with passionate and logical precision. But there will also be useless debates that only waste your energy and try to ensnare you. So steer clear of them. Instead, use your time and energy in the area of your passion and gifts. Don't allow Twisted to derail you into areas that are not your calling.

I'd also caution you to keep your pride in check. When you act in areas where God has gifted, you will find success. That's because it is *God's gift* that brings the success. If you are complimented, say a polite "thank you" and defer the glory to the Creator. Be wary of that inner desire for fame, power, and control. These are the very things that caused Lucifer himself to fall from heaven, and don't think you are beyond them.

For those who battle insecurities, think of it this way: Many insecurities are covered up either by extreme outward arrogance and displays of power or a form of insecure weakness. Neither of those comes from the one who created you. If you are struggling with insecurity, you are in chains. God is longing to release you. Here's a Scripture that will help: "If the Spirit of him who raised Jesus from the dead is living in you, he who raised Christ from the dead will also give life to your mortal bodies through his Spirit, who lives in you."[14] That means that the same Spirit that raised Christ from the dead is in you. The same Spirit that flowed through John the Baptist and King David is in you today. The same Spirit that flows through Billy Graham, Pope John Paul II, and me flows through you today. The question is not "What can I do?" but rather "What can I not do?" You can do all things through God who gives you strength.[15] *You* are a "walking revival," waiting for a place to happen! Once you get that truth inside you, your confidence will be transformed.

Because of those Bible truths, I'm confident in what I speak and write on purity today. I am dedicated to seeing teens experience a pure relationship with others in high school and college, rather than relationships that use and discard them for selfish purposes. I long for parents to have pure connections with their children and teens, to see them promoting better communication and better relationships and fewer damaging choices. I want to see schools purely educating teens and children on topics and in ways that truly respect them and empower them to have a healthy future. I pray for the church to take pure leadership again and move away from edifices built for recognition or control. I work to network with businesses that can add a voice of strength in their community as they promote purity and truth. And I challenge lawmakers to fight for pure legislation that promotes the value of every life and establishes abstinence education with character development as the foundation of national relationship education.

You are a "walking revival," waiting for a place to happen!

Yes, it's a big job. And yes, sometimes I'm incredibly weary. But I'm utterly convinced it's all worth it. And I'm not the only one.

An Ancient Revolutionary

The crowd surrounds you as you square off. A line has been drawn in the sand before you. You have been challenged by someone who disagrees with what you believe and what you stand for. "Fight!" some stranger yells. All eyes focus on you. Do you cross the line or not? If you walk away, they will label you. If you stay, you'll be in the thick of the battle.

Your heart is racing, and your hands turn clammy and cold. When you look around, all you can see is the faces of passersby, stopped to see what your decision will be. Each one chants in unison, *"Fight. Fight. Fight. Fight."*

A gap in the crowd opens and you see someone farther off, kneeling. His dark flowing hair and neat beard remind you of a man you've heard of years before. He holds a simple stick in his hand, and he is writing in the sand. You can't make out everything it says, but the words *life, calling,* and *purity* are legible.

The crowd presses in closer, continuing their crazed chant. This man underlines a word and turns to look at you. It is Jesus. His eyes pour into your soul a marvelous sense of power and purpose. Encouragement floods your heart. He winks, turns back to his lines in the sand, and the crowd blocks your view of him.

But *Didn't Jesus teach us to turn the other cheek?* you may wonder. *Doesn't he want us to back away from confrontation?*

Then a grin spreads across your face as the realization of Christ's existence takes on new meaning. He too had to cross a line once—a line that separated us from the Creator. And by the full expression of his life, he provided true freedom and renewed purity for each of us.

In the flash of an eye, it becomes clear to you what you must do.

In your mind you can see the faces of millions of teens and children. All are looking to you, calling for help, as Twisted strikes at their innocence, ripping away at their purity. He growls and glares over his shoulder at you, his eyes narrowing in anger.

Then a whisper moves and grows within you. And you know it's Jesus, speaking directly to your soul: *I've given you my blood, my name, my Word, and my Spirit. I will never leave you.*

A line is drawn. The crowd awaits. What will you do?

resources

The Home of Pure Revolution Events and Speaker/Author Doug Herman:
ReaLife Presentations, Inc.
P.O. Box 270510
Littleton, CO 80127-0010
(303) 973-4758
www.PureRevolution.com

BOOKS BY DOUG HERMAN
A Pure Revolution Project Manual. The comprehensive tool to successfully launch a community-wide Pure Revolution event in your city. Littleton, Colo.: ReaLife Presentations, Inc., 2003.

FaithQuake: Rebuilding Your Faith after Tragedy Strikes. Grand Rapids, Mich.: Baker Books, 2003.

What Good Is God? Finding Faith and Hope in Troubled Times. Grand Rapids, Mich.: Baker Books, 2002.

VIDEOS BY DOUG HERMAN
Sex Appeal. This presentation at a school assembly is a humorous and gripping journey into the sexual choices teens face. Littleton, Colo.: ReaLife Presentations, Inc., 2002.

I Don't Understand Why? The breathtaking story of Doug's wife and daughter's deaths to AIDS and the impact it had on his faith. Littleton, Colo.: ReaLife Presentations, Inc., 2000.

BOOK RESOURCES
Maher, Bridget, ed. *The Family Portrait: A Compilation of Data, Research and Public Opinion on the Family.* Washington, D.C.: Family Research Council, 2002.

Reisman, Judith A. *Kinsey: Crimes & Consequences.* Crestwood, Ky.: The Institute for Media Education, Inc., 1998 (revised 2000).

Meeker, Margaret J., M.D. *Restoring the Teenage Soul.* Traverse City, Mich.: McKinley and Mann, 1999.

Cole, Deborah D. and Maureen Gallagher Duran. *Sex and Character.* Richardson, Tex.: Foundation for Thought and Ethics, 1998.

ORGANIZATIONS

Ambassador Agency
1107 Battlewood Street
Franklin, TN 37069
(615) 370-4700
www.AmbassadorAgency.com

Centers for Disease Control
  and Prevention (CDC)
1600 Clifton Rd.
Atlanta, GA 30333
(404) 639-3311
www.cdc.gov

Christian Coalition of America
P.O. Box 37030
Washington, D.C. 20013-7030
(202) 479-6900
www.cc.org

Concerned Women for America
1015 Fifteenth St. N.W., Suite 1100
Washington, D.C. 20005
(202) 488-7000
www.cwfa.org

Eagle Forum
P.O. Box 618
Alton, IL 62002
(618) 462-5415
www.eagleforum.org

Family Research Council
801 G Street NW
Washington, D.C. 20001
(202) 393-2100
www.frc.org

Focus on the Family
8605 Explorer Drive
Colorado Springs, CO 80995
800-A-FAMILY
www.family.org

The Institute for Youth Development
P.O. Box 16560
Washington, D.C. 20041
(703) 471-8750
www.youthdevelopment.org

The Medical Institute
P.O. Box 162306
Austin, TX 78716-2306
(512) 328-6268
www.medinstitute.org

National Abstinence Clearinghouse
801 E. 41st Street
Sioux Falls, SD 57105
(605) 335-3643
www.abstinence.net

National Institutes of Health (NIH)
9000 Rockville Pike
Bethesda, MD 20892
(301) 496-4000
www.nih.gov

National Physicians Center
  for Family Resources
402 Office Park Drive, Suite 307
Birmingham, AL 35223
(877) 870-1890
www.physiciancenter.org

Traditional Values Coalition
139 "C" Street, SE
Washington, D.C. 20003
(202) 547-8570
www.traditionalvalues.org

endnotes

Introduction: Unlock Your Passion!

1. This story is told in Doug Herman, *FaithQuake: Rebuilding Your Faith after Tragedy Strikes* (Grand Rapids, Mich.: Baker Books, 2003), 21.

2. John Ayto, *Dictionary of Word Origins* (New York: Arcade Publishing, 1990), 443.

3. Throughout this book, most names are fictitious unless authorized by that individual.

Chapter One: Longing to Connect?

1. The term *man* is used in this book as it is the masculine form of the names of God. While the author understands this extends beyond issues of gender, he has selected it for ease of readability and clarity.

2. Rebecca Fowler, "Virgin Renaissance," *Sydney (Australia) Morning Herald,* 8 November 2002; <http://www.smh.com.au/articles/2002/11/07/1036308427650.html.>

3. Ibid.

4. 1 Corinthians 7:9

5. Deuteronomy 17:17

6. Lynn Harris, "How Many Men Have You Slept With?" *Glamour,* December 2002, 196–199.

7. Ibid.

8. Ibid.

9. Psalm 37:4

10. Margaret J. Meeker, M.D., *Restoring the Teenage Soul* (Traverse City, Mich.: McKinley & Mann, 1999), 23.

11. Ibid.

12. Matthew 6:33

13. See again Psalm 37:4.

14. Dale Kaufman, "Is Masturbation a Sin?" *Youthworker* (November/December 2001): 38.

15. Douglas Weiss, *Sex, Men, and God* (Lake Mary, Fla.: Siloam Press, 2002), 15.

16. Romans 5:8

17. Psalm 108:4

18. Psalm 89:1-2

19. Meeker, *Restoring the Teenage Soul,* 33.

20. Ibid., 34; emphasis added.

Chapter Two: Finding Beauty in a World of Ashes

1. Doug Herman, *What Good Is God? Finding Faith and Hope in Troubled Times* (Grand Rapids, Mich.: Baker Books, 2002), 26–27.

2. See 1 Samuel 13:14.

3. Genesis 1:27

4. See Galatians 5:22-23.

5. David R. Slavitt, trans., "Book III," *The Metamorphoses of Ovid* (Baltimore: Johns Hopkins University Press, 1994), 53.

6. Ibid., 54.

7. Ibid, 54–55.

8. Ibid, 55.

9. Rae Carruth's story is from Peter Richmond, "Flesh and Blood," *Gentlemen's Quarterly,* May 2001, 191–197.

10. Pitirim A. Sorokin, *The American Sex Revolution* (Boston: Porter Sargent Publishers, 1956), 88.

11. 1 Samuel 16:7

Chapter Three: The Great American Love Story

1. Genesis 3:1-7

2. Alan G. Hefner, "Baal," *Encyclopedia Mythica,* April 7, 2002; <www.pantheon.org/articles/b/baal.html>.

3. Ibid.

4. See Leviticus chapters 18 and 20.

5. Leviticus 18:3-5

6. Commentary note on Numbers 25:1-18 in *iLumina* [CD-ROM] (Wheaton, Ill.: Tyndale House Publishers, 2002).

7. "Baal-Karmelos," *Encyclopedia Mythica,* April 7, 2002; <www.pantheon.org/articles/b/baal-karmelos.html>.

8. 1 Kings 18:21

9. 1 Kings 18:24

10. 1 Kings 18:27

11. 1 Kings 18:28

12. "Moloch," *Encyclopedia Mythica,* April 7, 2002; <www.pantheon.org/articles/m/moloch.html>.

13. See Isaiah 7:14, for example.

14. See Matthew 1:25.

15. Glenn T. Stanton, "Don't Blame the Generation of 1968," *Family Policy* (January/February 1999): 1. Stanton was referring to the article "Sex O'Clock in America," *Current Opinion* 55 (1913): 113–114. The anonymous author of this essay borrowed the phrase from the editor of the *St. Louis Mirror,* William Marion Reedy.

16. Agnes Repplier, "The Repeal of Reticence," *Atlantic Monthly* 113 (1914): 298.

17. William E. Leuchtenburg, *The Perils of Prosperity: 1914–32* (Chicago: University of Chicago Press, 1958), 167.

18. Pitirim A. Sorokin, *The American Sex Revolution* (Boston: Porter Sargent Publisher, 1956), 19.

19. Ibid.

20. Judith A. Reisman, *Kinsey: Crimes and Consequences,* rev. ed. (Crestwood, Ky.: The Institute for Media Education, Inc., 1998, 2000), 1.

21. Ibid.

22. Ibid.

23. Stanton, "Don't Blame," 2.

24. Beth L. Bailey, *From Front Porch to Back Seat: Courtship in Twentieth-Century America,* (Baltimore, Md.: Johns Hopkins University Press, 1988), 17.

25. Stanton, "Don't Blame," 2–3.

26. James R. McGovern, "The American Woman's Pre-World War I Freedom in Manner and Morals," *Journal of American History* 55 (1968): 319.

27. Stanton, "Don't Blame," 3.

28. McGovern, "Manner and Morals," 322.

29. Steven Mintz and Susan Kellogg, *Domestic Revolutions: A Social History of American Family Life* (New York: Free Press, 1988), 112.

30. Linda Gordon, *Woman's Body, Woman's Right: A Social History of Birth Control in America* (New York: Grossman Publishers, 1976), 192.

31. Oswald Barrison Villard, "Sex, Art, Truth and Magazines," *Atlantic Monthly* (March 1926): 388–398.

32. Glenn T. Stanton, "A Deeper History of the Sexual Revolution," *Palmetto Perspective* (November 1998): 2–3, quoted in Villard, "Sex, Art, Truth," 392.

33. Villard, "Sex, Art, Truth," 388–398.

34. James Reed, *From Private Vice to Public Virtue: The Birth Control Movement and American Society Since 1830* (New York: Basic Books, 1978), 90.

35. Paul Robinson, *The Modernization of Sex* (New York: Harper and Row Publishers, 1976), 2–3.

36. Havelock Ellis, *Sex in Relation to Society,* vol. 2 of *Studies in the Psychology of Sex* (New York: Random House, 1936), 379, quoted in Stanton, "Sexual Revolution," 3.

37. Havelock Ellis, *Sex in Relation to Society,* vol. 2 of *Studies in the Psychology of Sex* (New York: Random House, 1936), 312–327.

38. Stanton, "Sexual Revolution," 4.

39. Ibid.

40. Reed, *Private Vice,* 87.

41. Ibid., 68.

42. Susan Wloszczyna, "Kinsey Film Will Keep Us Talking about Sexuality," *USA Today,* 22 November 2002, sec. E, p. 1.

43. James H. Jones, *Alfred C. Kinsey: A Public/Private Life* (New York: W.W. Norton, 1997), 75.

44. Reisman, *Kinsey,* 3.

45. Wardell Pomeroy, *Kinsey and The Institute for Sex Research* (New York: Harper and Row, 1972), 21.

46. June Reinisch, *The Kinsey Institute New Report on Sex: What You Must Know to Be Sexually Literate* (New York: St. Martin's Press, 1991), xvi.

47. Reisman, *Kinsey,* 17.

48. Jones, *Alfred C. Kinsey,* 514–515.

49. Reisman, *Kinsey,* 91.

50. Ibid., 109.

51. Ibid., 110.

52. Wardell Pomeroy, *Boys and Sex* (New York: A Pelican Book, 1981), 134–135. This book was reprinted recently and printed seven times prior to that. It recommends sundry forms of sexual deviation for children, including bestiality.

53. Reisman, *Kinsey,* 102.

54. Ibid., 37.

55. James H. Jones in "Kinsey Paedophiles," Yorkshire Television, United Kingdom, August 10, 1998, quoted in Reisman, *Kinsey,* 4.

56. Reisman, *Kinsey,* 4. If you are interested in hearing more about Dr. Reisman's investigation into Alfred Kinsey and his work, I strongly advise you to read *Kinsey: Crimes and Consequences.* It isn't easy reading, and it's graphic. But what you learn in this book will make you even more passionate about the fight to keep your kids pure.

57. Bill Moyers, "Mind and Body: The Brain," PBS, Washington, D.C., February 1993, quoted in Reisman, *Kinsey,* 176.

58. Reisman, *Kinsey,* 247. The *Roe v. Wade* decision includes a footnote citation to Draft No. 9 (May 8, 1959) of the ALI-MPC, which in turn states: "Major sources of Information on abortion include two sources: Calderone, *Abortion in the United States* (1958); Gebhard and others, *Pregnancy, Birth and Abortion,* chap. 8 (1958)."

59. Reisman, *Kinsey,* 178.

60. "Are You Going to Stand By; Will You?" SIECUS brochure, circa late 1980s.

61. "Talk about Sex," SIECUS, 1992.

62. Reisman, *Kinsey,* 171.

63. Romans 6:23

64. Margaret J. Meeker, M.D., *Restoring the Teenage Soul* (Traverse City, Mich.: McKinley and Mann, 1999), 21.

65. Rebecca Fowler, "Virgin Renaissance," *Sydney (Australia) Morning Herald,* 8 November 2002; <http://www.smh.com.au/articles/2002/11/07/1036308427650.html.>

Chapter Four: Intimate Encounters

1. Margaret J. Meeker, M.D., *Restoring the Teenage Soul* (Traverse City, Mich.: McKinley and Mann, 1999), 35.

2. Ibid., 34.

3. Leviticus 18:22 says, "Do not lie with a man as one lies with a woman; that is detestable."
4. Meeker, *Restoring the Teenage Soul,* 36–37.

Chapter Five: What Teens Wish Parents Knew about Sex and Love

1. Robert W. Blum, M.D., quoted in Anita M. Smith, ed., *Protecting Adolescents from Risk: Transcript of a Capitol Hill Briefing on New Finding from the National Longitudinal Study of Adolescent Health* (Washington, D.C.: Institute for Youth Development, 1999), 22.

2. Bridget Maher, ed., *The Family Portrait: A Compilation of Data, Research*

and Public Opinion on the Family (Washington, D.C.: Family Research Council, 2002), 152–153.

3. Tom W. Smith, "The Emerging 21st Century American Family," *General Social Survey,* (Chicago: National Opinion Research Center, November 24, 1999).

4. Princeton Survey Research Associates, *Newsweek,* April 20–28, 2000.

5. Gallup Poll, May 10–14, 2001.

6. "It's Your (Sex) Life; Your Guide to Safe and Responsible Sex" (Henry J. Kaiser Family Foundation and MTV, 2002), 4.

7. *General Social Survey* (Chicago: National Opinion Research Center, February 1–June 25, 2000) and Gallup Poll, May 10–14, 2001.

8. Margaret J. Meeker, M.D., *Restoring the Teenage Soul* (Traverse City, Mich.: McKinley and Mann, 1999), 41.

9. Ibid., 42.

10. Marilyn Morris, *Choices That Lead to Lifelong Success* (Dallas, Tex.: Charles River Publishing Company, 1998), 30–33.

11. Ibid., 27–29.

12. Psalm 139:13-16

Chapter Six: To Be Sexually Active—or Not?

1. "Newton's Laws of Motion," *The Physics Classroom*, December 30, 2002; <http://www.glenbrook.k12.il.us/gbssci/phys/Class/newtlaws/u2l4a.html>.

2. Centers for Disease Control, "Trends in Sexual Risk Behaviors among High School Students—United States, 1991–2001," February 9, 2003; < http://www.cdc.gov/mmwr/preview/mmwrhtml/mm5138a2.htm>, quoted in *Morbidity and Mortality Weekly Report* 51, no. 38 (September 27, 2002): 856–859.

3. Bridget Maher, ed., *The Family Portrait: A Compilation of Data, Research and Public Opinion on the Family* (Washington, D.C.: Family Research Council, 2002), 165–166.

4. Rebecca A. Maynard, ed., *Kids Having Kids: Economic and Social Consequences of Teen Pregnancy* (Washington, D.C.: Urban Institute Press, 1996), 2–5.

5. Maher, *Family Portrait,* 165–166.

6. Ibid.

7. Ibid.

8. Ibid.

9. John 15:13

10. Visit Pam's Web site at www.PamStenzel.com.

11. See Jeremiah 1:4-5 and Psalm 139:13.

12. "Surveillance Summaries," *Morbidity and Mortality Weekly Report* 49, no. 11 (December 8, 2000): 1–44; <http://www.cdc.gov/mmwr/preview/mmwrhtml/ss4911a1.htm>.

13. *Webster's New Collegiate Dictionary,* 1979 ed., s.v. "fetus."

14. See again Psalm 139:13.

15. M. Freundlich, "Supply and Demand: The Forces Shaping the Future of Infant Adoption," *Adoption Quarterly* 2, no. 1 (1998): 13–42.

16. K. A. Moore, et al., *Beginning Too Soon: Adolescent Sexual Behavior, Pregnancy, and Parenthood* (Washington, D.C.: ChildTrends, 1995).

17. K. S. Stolley, "Statistics on Adoption in the United States," *The Future of Children,* a publication of The David and Lucile Packard Foundation, 3, no. 1 (1995), 26–42; <http://www.futureofchildren.org/information2826/information_show.htm?doc_id=77449>.

18. Ecclesiastes 4:12

19. "Youth Risk Behavior Surveillance," *Morbidity and Mortality Weekly Report* 49, no. 5 (June 9, 2000).

20. American Social Health Association, "Sex on the Brain," May 28, 2002; <www.iwannaknow.org/brain2/index.html>.

21. See Galatians 5:22-23.

Chapter Seven: The Real Facts about STDs

1. "STDs: The Facts," a brochure (Austin, Tex.: The Medical Institute, 2001), 2.

2. Centers for Disease Control and Prevention (CDC), "Tracking the Hidden

Epidemics: Trends in STDs in the United States 2000," 1; <http://www.cdc.gov/nchstp/dstd/Stats_Trends/Trends2000.pdf>.

3. T. R. Eng and W. T. Butler, eds., *The Hidden Epidemic—Confronting Sexually Transmitted Disease* (Washington, D.C.: National Academy Press, 1997).

4. "It's Your (Sex) Life; Your Guide to Safe and Responsible Sex" (Henry J. Kaiser Family Foundation and MTV, 2002), 16.

5. CDC, "Tracking the Hidden Epidemics," 1.

6. "STDs: The Facts," 2.

7. Eng and Butler, *Hidden Epidemic.*

8. CDC, "Tracking the Hidden Epidemics," 8.

9. Deborah D. Cole and Maureen Gallagher Duran, *Sex and Character* (Richardson, Tex.: Foundation for Thought and Ethics, 1998), 71–73.

10. "STDs: The Facts," 2.

11. CDC, "Tracking the Hidden Epidemics," 4.

12. Ibid., 6.

13. Cole and Duran, *Sex and Character,* 69.

14. Ibid., 72.

15. CDC, "Tracking the Hidden Epidemics," 9.

16. Cole and Duran, *Sex and Character,* 72.

17. "STDs: The Facts," 2.

18. Cole and Duran, *Sex and Character,* 80.

19. Ibid.

20. Ibid., 2.

21. CDC, "Tracking the Hidden Epidemics," 2.

22. Ibid., 20.

23. Ibid.

24. Ibid., 22.

25. Ibid.

26. See the Web site <http://www.cdc.gov/nchstp/od/news/At-a-Glance.pdf>.

27. Centers for Disease Control and Prevention, "U.S. HIV and AIDS Cases Reported through December 2001," *HIV/AIDS Surveillance Report* 13, no. 2; <http://www.cdc.gov/hiv/stats/hasr1302.htm>.

28. CDC, "Tracking the Hidden Epidemics," 2.

29. Ibid., 18.

30. J. Walboomers et al., "Human Papillomavirus is a Necessary Cause of Invasive Cancer Worldwide," *Journal of Pathology* 189 (1999): 12–19; K. L. Wallin et al., "Type-Specific Persistence of Human Papillomavirus DNA Before the Development of Invasive Cervical Cancer," *New England Journal of Medicine* 341, no. 22 (1999).

31. CDC, "Tracking the Hidden Epidemics," 18.

32. American Social Health Association (ASHA), "HPV: Get the Facts"; <http://www.ashastd.org/hpvccrc/quickfaq.html>; L. A. G. Ries et al., eds., "SEER Cancer Statistics Review, 1973–1996" (Bethesda, Md.: National Cancer Institute, 1999); "Trends in Sexual Risk Behaviors among High School Students—United States, 1991–1997," *Morbidity and Mortality Weekly Report* 47 (1998): 749–752; Centers for Disease Control and Prevention, "U.S. HIV and AIDS Cases Reported through December 2001," *HIV/AIDS Surveillance Report* 13, no. 2; <http://www.cdc.gov/hiv/stats/hasr1302.htm>.

33. ASHA, "HPV: Get the Facts."

34. Cole and Duran, *Sex and Character,* 84.

35. CDC, "Tracking the Hidden Epidemics," 5.

36. Marilyn Morris, *Choices That Lead to Lifelong Success* (Dallas, Tex.: Charles River Publishing Company, 1998), 158. Morris's original source for this data was Rita Rubin, "News You Can Use—Birth Control Failure," data from The Alan Guttmacher Institute, *U.S. News and World Report,* 3 March 1997, 67.

Chapter Eight: When Is Enough, Enough?

1. This story is fictitious, but it is based on stories and reports from actual teens across the nation in grades six through eight. Although the story is graphic and may be considered highly offensive by some, it is intended to inform and motivate.

2. Margaret J. Meeker, M.D., *Restoring the Teenage Soul* (Traverse City, Mich.: McKinley and Mann, 1999), 75.

3. See John 10:10.

4. Rebecca Fowler, "Virgin Renaissance," *Sydney (Australia) Morning Herald,* 8 November 2002; <http://www.smh.com.au/articles/2002/11/07/1036308427650.html.>

5. See 2 Corinthians 1:6-7.

Chapter Nine: It Takes a Family First

1. Margaret J. Meeker, M.D., *Restoring the Teenage Soul* (Traverse City, Mich.: McKinley and Mann, 1999), 44.

2. Ibid.

3. William J. Bennett, John J. DiIulio Jr., and John P. Walters, *Body Count: Moral Poverty . . . and How to Win America's War Against Crime and Drugs* (New York: Simon & Schuster, 1996), 56.

4. 1 John 3:17

5. Bridget Maher, ed., *The Family Portrait: A Compilation of Data, Research and Public Opinion on the Family* (Washington, D.C.: Family Research Council, 2002), 198–199.

6. Ibid.

7. Ibid., 197.

8. Sara McLanahan and Gary Sandefur, *Growing Up with a Single Parent: What Hurts, What Helps* (Cambridge, Mass.: Harvard University Press, 1994), 137.

9. Maher, *Family Portrait,* 182–183.

10. Daniel J. Flannery et al., "Who Are They With and What Are They Doing? Delinquent Behavior, Substance Use, and Early Adolescents' After-School Time," *American Journal of Orthopsychiatry* 69 (April 1999): 247–253.

11. Maher, *Family Portrait,* 198–199.

12. Ibid.

13. Kristin Moore and Anne Driscoll, "A Statistical Portrait of Adolescent Sex, Contraception and Childbearing," National Campaign to Prevent Teen Pregnancy, March 1998, i.

14. Maher, *Family Portrait,* 182–183.

15. Meeker, *Restoring the Teenage Soul,* 70.

16. Ibid.

17. Ibid., 70–71.

18. Ibid., 71.

19. Maher, *Family Portrait,* 156.

20. Wayne Rice, "Understanding Your Teenager," (seminar presented at Littleton, Colorado, on October 5, 2002) quoting Wayne Rice, *Understanding Your Teenager* (Nashville, Tenn.: Word Publishing, 1999).

21. Meeker, *Restoring the Teenage Soul,* 16.

22. Ibid.

23. Robert W. Blum, M.D., quoted in Anita M. Smith, ed., *Protecting Adolescents from Risk: Transcript of a Capitol Hill Briefing on New Finding from the National Longitudinal Study of Adolescent Health* (Washington, D.C.: Institute for Youth Development, 1999), 43.

24. Anita M. Smith, ed., *Protecting Adolescents from Risk: Transcript of a Capitol Hill Briefing on New Finding from the National Longitudinal Study of Adolescent Health* (Washington, D.C.: Institute for Youth Development, 1999), 3.

25. Deuteronomy 4:9

26. Deuteronomy 30:19

27. Michael D. Resnick et al., "Protecting Adolescents from Harm: Findings from the National Longitudinal Study on Adolescent Health," *Journal of American Medicine* 278 (September 10, 1997): 823–832.

28. Les B. Whitbeck et al., "The Effects of Divorced Mothers' Dating Behaviors and Sexual Attitudes on the Sexual Attitudes and Behaviors of Their Adolescent Children," *Journal of Marriage and the Family* 56 (August 1994): 615–621.

29. James Jaccard, Patricia J. Dittus, and Vivian V. Gordon, "Maternal Correlates of Adolescent Sexual and Contraceptive Behavior," *Family Planning Perspectives* 28 (July/August 1996): 159–165, 185.

30. Meeker, *Restoring the Teenage Soul,* 17.

31. Ibid., 59.

32. Blum in Smith, *Protecting Adolescents,* 43–44.

33. Clea Sucoff, in Smith, *Protecting Adolescents,* 27.

34. Meeker, *Restoring the Teenage Soul,* 40.

35. Ibid., 59–60.

36. Ibid., 78.

37. Victor L. Strasburger, M.D., "Children, Adolescents, and Television," *Pediatrics Review* 13, no. 4 (April 1992): 144.

Chapter Ten: Get Ready to Fight!

1. Romans 7:15-19

2. 1 Thessalonians 4:3-5, 7

3. 2 Timothy 1:7

4. *Webster's New Collegiate Dictionary* (Springfield, Mass.: G. and C. Merriam Co; 1973, 1979), 929.

5. John Ayto, *Dictionary of Word Origins* (New York, N.Y.: Arcade Publishing, 1990), 390.

6. See Romans 3:23, Jeremiah 17:9, and Romans 5:12-21.

7. See Galatians 5:23.

8. Rebecca Fowler, "Virgin Renaissance," *Sydney (Australia) Morning Herald,* 8 November 2002; <http://www.smh.com.au/articles/2002/11/07/1036308427650.html.>

9. Marilyn Morris, *Choices That Lead to Lifelong Success* (Dallas, Tex.: Charles River Publishing Company, 1998), 149–150.

10. Ibid., 171–172.

Chapter Eleven: Drawing Lines in the Sand

1. Joshua 24:15

2. Bridget Maher, ed., *The Family Portrait: A Compilation of Data, Research*

and *Public Opinion on the Family* (Washington, D.C.: Family Research Council, 2002), 152–153.

3. Margaret J. Meeker, M.D., *Restoring the Teenage Soul* (Traverse City, Mich.: McKinley and Mann, 1999), 73.

4. Ibid., 78.

5. Robert W. Blum and P. M. Rinehart, *Reducing the Risk: Connections That Make a Difference in the Lives of Youth* (Minneapolis, Minn.: Division of General Pediatrics and Adolescent Health, University of Minnesota), 24.

6. Ibid., 34; emphasis added.

7. Maher, *Family Portrait,* 152–153.

8. Tom Minnery, *Why You Can't Stay Silent: A Biblical Mandate to Shape Our Culture* (Wheaton, Ill.: Tyndale House Publishers, 2001), 13. Quotes about Pastor Laybourne in *Why You Can't Stay Silent* were taken from Tom Hess, "Uprising in Vermont," *Focus on the Family Citizen*, December 2000/2001, 36.

9. Coalition for Adolescent Sexual Health, "What Parents *Really* Think about Sex Education: Significance of the January 2003 Zogby Poll Results." For further information about this survey or abstinence education, refer to www.whatparentsthink.com or e-mail Responsibility Education for Abstinence and Character (REACH) at reach@4abstinence.com

10. Maher, *Family Portrait,* 154–155.

11. Ephesians 6:12

12. Ephesians 6:10-11, 13-16

13. Zia Jaffrey, "Cry, the Beloved Country," *Vogue,* December 2000, 338.

14. Romans 8:11

15. See Philippians 4:13.

about the author

Doug Herman, an international speaker and author, has spent over 20 years in youth and family ministry. He has been a youth pastor at small country churches as well as one of the nation's largest multicultural churches. Then, after losing a wife and young daughter to AIDS through an infected blood transfusion, Doug emerged from this tragedy passionate about the message of purity, respect, and honor. He wants to offer students, families, and communities a Pure Revolution—one that would offer life rather than death.

The Pure Revolution Project was born, and it has been growing ever since. Doug's involvement as a high-school wrestling coach and substitute teacher has aided his effectiveness in the interactive and life-changing high-school assembly programs and Pure Revolution Events he conducts nationally each year. He is also the cofounder of CCARE (Colorado Coalition for Abstinence and Relationship Education) and a cofounder of the Community Advisory Board of The Children's Hospital of Denver for the Children's Hospital HIV Program.

Currently, Doug speaks over 100 days a year, giving 300 presentations annually to teens—and the adults who love them—about character development, sexual abstinence, and spiritual passion. In over 2,000 school assemblies and conferences, he has held diverse audiences of every size spellbound.

Doug has been interviewed on over 200 national radio and television programs, in addition to hosting his own radio program, "Pure Revolution Radio." His first two books—*What Good Is God? Finding Faith and Hope in Troubled Times* (Baker, 2002) and *FaithQuake: Rebuilding Your Faith after Tragedy Strikes* (Baker, 2003)—have received great reviews from a broad-based readership. He has published articles in *Leadership Journal, Youthworker, Living with Teenagers,* and *ParentLife.*

Now remarried to Stephanie, Doug enjoys balancing scuba diving, golf, and salsa dancing with his activities as father to Josh, Bri, and Luc.

To launch your own Pure Revolution Event in your community, or to schedule Doug as a speaker for your next event, simply call (303) 973-4758 or visit our Web site at **www.PureRevolution.com**

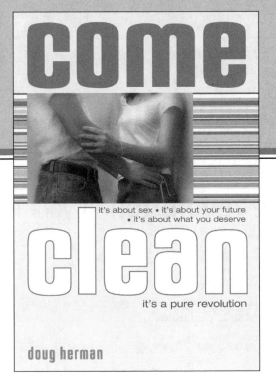

it's about sex • it's about your future • it's about what you deserve

it's a pure revolution

doug herman

Pick up a copy of *Come Clean.* . . . Doug Herman speaks to young people living in the pressures of today's world and gives them real and practical help to protect their future.

ISBN 0-8423-8358-1
Price: $10.99

www.pure**revolution**.com

Get the resources you need
for a **pure revolution** in your life!

- Don't forget to sign up for our monthly newsletter and upcoming activities in your state!

- Interact with other adults on issues of dating, whole-life purity, connecting with your children, spiritual journeys, and other great topics.

- Ask your vital question and read the top Q-&-A's asked by other adults.

- Visit our Research and Data pages for current statistics and other information.

- Get information on our international Pure Revolution Conferences.

- Want to do something about the impurity in your community? If you're fed up, here's the place to get all the resources you need! Our community manual will give you a simple plan to create a ripple effect in your city. Step-by-step instructions with options to customize an event for your city make Pure Revolution a wonderful project for your church, school, center, or organization.

- Long to see change in your local schools? School administrators can visit our School Administration page and get details on what can be done in the school setting—without legal danger. Our 20 years of work in schools makes this page effective in communicating our vision and allows you to print out resources as handouts.

Don't wait.

pure**revolution**.com